GREAT ARMIES

D1022471

GREAT ARMIES

Parragon

Bath • New York • Cologne • Melbourne • Delhi
Hong Kong • Shenzhen • Singapore • Amsterdam

This edition published by Parragon Books Ltd in 2016 and distributed by

Parragon Inc.
440 Park Avenue South, 13th Floor
New York, NY 10016
www.parragon.com

ISBN 978-1-4748-3206-9

Printed in China

CONTENTS

Decisive soldiers and tactics

Over the course of the centuries, history has often been decided on the battlefield. The difference between victory and defeat can be attributed to many factors: tactics, the composition of armies, weaponry, and even the courage of soldiers. Using detailed illustrations and computer graphics, this book delves into the tactics proposed by the boldest military geniuses and the soldiers who formed the most powerful armies in history. This magnificently illustrated book takes an impassioned look at the warriors, military leaders, and weapons that have become legendary.

Battle of Borodino
Waged in 1812 on the banks of the River Moskva, Napoleon's Grande Armée came face to face with the army of Alexander I of Russia.

INTRODUCTION

A MILITARY PERSPECTIVE ON OUR HISTORY

The 5,000 years of documented history on humanity entail, to a large part, a continuous narration of events related to violence: raids, sieges, invasions, and conquests have formed the destiny of civilizations since ancient times up to the modern day. The existence and longevity of governments, political systems, and entire societies have been determined, and often continue to be determined, by armies, the use of weaponry, and military strategies and tactics.

History is packed full of leaders who reached the heights of power only to lose it again. Kings, queens, and emperors were crowned and dethroned, and social organization systems emerged and disappeared. The main backdrop to all of these events has involved confrontations and battles, victories and defeats.

Thus, the chronicles and tales that make up the history of humanity are formed, and we might therefore be forgiven for believing that violence is inherent to the human race. However, whereas some fervently sustain such an idea on the basis of solid evidence, others state the contrary. It would be presumptuous on our part to even try to respond to the question debated for millennia and that will undoubtedly be debated for centuries to come. This book simply provides an overview—a summary of the events that, with the hindsight that time and history have provided, can be objectively assessed.

Anthropology and archaeology have demonstrated that during the Paleolithic period, over 125,000 years ago, mankind fought battles, whether to gain control of resources, to introduce new elements into their primitive societies, or to control certain hunting grounds. They did so using wooden, stone, or bone instruments; over time, these became more accurate and sophisticated. Tree branches were crafted into spears and javelins; stones into axes, arrowheads, or "hand axes" and flint "knives" used for cutting up game and, most probably, also used when battling their rivals. Scrapers, gravers, and then punches, daggers, projectile points, and spears made from bone, horns, or ivory were perfected as human society became increasingly more complex.

THE BIRTH OF ARMIES

Whereas the origins of war are attributable to survival, the need for food, resources, or land, the origins of armies are attributable to hierarchies, or primitive social organization. In principle, the role of the defender of a community falls on the strongest and most capable hunter; an animal hunter would be converted into a human hunter and, in turn, the person responsible for organizing the defense of tribal communities. His success would guarantee him, among other benefits, an increasingly more prominent role in society.

The discovery of the most primitive walled enclosures, built in Neolithic times, underscores this theory. This era is a period in humanity's history that precedes the formation of historical societies. Around 10,000 years ago, when humans abandoned a nomadic style of life in favor of permanent settlements, when we moved from being simple hunters and also turned our hand to farming, our weapons became more and more refined: handled axes and bows and arrows with sharpened flint tips gave way, in the Copper, Bronze, and Iron Ages, to the use of metals.

It is believed that the first and oldest civilization in the world flourished between the eighth and

fifth millennia BCE between the Euphrates and Tigris rivers. In Sumer, the first copper objects were fashioned; the wheel and the lathe were invented; the first writing system was developed; the principles of mathematics and astronomy were established; centralized governments and codes for the administration of justice were created; and social strata, slavery, and organized warfare all appeared for the first time. With the formation of the first city-states to which history refers, we can see, as described in the first chapter of this book, how the first armies were organized around the protection of an all powerful God-King.

From the Middle East, this model for social organization extended into Europe during the sixth millennium BCE, through the Balkans via the Sesklo culture, which is considered one of the first European cultures. In 1961, remains of such settlements were discovered in Thessaly and in regions of Greek Macedonia; these settlements featured walls containing bastions, such as the settlement of Nea Nikomedeia, which confirm the existence of "military powers" capable of attacking and defending themselves from their enemies. In fact, it is believed that the Sesklo culture may have disappeared as a result of an invasion by the Dimini culture, whose settlements in the third millennium BCE were a distinct mix of military and agriculture: the village grew around a small hill protected by walls, and a primitive megaron was erected at the top of the hill, probably as a place of residence for the local chief.

TACTICS AND STRATEGY

Two thousand years later, while Sumer started to document its history, the Minoan culture flourished in Crete while ancient Egypt was at the height of the Protodynastic Period; between 3300 and 3100 BCE, cultures also started to develop in other parts of the world, such as the Indus Valley, China, and South America. There, armed confrontations went much farther than simple primitive ritual confrontations. Dating back to this period, the fourth century BCE, is *The Art of War*, a Chinese military treatise that is still considered fundamental to strategy learning to this day. The book's author, Sun Tzu, wrote about considerations such as "the supreme art of war is to subdue the enemy without fighting" or "the ability to gain victory by changing and adapting according to the opponent is called genius." The pinnacle of genius, inventiveness, innovation, and brute strength determine the tactics—the art of deploying troops in battle—and the strategy in converting a plan into obtaining an objective. From here on, societies,

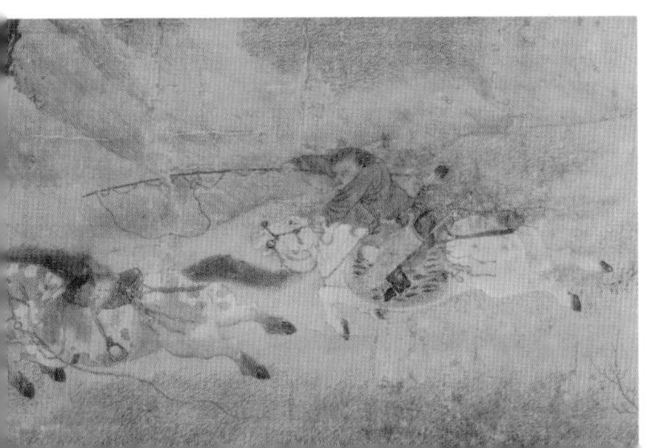

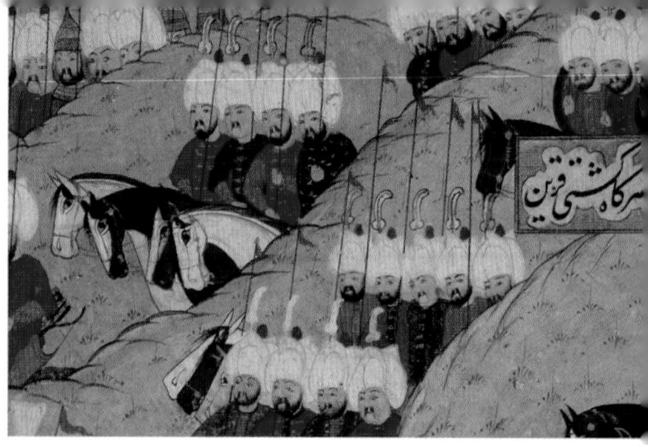

equipped with weapons, a commander, organization, logistics, and communication channels made the next step–the creation of armies as we know them today.

The first armies for which evidence exists appeared in ancient Sumer, such as the army commanded by Sargon of Akkad (who died in 2284 BCE); he was victor in 34 battles and, at the head of an army of 5,400 men, conquered all the city-states of Mesopotamia. Another example is the army of Hammurabi (who is believed to have been born in 1763 BCE) and who, at war against King Rim-Sin I of Larsa, diverted the course of the river that provided the city with water and obtained control, by means of fortifications, of an area that stretched from Syria to the Persian Gulf. By this time, troops were recruited and trained, and military formations were equipped with siege machines, in addition to primitive weapons and an element that would be a deciding factor in the first battles of which evidence remains: horse-drawn chariots of war.

Nonetheless, it was the western take on warfare from the fifth century BCE, with the Greek hoplites whose formations later inspired the powerful legions of Rome, that would determine the configuration of armies and inspire their actions for the following 2,000 years. The West laid the foundations on which these armies were built: discipline, regular training, and trust in technology. These three characteristics bestowed a notable continuity on Western military tradition. For example, take the fact that at the height of the nineteenth century, Napoleon III and Prussian General Helmuth von Moltke independently translated the chronicles of Julius Caesar's campaigns, written almost 2,000 years previously.

Take a young George Washington as another example; in the eighteenth century, he owned an annotated copy of *De Re Militari*, a brief summary of Roman military practices written around 390 CE by Publius Flavius Vegetius Renatus. Editions of this compendium date back to the eighth, ninth, and twelfth centuries CE and between the thirteenth and eighteenth centuries it was translated into English, Spanish, French, Italian, and German. In fact, many of the biggest battles of the twentieth century, such as those set out as part of the Germans' "Schlieffen Plan" in order to conquer France during World War I, were based on the old "pincer movement" tactic, the creation of which was attributed by ancient Roman authors to Carthaginian General Hannibal during the Battle of Cannae in 216 BCE.

SURRENDER OR ANNIHILATION

It could be said that of the two different strategies used by armies to gain victory throughout history—either tiring enemies into surrender, or their complete annihilation—it was the second, certain notable exceptions aside, that dominated military formations for a little over the past hundred years. At the beginning of the nineteenth century, Prussian militarist Carl von Clausewitz affirmed this in his famous work *On War*: "Direct annihilation of the enemy's forces must always be the dominant consideration," as "the destruction of the enemy's force is the firstborn son of war." This theory was demonstrated, just a few years before this work was published, by the military actions of Napoleon Bonaparte, whose army conquered almost all of Europe. It was confirmed, almost two centuries later, when the Allied Forces dropped two atomic bombs over the Japanese towns of Hiroshima and Nagasaki, effectively ending World War II.

The work of von Clausewitz, in which he maintains that war is "the continuation of politics by other means," is still studied to this day at most military academies worldwide. However, since the second half of the twentieth century, as a result of the Cold War and the proliferation of nuclear weapons, in most countries of today's global society, armies are no longer the main actors in politics, but an instrument which, in the hands of civilians, serves to fulfill certain goals. These goals are ultimately the same as those fought for in the early days of humanity—food, resources, and land.

The nature of human beings has barely changed over thousands of years, although perhaps one aspect could be pointed out today that distinguishes modern civilization from that of our ancestors: most societies no longer tolerate sacrificing lives to fulfill certain goals. Today, the military and citizens are called on for dialog and for the permanent control of the weapons' potential, which, due to developments in technology, have obtained an immense power capable of massive destruction.

It is true, as asserted by U.S. international relations expert and political scientist, John Mueller, in his work *The Remnants of War*, published in 2004, that war, in a classical sense, may be in decline. However, it is also true that it is impossible to permanently rule out the possibility that a new conflict of significant proportions could ignite the world once again.

Our future lies in the rule of reason.

CHAPTER 1

ANCIENT TIMES

1 INTRODUCTION

THE FIRST ARMIES

The first recorded evidence of the existence of complex societies comes from around 4,500 years ago, in Mesopotamia, the Eastern Mediterranean, the Indus Valley, and China; they were sedentary populations organized around the land on which they practiced an intensive form of irrigated agriculture. The protection and conquest of these lands were responsible for the creation of the first armed forces, when populations that were self-sufficient became stronger and started to grow.

This was the case in ancient Egypt around 2500 BCE and in the Sumerian city-states of Ur, Babylon, and Assur, where forces could be found on foot, armed with spears, axes, and wooden and bronze daggers. They fought in formation and protected themselves with helmets and animal skins. This is how they are depicted in the Stele of the Vultures, which narrates the victory of Eannatum, the sovereign of Lagash, a Sumerian city, over Umma in 2450 BCE. The relic owes its name to the fact that the former army walked over the bodies of their enemies, who attracted the vultures. This stele and the Standard of Ur (around 2500 BCE), on which donkey-drawn chariots of war appear, are the first known depictions of armies from ancient times.

The formations were not large in size. They served sovereigns as personal bodyguards and it was not until well into the Middle Kingdom of Egypt (between 2055 and 1640 BCE), that armies incorporated "professional" warriors, such as the case of the Medjay, Nubian mercenaries who reported to the kings of Memphis. Their weapons were rudimentary: wooden shields covered in hippopotamus or cow skin, spears with copper tips, and simple bows and arrows with tips made from bone or stone, in addition to maces, daggers, axes, and bronze swords.

The Hyksos, from Assyria, were responsible for introducing the horse and cart into Egypt as weapons of war. They used light armor made from bronze plates and compound bows, and while the Egyptians attached their axes to wooden handles and tied them with string, the Hyksos drilled holes into the metal before attaching the handle. They dominated Egypt for centuries before they were expelled by Ahmose I, who laid the foundation stones of the New Kingdom (1570–1070 BCE). Thereafter, the dynasties made lightweight chariots of war their main weapon, as demonstrated at the Battle of Kadesh between the Egyptians and the Hittites (around 1275 BCE).

Mesopotamian, Assyrian, Babylonian, and Persian cultures, who dominated the Middle East from the ninth to the fifth centuries BCE, used heavy chariots and cavalry, in addition to siege equipment, as can be seen in a number of reliefs at the Palace of

Sennacherib at Nineveh. The Assyrians undermined walls and built ramps to access fortified cities. Their armies were led by professionals, and used a well-organized supply system.

In Mycenaean society (1600–1200 BCE), wars were no different from those fought by the palatial monarchies of the Mediterranean and Asia. In Greece, around 800 BCE, the hoplites were born from a group of small subsistence, landowner farmers. These infantry soldiers were armed with a spear 6 ft 6 in/2 m long and a shield: they used protective helmets, bronze breastplates, and a round, bronze-covered wooden shield known as a *hoplon*, and fought in a phalanx formation. These compact groups, of between eight and sixteen soldiers, fought to defend their cities and social status; members considered themselves as being equals. There was no body of officers, they did not believe in tactics, strategy, or training, and on the battleground they fought always in clashes between closed formations.

This type of warfare was transformed during the Greco-Persian Wars (490, 480–478 BCE). Thereafter, warfare incorporated the use of fighting on horseback and with light troops, garrisons in mountain passes, raids, sieges and countermures, and naval attacks using vessels equipped with large spurs. The wars against Darius the Great and his successor, Xerxes, represent the first known conflict in which large-scale naval operations were mounted.

The Macedonians added an elite armored cavalry, light infantry, archers, javelin throwers, and slingers to the phalanx. Furthermore, they lengthened their spears to almost 15 ft/4.5 m, and made tactics and strategy the cornerstone of warfare, which was now seen as a political tool. At the Battle of Gaugamela (331 BCE) in which Alexander the Great fought Darius III of Persia, the Macedonian's strategy was key to his victory.

Just three years after the death of Alexander, in 323 BCE, the first unified Indian Empire was born; ruled by the Mauryan Dynasty (320–180 BCE), it would eventually encompass the north and center of the country, in addition to Afghanistan and Pakistan. During its period of splendor, the dynasty's army, comprising chariots, elephants, infantry, and archers, grew to 750,000 warriors, some of whom were particularly unusual, such as the nagas, a mystic group that used cobras in combat, and 9,000 armor-covered

elephants. Soldiers fought using javelins, spears, 10-ft/3-m spikes, tridents, and pole weapons from the elephants' backs.

Rome copied the Greek model, and the phalanx formation, which was the main form of battle during the fourth and third centuries BCE, was organized into smaller units; it became more mobile and had an excellent capacity for adapting to the environment. The Romans, who replaced the spear and round shield with a rectangular, curved shield and a double-edged sword, achieved the perfect balance between traditional Greek and Macedonian warfare. The Roman army was made up entirely of professional fighters, and its organizational capacity and buoyant economy assisted it in assuming an unbeatable infrastructure.

In Western Europe, the Celts, experts in close combat and charging en masse, employed ambushes and distraction and guerrilla techniques. They were very skilled at forging bronze and iron and were able to use chariots; in the second and first centuries BCE, they started to use cavalry in their armies, developing animal-skin armor, materials made from light bronze, armor plates and coats of mail and scale armor that covered their entire body. Initially, their metal helmets were bare, like the *coolus* used by the Romans. However, they would later incorporate the use of metal wings or horns and animal antlers. Their swords, long in England and double-edged on the Iberian Peninsula, were particularly well manufactured.

Between the third and the first centuries BCE, the first professional army in China was created. The Qin (255–206 BCE) and Han (206 BCE–9 CE) Dynasty warriors, whose uniform changed depending on their title and rank, used the most sophisticated weapons of the period, such as steel chariots and swords, in addition to springs and stirrups on horses. The 8,000 figures of the Terracotta Army are a testament to this; these life-size figures were found in 1974 at the tomb of Emperor Qin Shi Huang, who unified China, and depict lancers, archers, crossbowmen, charioteers, and various high-ranking officers.

The last of the great armies of ancient times was that of the Gupta Empire (India, 320–550 CE), which used elephants and cavalry charges; the army developed powerful metal crossbows which used metal and incendiary arrows. Its archers were protected by infantry units that, in addition to spears, used long or curved swords made from superior metals. The Khanjar, a long double-edged sword with a blunt tip, was especially devastating.

Chronology and Main Battles

Almost 3,200 years passed between the foundation of the Old Kingdom of Egypt, in 2686 BCE, and 476 CE, when Odoacer, king of the Herulians, brought an end to the Western Roman Empire. During this period, armies moved from being small formations at the service of godlike sovereigns, to large professional units with a range of different and well-defined ranks and titles. From the chaos of ancient times came training, strategy, tactics ... and politics.

2686 BCE Old Kingdom of Egypt (to 2160 BCE)

2300 BCE Sargon of Akkad conquers all the city-states of Mesopotamia

2055 BCE Middle Kingdom (to 1640 BCE) and reunification of Egypt

1875 BCE Sargon I of Assyria extends his territory to Cappadocia

1793 BCE Hammurabi, king of Babylonia

1680 BCE Labarna I extends his reach to Anatolia and inaugurates the Old Hittite Kingdom

1570 BCE Ahmose I takes up the throne and expels the Hyksos from Egypt

1551 BCE New Kingdom of Egypt (to 1070 BCE)

1500 BCE The Aryans invade the Indus Valley

1275 BCE Battle of Kadesh. Ramesses II defeats the Hittites

1200 BCE Iron metallurgy starts in the Middle East

1126 BCE Nebuchadnezzar succeeds to the Babylonian throne

2686 BCE

1000 BCE

911 BCE Adad-Nirari overcomes Babylonia and marks the beginning of the New Assyrian Empire

844 BCE The Medes settle in northeast Iran and the Persians to the south

841 BCE King Li is defeated and recorded history in China begins

800 BCE The Celts appear on the Iberian Peninsula

721 BCE King Sargon II of Assyria destroys the Kingdom of Israel

612 BCE Fall of Nineveh and the end of the Assyrian Empire

559 BCE Cyrus establishes the Persian Empire

525 BCE The Persian king, Cambyses, conquers Egypt

510 BCE Rome recognizes the maritime monopoly of Carthage

508 BCE Democracy is installed in Athens

Assyrian King, Sargon II.

SUN TZU AND THE ART OF WAR

Sun Tzu, a Chinese general during the fifth century BCE, wrote the oldest military treatise, the text of which notably influenced war strategists in the East.

A serious matter
The Art of War begins by stating: "War is a matter of vital importance [...]. It is mandatory that it be thoroughly studied."

480 BCE
2nd Greco-Persian War, Battles of Thermopylae and Salamis

479 BCE
The Persians are defeated by the Greeks at the Battle of Plataea

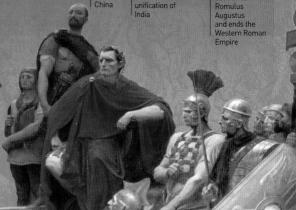

333 BCE
Alexander the Great defeats the Persians at the Battle of Issus

332 BCE
Alexander the Great conquers Syria and Palestine and brings Egypt under his control

331 BCE
The Persians are defeated by the Macedonians at the Battle of Gaugamela

221 BCE
China is unified under the Qin Dynasty

149 BCE
Third Punic War

146 BCE
Destruction of Carthage

58 BCE
Julius Caesar begins the Gallic Wars

52 BCE
Battle of Alesia between the Romans and the Gauls

43 CE
Rome invades Britannia

117 CE
The Roman Empire reaches its greatest extent

330 CE
Constantinople becomes the capital of the Roman Empire

395 CE
The Roman Empire is divided between the East and the West

452 CE
Attila, king of the Huns, invades Italy

500 BCE — **476 CE**

490 BCE
The Persians are defeated by the Greeks at Marathon in the First Greco-Persian War

431 BCE
Peloponnesian War between Athens and Sparta

303 BCE
Chandragupta inaugurates the Mauryan Dynasty

264 BCE
First Punic War between Rome and Carthage

218 BCE
Second Punic War

216 BCE
Battle of Cannae

215 BCE
Work begins on the construction of the Great Wall of China

44 BCE
Assassination of Julius Caesar

220 CE
End of the Han Dynasty in China

320 CE
Start of the Gupta Dynasty and the unification of India

476 CE
Odoacer, king of the Herulians, dethrones Romulus Augustus and ends the Western Roman Empire

The Roman fleet defeats the Carthaginian fleet at Ecnomus, off the Carthaginian coast, during the First Punic War, 256 BCE.

Military Leaders of Ancient Times

These were the protagonists of the great military battles and, in many cases, genuine pioneers in the art of war, putting never-before-seen strategies and tactics into practice. Leading their armies, whether large military formations or small groups of men, they significantly expanded the spheres of influence of their kingdoms, empires, and societies. They lived thousands of years ago, but they are considered some of the most famous warriors in history.

2300-2215 BCE

SARGON OF AKKAD
His background is unknown. Sargon himself recounted that a priestess abandoned him in a basket on the Euphrates. He entered the court of the king of Kish, against whom he rebelled. He founded Akkad, the capital of his empire. He brought Mesopotamia under his control following the Battle of Uruk.

1326-1234 BCE

RAMESSES II
He succeeded to the throne in 1301 BCE and constructed the temples at Luxor and Abu Simbel, in honor of the gods, himself and one of his wives, Nefertari. In his most important military feat, he faced the Hittites at the Battle of Kadesh, from which he emerged victorious.

540-480 BCE

LEONIDAS
King of Sparta from 488 BCE, who became a legendary figure following his death at the Battle of Thermopylae, during which he led a group of 6,000 Greeks against the armies of Xerxes I, numbering around 210,000 men. His sacrifice enabled the Greeks to defeat the Persians at Salamis.

519-465 BCE

XERXES I
King of Persia from 485 BCE, he was the protagonist of the Second Greco-Persian War. He invaded Greece through the passage of Thermopylae, vanquishing the Spartans, and then razed Athens to the ground. He was defeated by the Greek fleet at Salamis. He was assassinated by his vizier, Artabanus.

"Men in general are quick to believe that which they wish to be true."

Gaius Julius Caesar, the *Gallic War Commentaries*, Book III, 18. 58 BCE

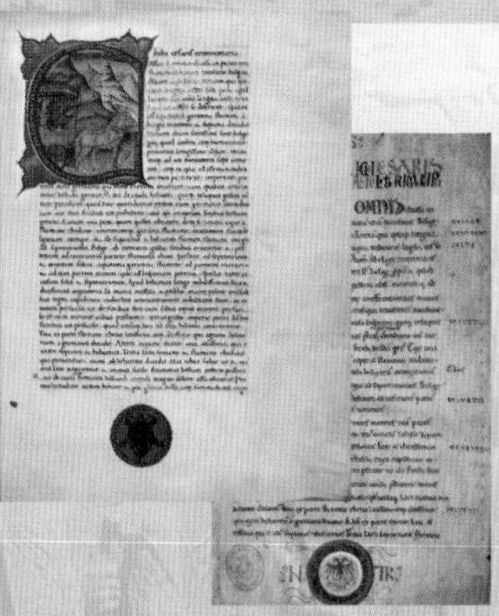

NINE YEARS OF WAR
The *Gallic War Commentaries*, written in the third person by Julius Caesar between 58 and 50 BCE, consist of eight books in which Caesar recounts the battles and schemes involved in his campaigns against his fiercest enemies—the Gauls.

356-323 BCE

ALEXANDER THE GREAT
Real name Alexander III of Macedonia, he died age 33. He was crowned age 20 following the assassination of his father, Philip II, and reigned for 13 years. During this period, he conquered the entire Persian Empire and reached the Indian border. He died in Babylonia under strange circumstances.

247-183 BCE

HANNIBAL
At 25, Hannibal was named Commander of the Carthaginian army in Hispania, and it did not take him long to challenge Rome during the Second Punic War. He reached Rome, but decided against attacking the city. After the defeat of Carthage, he went into exile in Asia, where he eventually committed suicide.

100-44 BCE

JULIUS CAESAR
He expanded the Roman Empire to include Gaul and the territories of Britannia and Germania. He inaugurated the Great Roman Civil War, following which he appointed himself perpetual dictator and ended the Republic. He was assassinated by Brutus and Cassius, stabbed 23 times.

c. 80-46 BCE

VERCINGETORIX
Leader of the Arverni tribe, Vercingetorix led the revolt of the Gallic tribes against the Romans in 52 BCE. Having been beaten by Julius Caesar at Alesia, he was held as a prisoner in Rome. A few years later, he was displayed at Caesar's victory parade before being strangled in public.

Weapons of Ancient Times

The discovery of metals during the third millennium BCE resulted in the replacement of primitive stone weapons with more effective and deadlier weapons—first using copper and bronze then, from 900 BCE, iron. Ancient armies used bows and javelins as throwing weapons, and maces, axes, spears, and swords in close combat.

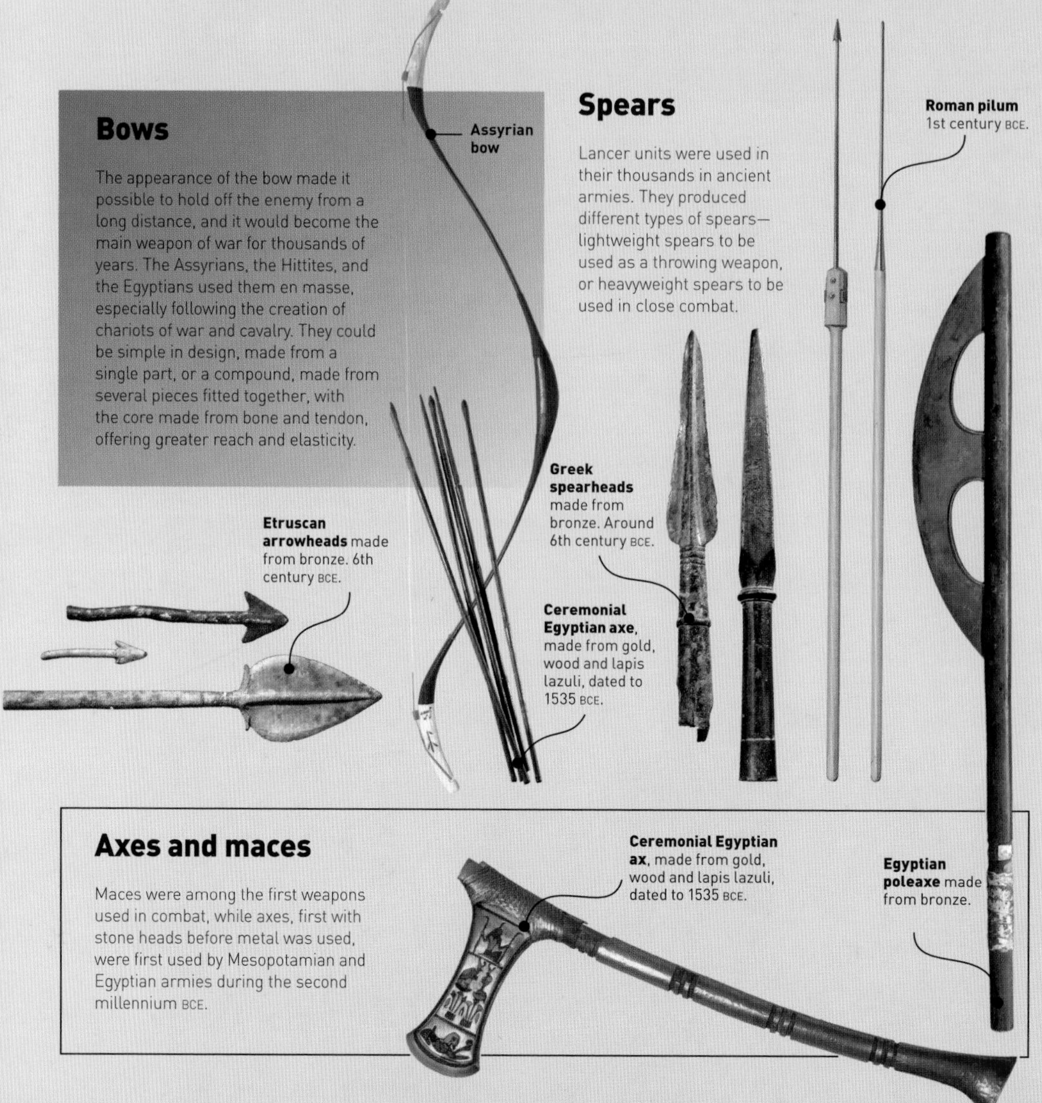
Assyrian bow
Roman pilum 1st century BCE.
Greek spearheads made from bronze. Around 6th century BCE.
Etruscan arrowheads made from bronze. 6th century BCE.
Ceremonial Egyptian axe, made from gold, wood and lapis lazuli, dated to 1535 BCE.
Ceremonial Egyptian ax, made from gold, wood and lapis lazuli, dated to 1535 BCE.
Egyptian poleaxe made from bronze.

Bows

The appearance of the bow made it possible to hold off the enemy from a long distance, and it would become the main weapon of war for thousands of years. The Assyrians, the Hittites, and the Egyptians used them en masse, especially following the creation of chariots of war and cavalry. They could be simple in design, made from a single part, or a compound, made from several pieces fitted together, with the core made from bone and tendon, offering greater reach and elasticity.

Spears

Lancer units were used in their thousands in ancient armies. They produced different types of spears—lightweight spears to be used as a throwing weapon, or heavyweight spears to be used in close combat.

Axes and maces

Maces were among the first weapons used in combat, while axes, first with stone heads before metal was used, were first used by Mesopotamian and Egyptian armies during the second millennium BCE.

Daggers and swords

Although daggers were employed by the first ancient warriors as an auxiliary weapon, the increase in importance given to swords is attributable to the mastering of metalwork techniques. With the discovery of hot hammering and iron tempering around 1200 BCE, sharper and deadlier blades capable of penetrating armor were produced. Romans and Celts (who were master manufacturers) made these weapons their first choice of arms.

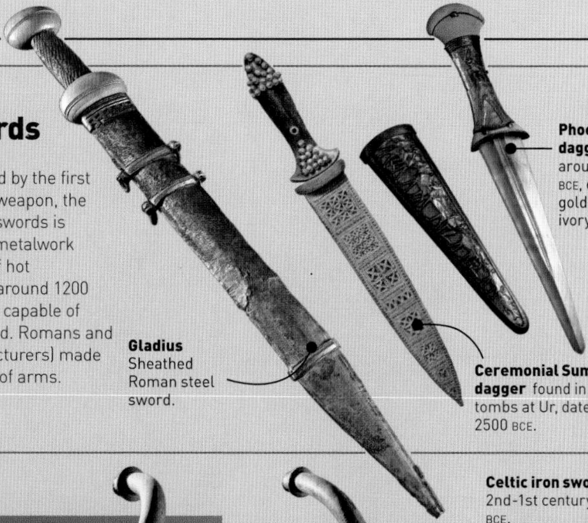

Gladius Sheathed Roman steel sword.

Ceremonial Sumerian dagger found in the tombs at Ur, dated to 2500 BCE.

Phoenician dagger, from around 1800 BCE, covered in gold, silver, and ivory.

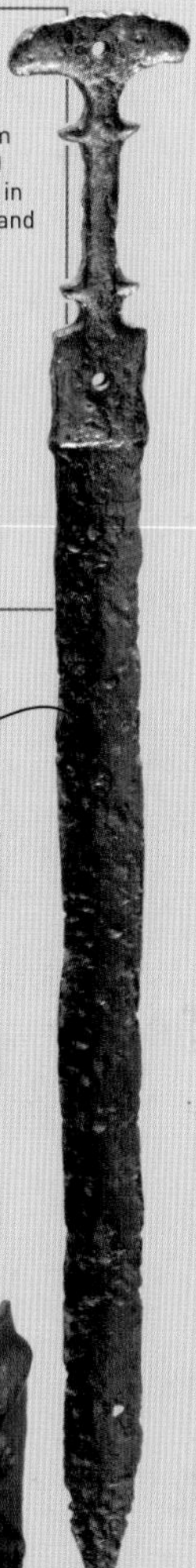

Celtic iron sword 2nd-1st century BCE.

Helmets and armor

Ancient armies found a way of offering the greatest level of protection possible to warriors, without compromising their ability to move. They wore bronze and iron helmets, in addition to metal plate armor that protected their torso and the most vulnerable parts of their body.

Etruscan bronze sword dated to around the 6th century BCE.

Bronze Celtic helmet 800-400 BCE.

Phoenician bronze plate armor 3rd century BCE.

Helmet of a Roman centurion fitted with cheek protection.

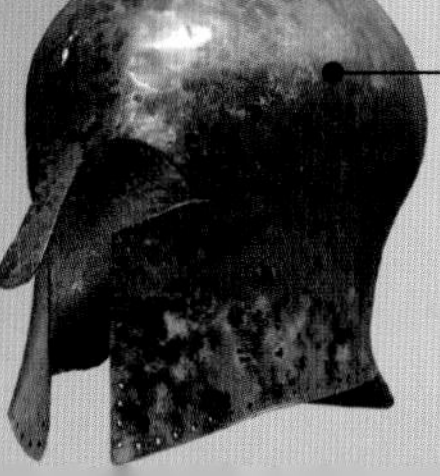

Greek greaves, leg protection worn by the hoplites, 5th–4th century BCE.

Corinthian Greek helmet from the 7th century BCE.

The Assyrian Army

From the end of the tenth century to the beginning of the seventh century BCE, Assyria was one of the most powerful states in western Asia. Its ability to expand its territories throughout the Middle East, from Mesopotamia to Egypt, was attributable to its military power. This was built around a very well-organized army, led by professional generals, who were efficient in attack and who used advanced siege techniques. The army was made up of around 100,000 men, among whom its powerful cavalry and archers were of particular importance.

Military superiority

Well known for their courage and cruelty, the Assyrians owed their military superiority to several factors. They were the first to establish military schools, organizing their armies perfectly, and they used iron instead of bronze, thus enhancing the resistance and durability of their weapons and shields. Equally, the capacity of their archers on horseback to shoot while galloping should not be overlooked.

CHARIOTS OF WAR
The Assyrians improved the chariots of war that were already commonplace in Asia Minor. The larger sized wheels and axles were capable of moving larger and heavier chariots transporting a charioteer, an archer, and two squires to protect them.

Cavalry The Assyrian army was the first to employ cavalry squadrons that included horseback archers.

Heavy infantry Formed by native Assyrians equipped with spear, shield, helmet, and armor, they represented the core of the army.

Siege machines

The invincibility of the Assyrian army led its enemies to reject out-and-out battles in open spaces, tending to take refuge in their fortresses. However, the Assyrians developed advanced techniques and siege machines that would become their most feared weapons. They constructed ramps on which battering rams and gabions were raised to undermine the walls.

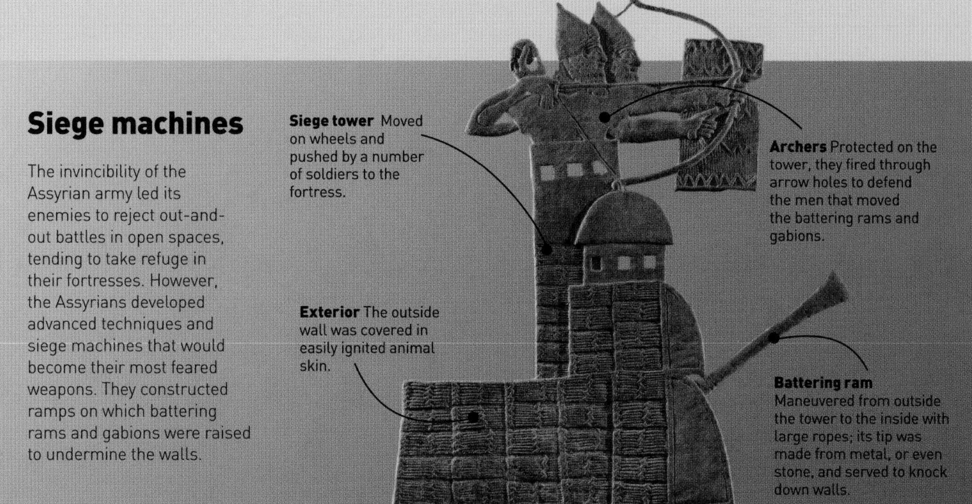
Siege tower Moved on wheels and pushed by a number of soldiers to the fortress.
Archers Protected on the tower, they fired through arrow holes to defend the men that moved the battering rams and gabions.
Exterior The outside wall was covered in easily ignited animal skin.
Battering ram Maneuvered from outside the tower to the inside with large ropes; its tip was made from metal, or even stone, and served to knock down walls.

Horses Initially two, then up to three or four, they catalyzed the Assyrians' power of attack. They were protected by thick fabric armor.

Uniform They wore scale armor made from metal to cover their torso, and a conical iron helmet.

Archers They traveled either on foot or on horseback. Their arrows had iron tips and had a reach of 2,130 ft/650 m.

Light infantry They served to support the heavy infantry and could use spears, bows, or slingshots.

Macedonian Army

Between 334 and 323 BCE, the Macedonian king, Alexander the Great, accomplished the greatest feat ever witnessed at the time: he conquered the apparently unassailable Persian Empire and created an even greater empire, the limits of which would reach the edges of the known world. His achievement was not only attributable to his strategic and tactical genius and his incomparable charisma and leadership, but also to the greatest army of the time, a military machine created by his father, Philip II, and perfected by Alexander himself.

Philip's legacy

To impose his authority on Macedonia and fortify his weak borders, King Philip II decided to transform his army, little more than a royal guard, into a highly efficient and prepared unit of men. He recruited all men of fighting age and submitted them to a strict training regime led by mercenary generals, involving both physical and tactical and strategic elements. The Macedonian phalanx, perfected by Alexander the Great, became the most powerful combat unit of the period.

LIKE A HEDGEHOG
The *sarissa*, an 18–21-ft/6–7-m long spear with a butt-spike at the end, was the weapon most commonly used by the Macedonian phalanx. The first lines lowered their sarissas to keep the rival infantry at bay, while the following lines progressively raised the tilt of their spears to deflect arrows and block the cavalry.

Leading from the front
Alexander was always at the head of the cavalry unit, at a position of great risk.

Battle formation

Alexander's army comprised three main bodies. The right flank was made up by the elite cavalry, the *hetairoi*, or Companions, who performed decisive maneuvers during battle. The center was made up by the Macedonian phalanx: a containment unit with 16 lines of *hoplites* armed with *sarissas*, accompanied by light troops, the *pezhetairoi*, and the *hypaspists* and *peltasts*, who protected the flanks. Finally, the light cavalry were responsible for defense on the left flank.

Hetairoi
The elite cavalry organized into squadrons of 250 units in a wedge formation.

Hypaspist
The royal guard protected the flanks of the phalanx.

Peltast
Light mercenary infantry employed in skirmishes.

Hoplite
Heavy infantry that formed the center of the phalanx.

Other weapons
In addition to sarissas, the Macedonian army used knives with forward-curving blades (*kopides*) for close combat and small bronze shields (*aspis*).

Mobile walls
Against the Persians and Indians, the Macedonians faced a formidable enemy: elephants. They overcame these giants with sarissas and other throwing weapons.

The Persian Army

For almost two hundred and fifty years (560–330 BCE), from the times of Cyrus the Great to Darius III, the Achaemenid Persian army comprised warriors recruited from different parts of the vast empire, in addition to a large number of Greek mercenaries. The army itself was immense, but it was poorly organized and too heterogeneous.

Decimal system

The Persian army was organized into units of 10,000 soldiers (*baivarabam*), divided into groups of 1,000 (*hazarabam*), 100 (*sataba*) and finally 10 (*dathaba*). The most important combat unit was the light cavalry, which was located on the flanks with the task of surrounding and attacking the enemy army. The most important infantry units were the archers, tasked with weakening the rival's defenses with a constant barrage of arrows, with the experienced Greek hoplite mercenaries located at the center of the line.

Heavy Infantry
Spears and shields were its weapons of choice. Its most revered units were made up of Greek mercenaries.

Heavy cavalry
They used javelins and a short sword, or different types of ax, as contact weapons.

Archers
They served to support cavalry attacks and tended not to enter close combat.

Light cavalry
The speed of its horses and the skill of its riders favored the use of surprise attacks.

Sparabara These Persian shieldbearers used light rectangular animal wicker shields that offered them ankle-to-shoulder protection. The sparabara were located on the front line and used 6 ft-6 in/2-m long spears.

Armorless Although they evolved over time, Persian warriors were basically great horsemen and skilled archers. The fact that they did not usually use armor can be attributed to this preference for long-range weapons over close combat.

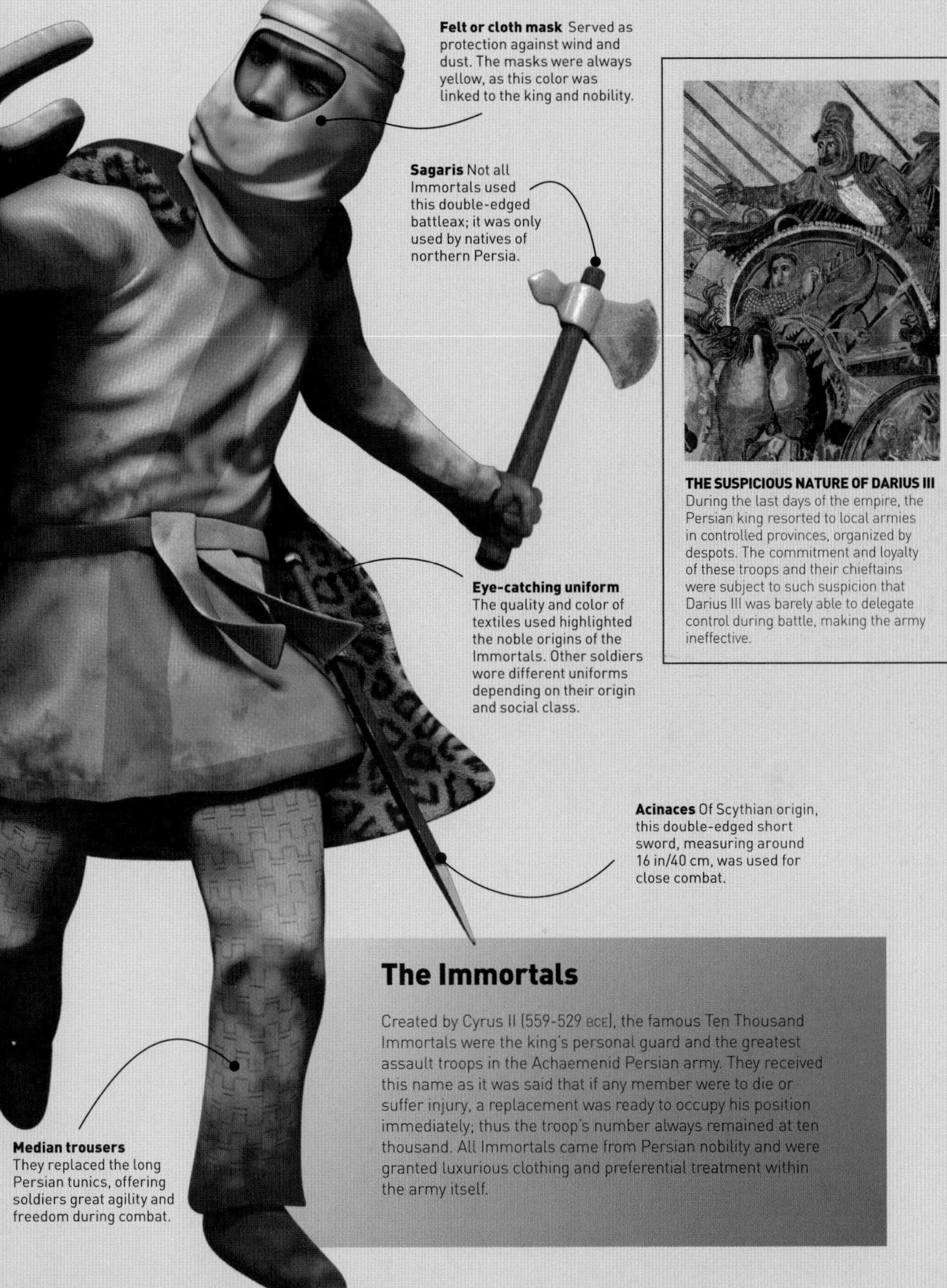
Felt or cloth mask Served as protection against wind and dust. The masks were always yellow, as this color was linked to the king and nobility.
Sagaris Not all Immortals used this double-edged battleax; it was only used by natives of northern Persia.
Eye-catching uniform The quality and color of textiles used highlighted the noble origins of the Immortals. Other soldiers wore different uniforms depending on their origin and social class.
Acinaces Of Scythian origin, this double-edged short sword, measuring around 16 in/40 cm, was used for close combat.
Median trousers They replaced the long Persian tunics, offering soldiers great agility and freedom during combat.

THE SUSPICIOUS NATURE OF DARIUS III
During the last days of the empire, the Persian king resorted to local armies in controlled provinces, organized by despots. The commitment and loyalty of these troops and their chieftains were subject to such suspicion that Darius III was barely able to delegate control during battle, making the army ineffective.

The Immortals

Created by Cyrus II (559-529 BCE), the famous Ten Thousand Immortals were the king's personal guard and the greatest assault troops in the Achaemenid Persian army. They received this name as it was said that if any member were to die or suffer injury, a replacement was ready to occupy his position immediately; thus the troop's number always remained at ten thousand. All Immortals came from Persian nobility and were granted luxurious clothing and preferential treatment within the army itself.

The Battle of Gaugamela

Fought in 331 BCE, Gaugamela was pivotal in deciding the fate of the Persian Empire. Having been defeated at Issus by the phalanx of Alexander the Great, Darius III gathered together a formidable army on a large plain close to the River Tigris. In theory, the land on which the battle was to be fought should have favored the Persian army, which included elephants and 200 crescent-shaped chariots. However, the Battle of Gaugamela would be the first historic example that power in numbers did not always guarantee victory.

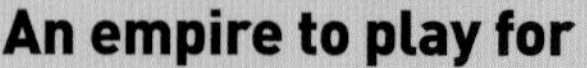

An empire to play for

Alexander knew that if he defeated Darius, the Persian army would crumble. The challenge facing Alexander could be seen in the significant difference in army numbers: Darius had created an army of 200,000 infantrymen, 40,000 horsemen, 200 chariots armed with scythes, and 15 elephants. The Macedonian army, meanwhile, numbered just 7,000 horsemen and 40,000 infantrymen. Battle began at dawn on October 1, 331 BCE and ended with Alexander's convincing victory; he masterfully guided his army against a disorganized and chaotic Persian army.

Alexander
Although he came within a few feet of Darius, he was unable to capture him.

1 Cavalry attack
Alexander launched a diagonal attack using his elite cavalry, in a wedge formation, on the left flank of the Persian army, which turned in defense. He was thus able to open an important gap in the enemy line.

Persian army

Macedonian army

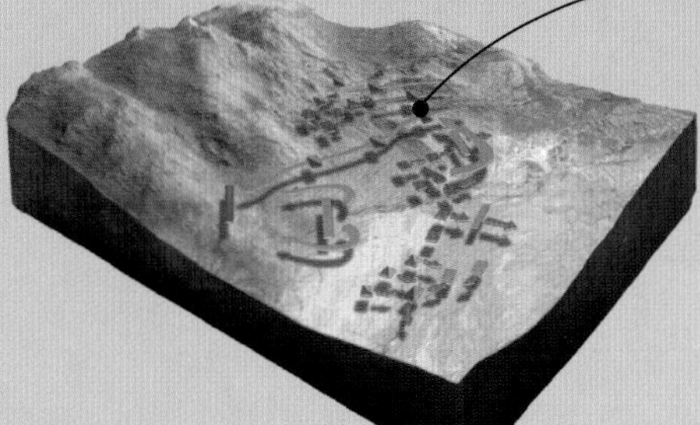

2 Decisive moment
The Macedonian general, Parmenion, had to contain the attack on his flank, while waiting for Alexander to provide assistance; although a large part of the Persian cavalry was able to reach the Macedonian camp, it was eventually turned back.

THE OUTCOME
Having destroyed the left flank of the Persian army, Alexander went in pursuit of Darius, who had escaped from the battlefield. This resulted in his army becoming despondent, thus leading to the destruction of its central core. Finally, Alexander came to the aid of Parmenion and sealed the fate of the Persians.

INVASION OF THE PERSIAN EMPIRE
Alexander defeated the Persians for the first time in May 334 BCE, during the Battle of the Granicus. He defeated Darius III yet again during the Battle of Issus (333 BCE), thus assuming power over Babylonia. He located and captured the Phoenician city of Tyre (332 BCE), and at the end of that same year, he conquered Egypt. Finally, the victory at Gaugamela granted Alexander control of the entire Persian Empire. His empire would eventually reach India.

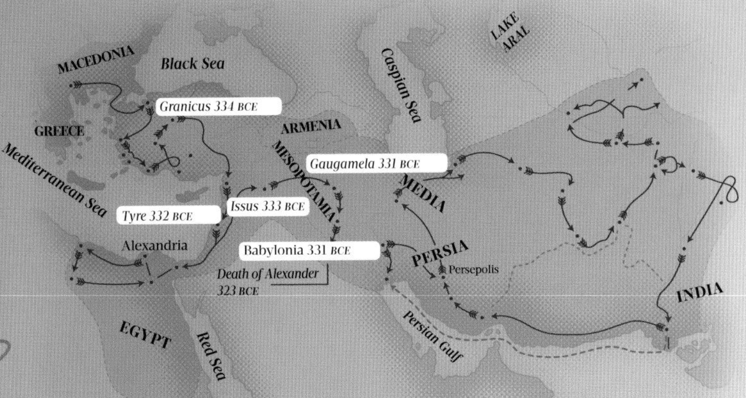
MACEDONIA
Black Sea
Caspian Sea
LAKE ARAL
Granicus 334 BCE
GREECE
ARMENIA
Mediterranean Sea
MESOPOTAMIA
Gaugamela 331 BCE
MEDIA
Tyre 332 BCE
Issus 333 BCE
Alexandria
Babylonia 331 BCE
PERSIA
Persepolis
Death of Alexander 323 BCE
INDIA
EGYPT
Red Sea
Persian Gulf

Lucky Darius He was able to escape from Gaugamela with his life, although just months later he would be betrayed and assassinated in Bactria.

Persian chariots They were an important part of Darius's plan, but they failed miserably. Nor were the elephants able to prevent defeat.

Persian infantry Greater in number, but less prepared. It comprised thousands of temporary recruits and peasants with little military training.

Hetairoi The skill of the Macedonian elite cavalry, commanded by Alexander, was crucial to the battle's outcome.

CUNNING
Aware that there were Persian spies among his ranks, Alexander spread the rumor that they would attack during the night, before the day of the battle. This kept the Persians awake and allowed his men to arrive at the battlefield in better condition.

The Carthaginian Army

Carthage was founded in 814 BCE in North Africa, close to modern-day Tunis. Between the fifth and third centuries BCE, it expanded throughout North Africa before colonizing the south of the Iberian peninsula, taking control of western Sicily and extending its territories to Corsica and Sardinia, creating an empire based on maritime trade in the Mediterranean. It would not take long for the empire to come into conflict with the other expansionist power—Rome. Despite its eventual defeat at the hands of the Romans, the legacy of the Carthaginian army has not been forgotten.

A unit of mercenaries

The Carthaginian army was built around mercenaries, the majority of whom were Greek or Italian, and soldiers recruited from allied or supporting populations. Among the Carthaginian generals, Hannibal, famed for being able to capitalize on such a hotchpotch army, is worth a particular mention. Far from creating a unified front, he assigned each group a specific role on the battlefield, depending on their own particular abilities and in line with his preconceived strategy.

THE CARTHAGINIAN FLEET
Control of the Mediterranean involved retaining a powerful mercantile and military fleet. The "quinquereme" (a boat with five banks of oarsmen) was the backbone of the Carthaginian armada. Its crew included up to 420 men, 270 of whom were oarsmen.

The leader The cohesion of the Carthaginian army was based around loyalty to the leader and the determination of its members to obtain their share of the spoils.

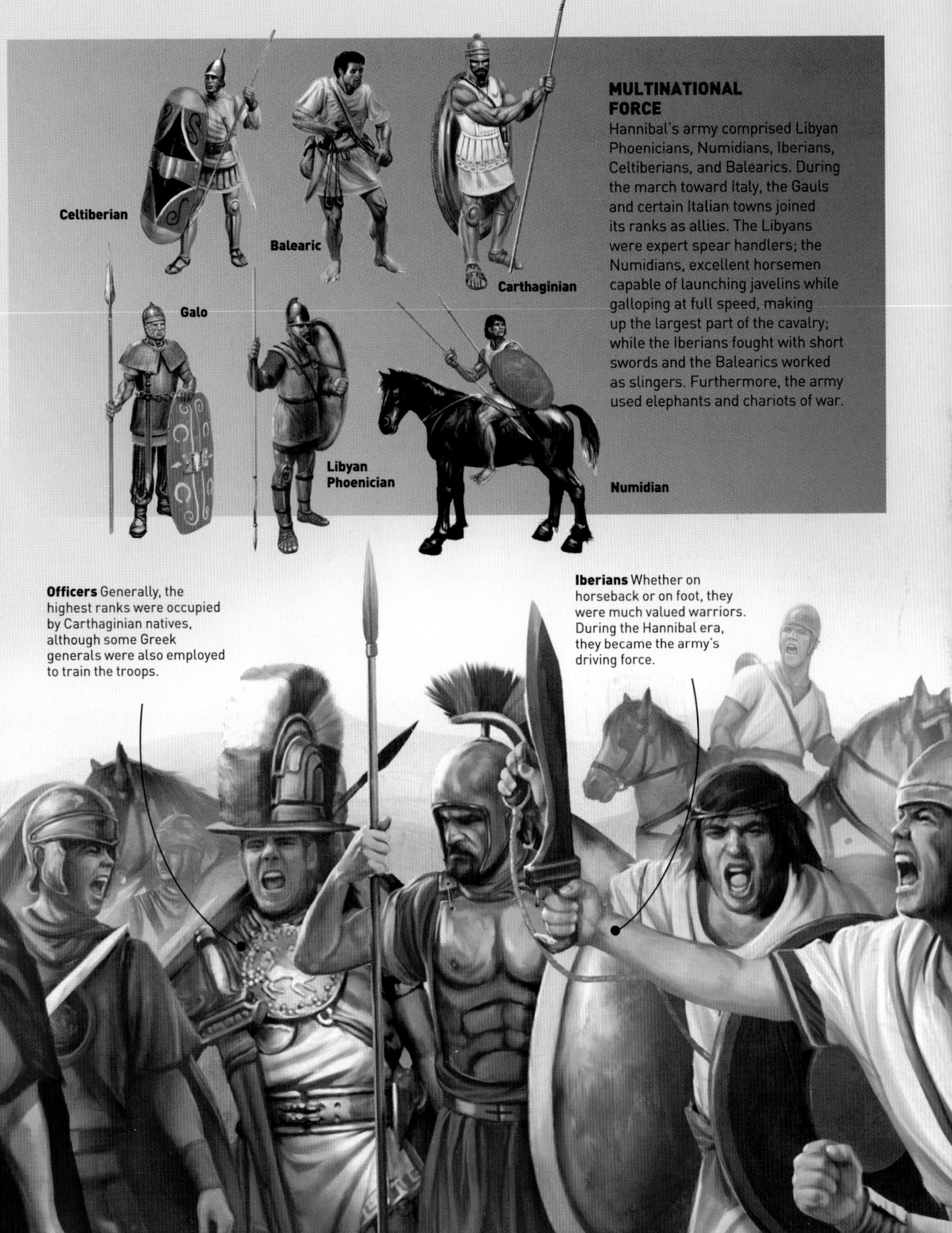
Celtiberian
Balearic
Carthaginian
Galo
Libyan Phoenician
Numidian

MULTINATIONAL FORCE

Hannibal's army comprised Libyan Phoenicians, Numidians, Iberians, Celtiberians, and Balearics. During the march toward Italy, the Gauls and certain Italian towns joined its ranks as allies. The Libyans were expert spear handlers; the Numidians, excellent horsemen capable of launching javelins while galloping at full speed, making up the largest part of the cavalry; while the Iberians fought with short swords and the Balearics worked as slingers. Furthermore, the army used elephants and chariots of war.

Officers Generally, the highest ranks were occupied by Carthaginian natives, although some Greek generals were also employed to train the troops.

Iberians Whether on horseback or on foot, they were much valued warriors. During the Hannibal era, they became the army's driving force.

Chariots of War

Around the second millennium BCE, Mesopotamian warriors used chariots of war for military purposes, pulled by draft animals. Initially, chariots of war charged and broke the lines of the enemy infantry, pursuing troops in retreat. However, as their design became lighter, quicker, and more maneuverable, they became a key tactical weapon in battle. They would eventually be used throughout the Near East.

The Sumerians

They are credited with having invented the chariot of war, in addition to using it for transportation purposes. Its use became more general in wars fought by the city-states of the region.

Type of wheels ▸ Solid wood

Number of wheels ▸ 4

Driven by ▸ 4 wild donkeys

Manned by

The Hittites

Modern-day Anatolia was the heart of this civilization between the eighteenth and twelfth centuries BCE. The Hittites perfected the light chariot and made it their main weapon.

Type of wheels ▸ Made from wood and iron

Number of wheels ▸ 2

Driven by ▸ 2 horses

Manned by

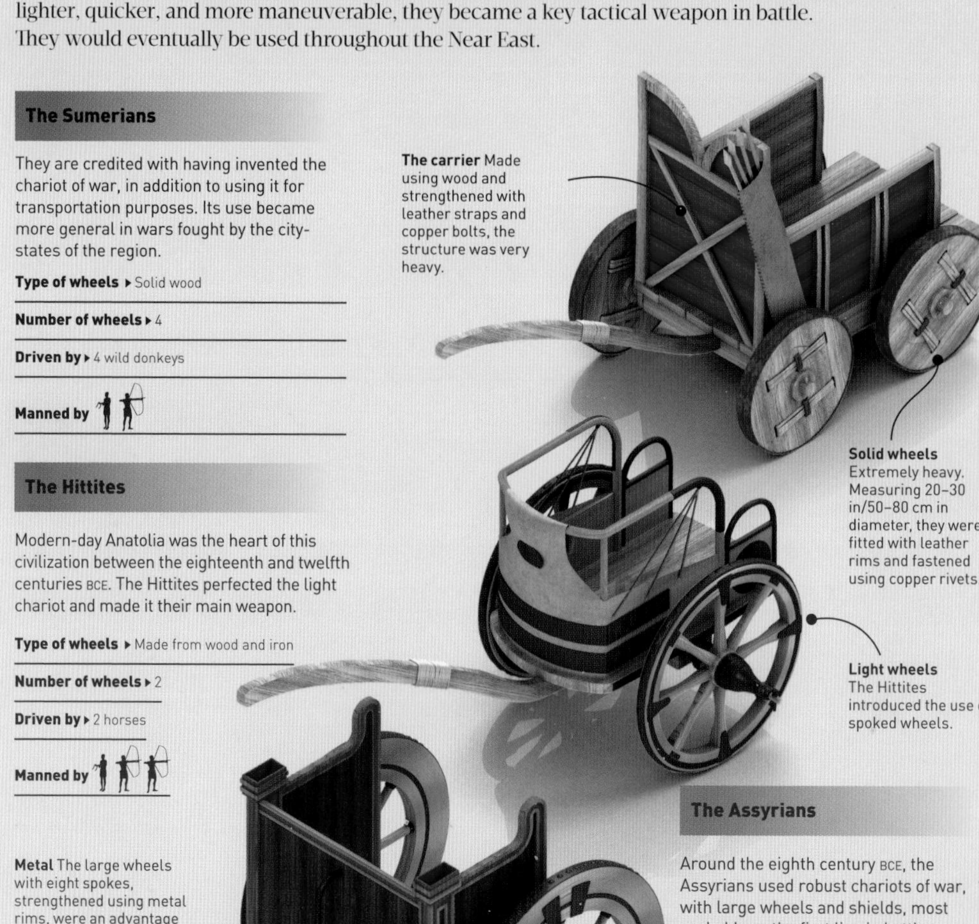
The carrier Made using wood and strengthened with leather straps and copper bolts, the structure was very heavy.
Solid wheels Extremely heavy. Measuring 20–30 in/50–80 cm in diameter, they were fitted with leather rims and fastened using copper rivets.
Light wheels The Hittites introduced the use of spoked wheels.
Metal The large wheels with eight spokes, strengthened using metal rims, were an advantage when facing the enemy.

The Assyrians

Around the eighth century BCE, the Assyrians used robust chariots of war, with large wheels and shields, most probably as the first line in battle.

Type of wheels ▸ Made from wood and iron

Number of wheels ▸ 2

Driven by ▸ 2, 3, or 4 horses

Manned by

The Egyptians

The Egyptians perfected the chariots employed by Hyksos invaders, converting them into versatile mobile platforms for shooting arrows and spears.

Type of wheels ▸ Made from wood and iron

Number of wheels ▸ 2

Driven by ▸ 2 horses

Manned by

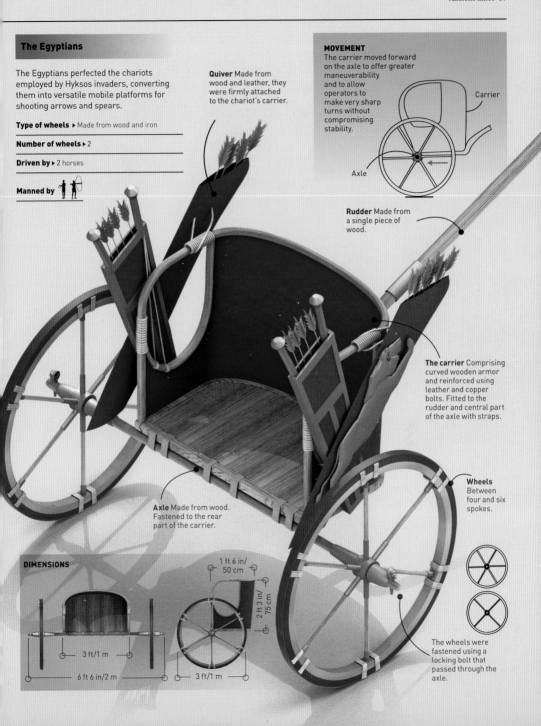

Quiver Made from wood and leather, they were firmly attached to the chariot's carrier.

MOVEMENT
The carrier moved forward on the axle to offer greater maneuverability and to allow operators to make very sharp turns without compromising stability.

Carrier

Axle

Rudder Made from a single piece of wood.

The carrier Comprising curved wooden armor and reinforced using leather and copper bolts. Fitted to the rudder and central part of the axle with straps.

Wheels Between four and six spokes.

Axle Made from wood. Fastened to the rear part of the carrier.

DIMENSIONS

1 ft 6 in/ 50 cm

2 ft 3 in/ 75 cm

3 ft/1 m

6 ft 6 in/2 m

3 ft/1 m

The wheels were fastened using a locking bolt that passed through the axle.

IN THE SERVICE OF THE PHARAOH

There is no evidence for the existence of an army as such in the Egyptian Old Kingdom. In this period (2686–2160 BCE) the troops formed a garrison to protect the pharaoh, whom the Egyptians considered a god. Their weapons were very basic–spears and maces with stone and bone tips–although the sovereign had groups of Nubians and Libyans who used simple bows. In the event of war, citizens in the provinces were enlisted.

Only in the Middle Kingdom (2055–1640 BCE), when the Egyptians ruled over all of Nubia and a large part of the Mediterranean Levant, was there a permanent army in which the soldiers were military men and not simple citizens. The warriors didn't mix with the civilian population, and the Theban pharaohs distinguished generals and soldiers by giving them weapons and symbols of honor such as the "royal golden prize," which was worn as a necklace. By then, the pharaohs appeared depicted as warriors, always accompanied by soldiers of noble rank who had weapons of copper. They used spears and axes made of copper, and bows and daggers, and they already had arsenals of darts and wooden shields, and a quartermaster to ensure the troops were provisioned.

Around the time of the invasion of the Hyksos, around 1700 BCE, iron, horses, and chariots were introduced into Egypt, although it wasn't until the New Kingdom (1551–1070 BCE) when these innovations were implemented by the armies.

There then arose a hereditary military aristocracy, and the army was organized into four armed forces under the protection of the great gods: Amun, Ra, Ptah, and Seth. Each unit had ten thousand men who went into combat surrounded by light chariots pulled by two horses, which made them practically invincible. They wore helmets, held shields, and had armor made from sheets of metal. They also used swords (the *khopesh*) and implemented the first war tactics: they chose the ground for the battle, lined up the troops, and attacked in square formations of one hundred by one hundred men, protected by chariots with one or two archers. The nobility and professional military men had bows made from pieces of wood fastened together with fibers and horn.

The most famous battle from this period was the Battle of Kadesh (1275 BCE), in which the troops of Ramesses II fought against the Hittites for the control of Syria and Lebanon. Ramesses recorded the event on numerous temple walls extolling their involvement in the combat, but it is certain that Kadesh remained in the power of his enemies after a peace treaty was agreed, the first ever recorded in history.

Egyptian Soldiers

For centuries, Egypt's geography acted as a natural form of defense. The Egyptian soldiers were conscripted farmers, but the invasion of the Hyksos (in the seventeenth century BCE), and the relative ease with which Lower Egypt fell, demonstrated the need to have a professional army. Upper Egypt learned its lesson. The expulsion of the Hyksos and the foundation of the New Kingdom brought with it a new well-trained and well-equipped army, which faced powerful rivals such as the Hittites and the Mitanni.

Arrows and spears

The Egyptian armies of the New Kingdom were made up of enormous formations of spearmen, supported by a similar number of archers, plus a formidable weapon of the time—the chariot. The way battle was fought by the Egyptian infantry was rather simple. The archers launched a hail of arrows at the enemy, after which the spearmen charged. After throwing their spears, they resorted to their handheld weapons, axes, swords, and maces, for hand-to-hand combat.

SYMBOLS OF WAR

The standard-bearer (*tay seryt*) announced the departure of the troops, carrying the insignias of each of the companies. The most common standard was in the shape of a fan.

Its function was to keep the troops organized.

It would usually take the image of a sacred animal.

MERCENARIES

The Pharaoh armies had mercenaries, the majority of whom were Nubians (below), famous for their skill as archers, and Libyans. The Nubians used special arrows with flint tips. The Sherden, one of the groups of Sea Peoples, acted as the pharaoh's personal guard.

OTHER WEAPONS

The Egyptian soldiers were trained to use all types of weapons, but they specialized in one in order to form companies.

Bow The compound bow, inherited from the Hyksos, was highly valued in the New Kingdom.

Dagger With a stone or bronze blade, it was a handheld weapon used by the archers.

DEPARTURE, CONSTRUCTION, AND COMBAT

The recruited soldiers were seen off from their native place as if they had already died because they knew they would never be seen again. They expected a tough period of training, marches in the desert, and hand-to-hand combat.

Spear Troops regularly used wooden javelins as tall as a man.
Armor Was made of several layers of flax, reinforced to protect against arrows.
Sword The khopesh was made of bronze and had a partially convex blade.
Arrows The tips of the arrows were made of flint or bronze.
Protection Made of toughened flax, it was rigid and as resistant as leather.
Shield Made from wood, it was reinforced at the front with leather and a bronze plate.
Ax One of the most common models used was the ax in the shape of an epsilon with a bronze blade.
Marches On campaigns, the troops marched an average of 11 miles/ 19 km daily in desert terrain.
Spear During the New Kingdom the tips were made of bronze or flint.

The Battle of Kadesh

In 1275 BCE, the battle of Kadesh took place between the powerful Egyptian empire and an alliance led by the Hittite kingdom. The objective was to dominate the routes and trade of the region, now modern-day Syria. Thousands of infantrymen and chariots did battle close to the city of Kadesh. There was no clear victory for either party, but it passed into history as being the first known great battle to use combat vehicles.

Risky maneuvers

The pharaoh Ramesses II, believing that he would find the Hittites more to the north, advanced with the Amun division. The Hittites, led by King Muwatalli, made a surprise attack on Ramesses' encampment and the unsuspecting Egyptian divisions. However, thanks to their quick reactions and their lighter, more maneuverable chariots, the Egyptians were able to repel the Hittite attack.

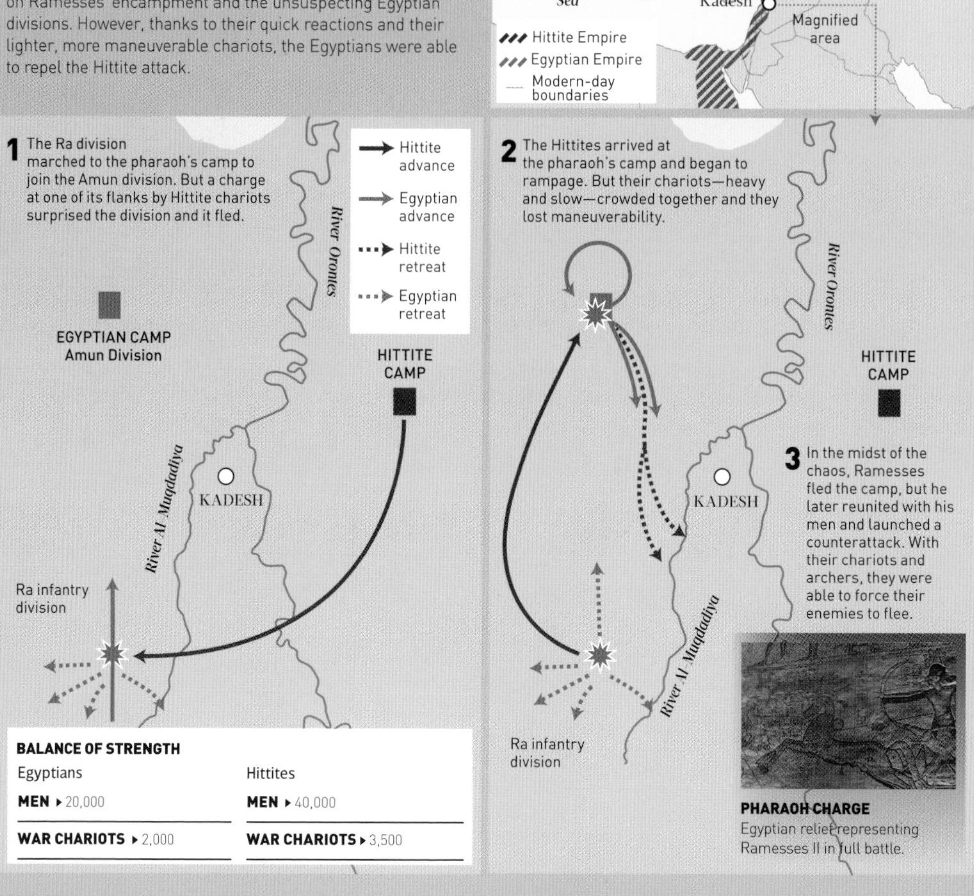

Mediterranean Sea
Kadesh
Magnified area
Hittite Empire
Egyptian Empire
Modern-day boundaries
1 The Ra division marched to the pharaoh's camp to join the Amun division. But a charge at one of its flanks by Hittite chariots surprised the division and it fled.
Hittite advance
Egyptian advance
Hittite retreat
Egyptian retreat
River Orontes
EGYPTIAN CAMP
Amun Division
HITTITE CAMP
KADESH
River Al-Muqdadiya
Ra infantry division
2 The Hittites arrived at the pharaoh's camp and began to rampage. But their chariots—heavy and slow—crowded together and they lost maneuverability.
River Orontes
HITTITE CAMP
KADESH
3 In the midst of the chaos, Ramesses fled the camp, but he later reunited with his men and launched a counterattack. With their chariots and archers, they were able to force their enemies to flee.
River Al-Muqdadiya
Ra infantry division

BALANCE OF STRENGTH

Egyptians	Hittites
MEN ▸ 20,000	**MEN** ▸ 40,000
WAR CHARIOTS ▸ 2,000	**WAR CHARIOTS** ▸ 3,500

PHARAOH CHARGE
Egyptian relief representing Ramesses II in full battle.

The result

Although the Egyptians were able to force the Hittites to flee, they were unable to take control of Kadesh. Some fifteen years later, both parties met again in the city to sign the first ever known peace treaty.

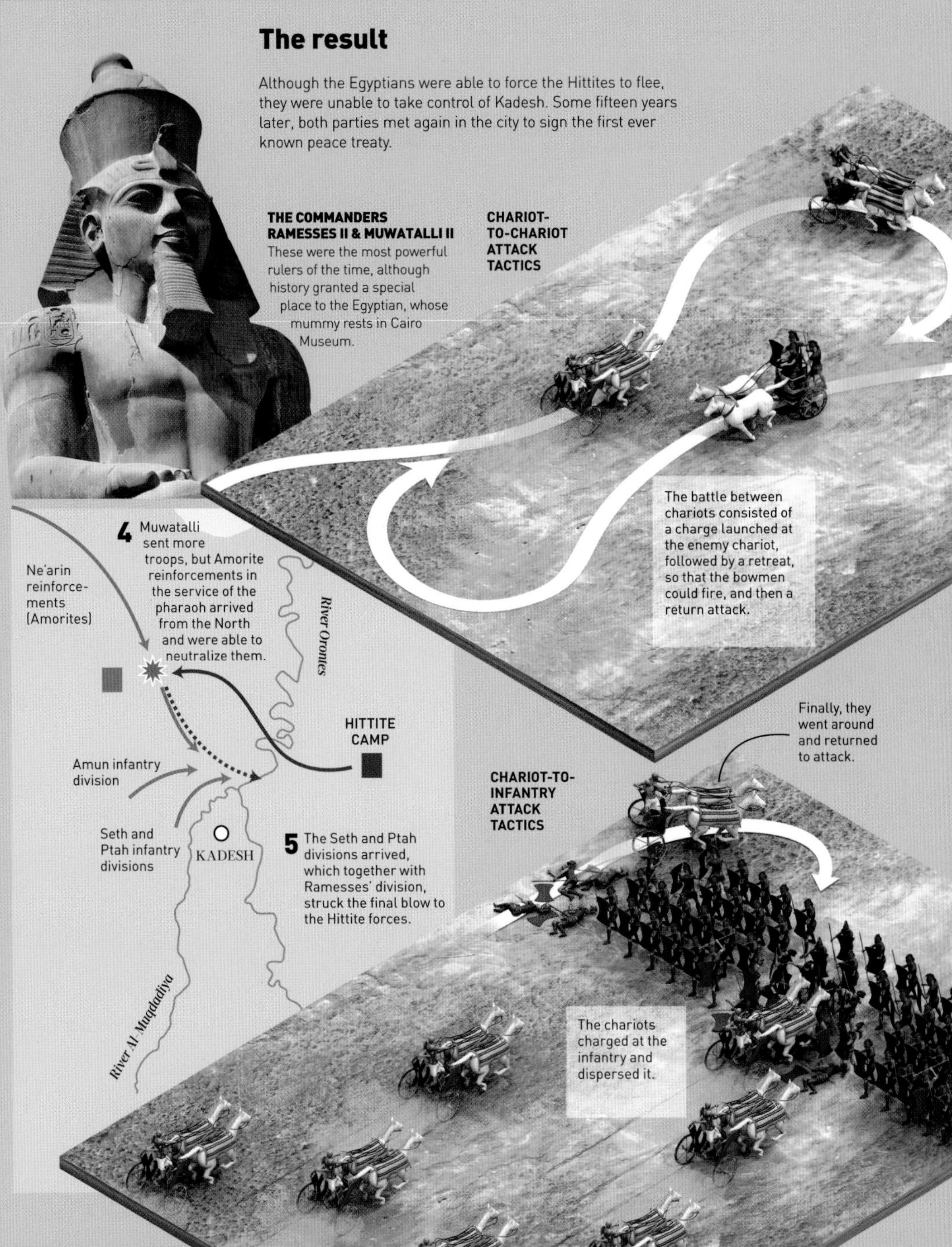
THE COMMANDERS RAMESSES II & MUWATALLI II
These were the most powerful rulers of the time, although history granted a special place to the Egyptian, whose mummy rests in Cairo Museum.
CHARIOT-TO-CHARIOT ATTACK TACTICS
The battle between chariots consisted of a charge launched at the enemy chariot, followed by a retreat, so that the bowmen could fire, and then a return attack.
4 Muwatalli sent more troops, but Amorite reinforcements in the service of the pharaoh arrived from the North and were able to neutralize them.
Ne'arin reinforcements (Amorites)
River Orontes
HITTITE CAMP
Amun infantry division
Seth and Ptah infantry divisions
KADESH
5 The Seth and Ptah divisions arrived, which together with Ramesses' division, struck the final blow to the Hittite forces.
River Al-Muqdadiya
Finally, they went around and returned to attack.
CHARIOT-TO-INFANTRY ATTACK TACTICS
The chariots charged at the infantry and dispersed it.

THE FEARSOME HOPLITES

From the eighth century BCE, with the emerging culture of *polis* (city-states), there arose in Greece the military practice as we know it in the West today. The Greeks, then organized into city-states, constituted a unique partnership of farmers and voting landowners, from among whom the hoplites emerged. They were, for military purposes, a society of equals, and were arranged into phalanxes, comprising rows of armored men who bought their own armor consisting of a helmet, greaves (pieces of bronze to protect the legs), a round, concave shield, body armor, a double-tipped javelin (the sarissa, which could be reused if it broke), and a short sword.

The hoplite fighting method of attacking, en masse and in hand-to-hand combat in the field, remained unchanged until the Greco-Persian Wars against the Persians (490, 480–478 BCE), of which the following battles are particularly noteworthy: the Battle of Marathon (490 BCE), in which Darius I was defeated on the coastal plain of Attica; the Battle of Thermopylae (480 BCE), in which the Spartans were defeated by Xerxes I; the Battle of Salamis (480 BCE), one of the great naval battles of the time in which the Greek triremes, fitted with a metal battering ram at the bow, destroyed the Persian army; and the Battle of Plataea (479 BCE), in which the Greeks lined up almost 70,000 warriors.

The size of the Greek phalanx varied: in the beginning, the Athenians, Thebans, and Macedonians fought with 16 rows of 256 men, which was a compact mass of 4,096 men; the Spartans fought with four, six and then eight rows, and, from the fourth century, they incorporated a body of light infantry–the peltasts–who fought in the wings or in the rearguard of the phalanxes, and psiloi–archers, slingers, and explorers who opened the battle, to cause skirmishes.

The Greek cavalry didn't arrive until much later. In fact, it was thought, in the words of Xenophon, that "only people of weaker constitutions and less desire for glory" rode horses, and the cavalrymen, usually aristocrats, were always at the service of the infantry, a tradition that would persist in the West for over one thousand years. It is known that in 476 BCE, Athens had 300 hoplites on horseback, in battle, flanking the footmen.

In the time of Philip II, the Macedonians had already incorporated special corps of men into the army, who built war machines such as movable bridges, called "ravens," to break the besiegers' rams, large assault towers on rollers with battering rams, and ballistae, from which they launched projectiles with burning cloth. Alexander the Great later introduced squadrons of 64 horsemen, called "cataphracts," into his army.

The Hoplites

The hoplites were warriors from Classical Greece, the soldiers who made up the typical formation of heavy infantry–called a "phalanx"–that dominated the ancient battlefields for centuries. The name comes from the hoplon (shield) they carried. Except for the "professional" Spartans, trained from childhood by the state in strict military discipline, the other Greek hoplites were volunteers who answered the call to arms when their city-states were threatened or exposed to armed aggression.

City warriors

The wealthier citizens, who could afford to pay for the military panoply, became the heavy infantrymen. Those with few resources fought as light infantrymen, harassing the enemy with javelins and slingshots. The value of the hoplites as soldiers and of the phalanx as a battle formation is evident in the wars against the Persians of the fifth century BCE, where their discipline and comradeship were key to defeating armies increasingly greater in number.

CLOSED PHALANX
A phalanx was between eight and twelve rows deep. Each hoplite covered himself and his comrade's side.

THE IMPORTANCE OF THE SHIELD
The strength of the phalanx was in the closed formation with shield against shield, where everything depended on the discipline and courage of each soldier. It was shameful to break the line of the shield in the field as it was seen as a breakdown of hoplite courage. Whoever broke the line left their partner defenseless.

Hoplon Had a layer of leather, one of wood, and one of bronze. It weighed up to 15 lb/7 kg.

THE SPARTAN EXCEPTION

The military state of Sparta immersed its men into a methodical military discipline from childhood. Professionals in war throughout their lifetimes, the Spartan hoplites were distinguished by their red cloaks and the letter lambda on their hoplons.

Sword The most common was the "xiphos," a double-edged sword with a straight blade.
Hair The Spartans were the only Greeks who had beards and wore their hair long.
Dory The spear measured between 6–13 ft/2–4 m. Rather than for throwing, it was used for thrusting. It had a leaf-shaped iron tip and a cone-shaped head to finish off enemies.
Kranos The helmet was made of bronze and the plume was of horsehair.
Tribon A red cloak, made of cotton or wool, used on marches and as a shelter.
Linothorax This armor was made from thickly layered linen reinforced with metal scales.
Handle It had a bronze clasp in the centre and handles made of cord or leather at the edges.
Pteruges This is what they called the strips of leather that protected the genitals.
Knemides The greaves were made of bronze and the insides were lined.
The letter "lambda" symbolized Laconia, the region of which Sparta was the capital.

The Battle of Thermopylae

In 480 BCE, one of the most famous battles in history took place. In the Thermopylae Gorge, in what is now Greece, a small army of 7,000 men, made up of an alliance of Greek city-states led by Athens and Sparta, defended this natural pass from the powerful forces of over 200,000 men of the Persian king Xerxes. The Greeks were eventually defeated, but the battle served to slow the invasion advance for three days, inflicting heavy casualties.

The price of glory

Knowing they were outnumbered, the Greeks forced the Persians to fight in the narrow gorge. Led by the Spartan king Leonidas, they managed to hold the position for two days, until they were attacked from the rear. Xerxes won, but his plans to invade Greece were frustrated for good after the naval defeat at Salamis that same year, and again the following year at Plataea.

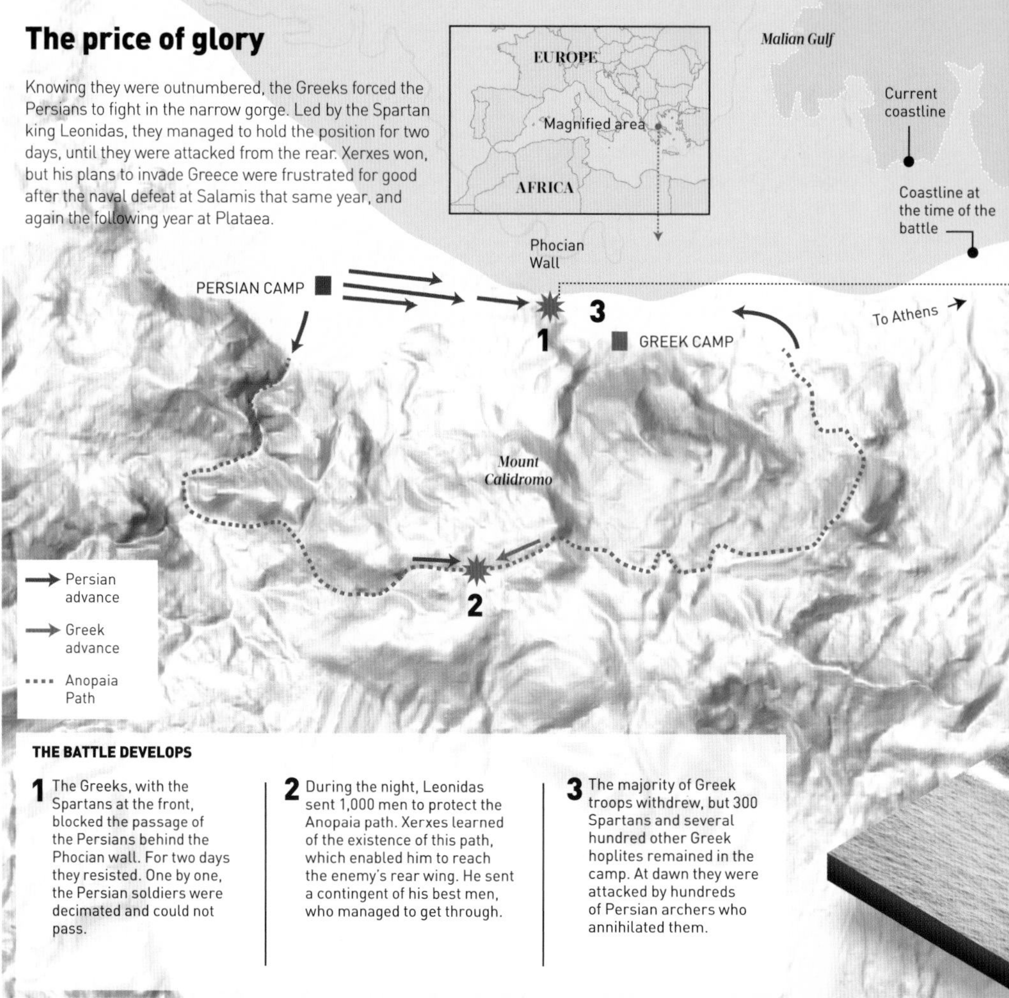
EUROPE
Magnified area
AFRICA
Malian Gulf
Current coastline
Coastline at the time of the battle
Phocian Wall
PERSIAN CAMP
3
1
GREEK CAMP
To Athens
Mount Calidromo
2
Persian advance
Greek advance
Anopaia Path

THE BATTLE DEVELOPS

1 The Greeks, with the Spartans at the front, blocked the passage of the Persians behind the Phocian wall. For two days they resisted. One by one, the Persian soldiers were decimated and could not pass.

2 During the night, Leonidas sent 1,000 men to protect the Anopaia path. Xerxes learned of the existence of this path, which enabled him to reach the enemy's rear wing. He sent a contingent of his best men, who managed to get through.

3 The majority of Greek troops withdrew, but 300 Spartans and several hundred other Greek hoplites remained in the camp. At dawn they were attacked by hundreds of Persian archers who annihilated them.

LEONIDAS
The brave Spartan king ruled his people for less than ten years. He was about 60 years old when he died at Thermopylae.

XERXES
Son of Darius I, he resumed the invasion of Greece, which his father had to abandon after being defeated by the Greeks at Marathon a few years earlier. He was about 40 years old at the time of the battle.

XERCES
PERS. REX

BALANCE OF STRENGTH

GREEKS

Men ▸ 7,000

Spartans ▸ 300

PERSIANS

Men ▸ 200,000

Immortals ▸ 10,000

Archers ▸ 5,000

A strategic pass

The Greeks chose the Thermopylae pass to neutralize the numerical superiority of the Persians. The narrowness of the land did not allow Xerxes to launch a large mass of soldiers or use their powerful cavalry.

Extended area (inverted)

Archers According to Herodotus, there were so many of them that their arrows "obscured the light of the Sun."

Phocian Wall In the Thermopylae pass there was an old stone wall. Leonidas ordered it to be rebuilt to protect the forces behind it. However, on the last day of battle it was almost destroyed.

196 ft/ 60 m

The Spartans Were a purely warrior people. Their long spears, helmets, and shields gave them the advantage over the Persian infantry.

The Immortals Xerxes' elite forces. They were decimated by the Spartans.

Malian Gulf

The Greek Triremes

Equipped with three lines of oars (hence the name *trireme*), Greek ships dominated the Mediterranean from the sixth century to the fourth century BCE. These warships were decisive in battles against the Persians. Thanks to their lightness and speed, they could easily maneuver into position to ram enemy ships and board them. In the decisive Battle of Salamis (480 BCE), some 360 Greek triremes defeated a Phoenician-Persian squadron of more than 700 ships.

The crew

Each ship was commanded by a *trierarch* (a wealthy citizen who was responsible for hiring and paying the crew). The crew consisted of 200 men, 170 of whom were oarsmen. On board, in addition to the officers and seamen, there were usually 14 soldiers: 10 heavy infantrymen and 4 archers. There was little space for provisions; therefore, they could only carry sufficient food and drink for three days.

Technical data

Length ▸	118–121 ft/36–37 m
Breadth ▸	11 ft/3.6 m
Weight ▸	46 tons
Length of oars ▸	14 ft/4.5 m
Average speed ▸	5 mph/9 km/h
Maximum speed ▸	9 mph/15 km/h

THE BOW
In naval combat, the ship rammed enemy ships with a bow ram, consisting of three bronze-covered wooden teeth. This opened a waterway or cut off the oars of oarsmen.

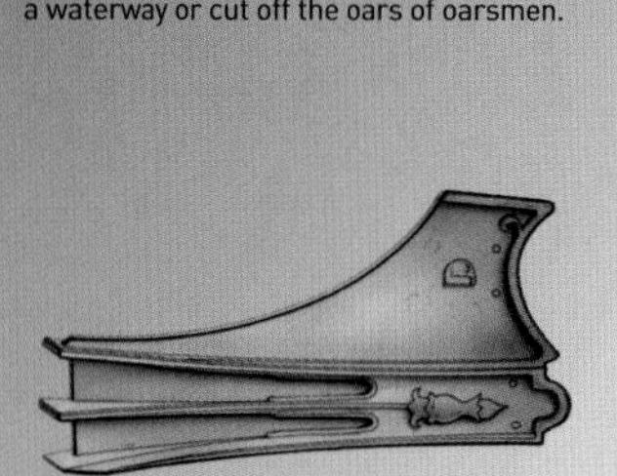

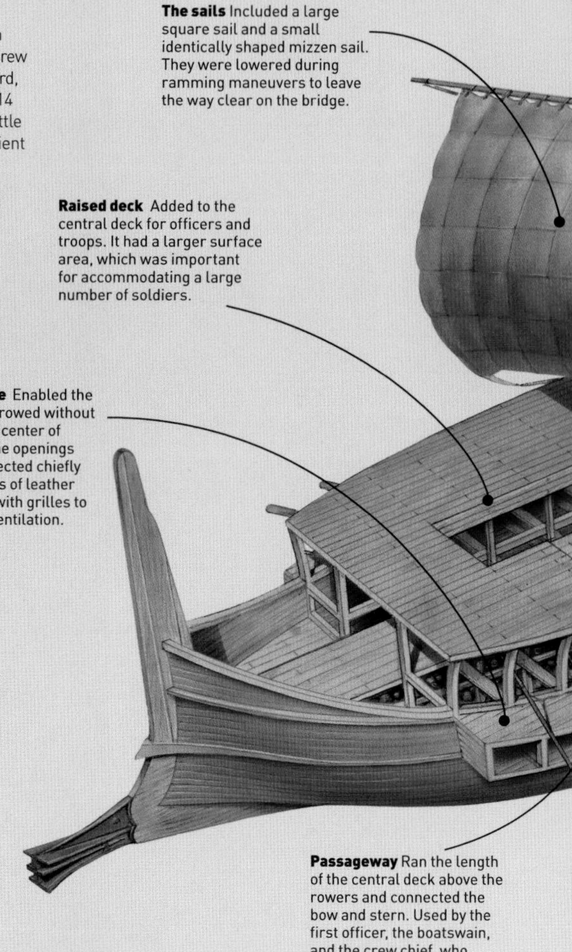
The sails Included a large square sail and a small identically shaped mizzen sail. They were lowered during ramming maneuvers to leave the way clear on the bridge.
Raised deck Added to the central deck for officers and troops. It had a larger surface area, which was important for accommodating a large number of soldiers.
Edge piece Enabled the ship to be rowed without raising its center of gravity. The openings were protected chiefly with pieces of leather and later with grilles to improve ventilation.
Passageway Ran the length of the central deck above the rowers and connected the bow and stern. Used by the first officer, the boatswain, and the crew chief, who regulated the rhythm of the rowing.

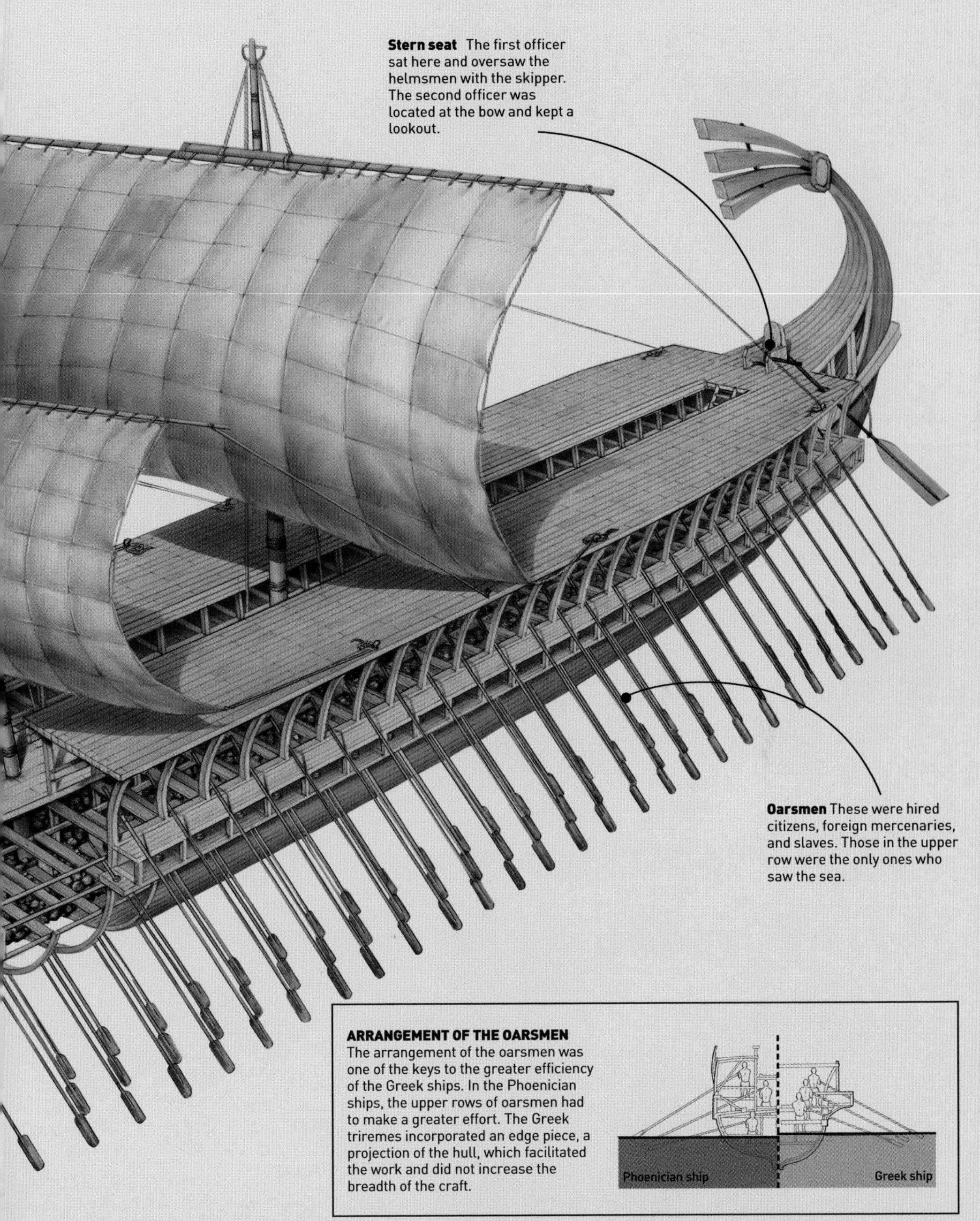
Phoenician ship
Greek ship

Stern seat The first officer sat here and oversaw the helmsmen with the skipper. The second officer was located at the bow and kept a lookout.

Oarsmen These were hired citizens, foreign mercenaries, and slaves. Those in the upper row were the only ones who saw the sea.

ARRANGEMENT OF THE OARSMEN

The arrangement of the oarsmen was one of the keys to the greater efficiency of the Greek ships. In the Phoenician ships, the upper rows of oarsmen had to make a greater effort. The Greek triremes incorporated an edge piece, a projection of the hull, which facilitated the work and did not increase the breadth of the craft.

THE FORCE OF AN EMPIRE

It could be said that Rome, which grew from a small city-state to form a giant empire in just 500 years between the fourth and first centuries BCE, was always at war: first with the tribes that inhabited Italy, then with Carthage and European peoples of the north, south, and west of its frontiers and finally with the Hellenistic kingdoms on the eastern Mediterranean. Its army, which initially consisted of military citizens, became professional over the years and had career soldiers equipped and paid by the state, and trained with strict discipline. They took the Etruscan phalanx model, and from this, during the fourth and third centuries BCE, they created the core of its legions.

The Roman army constantly evolved over almost one thousand years, and its structure became more and more complex over time, although the infantry was always its most formidable weapon. A legion had a total of 4,200 to 6,000 men who were divided into ten blocks, or "maniples," and arranged in three lines. First came the *hastati* (young men), in the middle, the *principes* who were middle-aged and, lastly, the *triarii*, who were the oldest and fought in the third position. They were equipped with armor, helmets with plumes, and a shield with a centerpiece of iron. The hastati and the principes were equipped with the *pilum*, a javelin made of wood and iron almost 9 ft/3 m long, and they all carried a short sword. The legions also used cavalry, made up of aristocrats, although this force would not become a secondary formation for a long time; one of its main functions was to act as the vanguard and rear guard of the legions while on the march.

The Romans were also experts in defining the roles of soldiers and officers, who were subject to a strict hierarchy. Generals, tribunes, consuls, prefects, centurions, and captains had clearly defined responsibilities—and through their training, discipline, remarkable strategy, and perfect logistics fostered by a growing economy, their military superiority was undisputed for centuries. They had roads, ports, fixed and mobile encampments, hospitals, doctors, and support services, as well as weapons and armor in great numbers. They also built a wide range of different siege engines such as towers, battering rams (nicknamed "tortoises"), and galleries to protect themselves from missiles. They used launching devices, which were very sophisticated for the time, such as catapults, onagers, and ballistae, capable of launching spears or weights of 110–220 lb/50–100 kg for distances of 1,300–1,650 ft/400–500 m. Added to this was the vast naval fleet, whose main ports were Misenum on the Bay of Naples and Ravenna, at the mouth of the River Po. From its ships, equipped with a tower on the deck, soldiers could launch projectiles at enemy ships.

The Roman Legions

The legions formed the heart of the conquering army that maintained the Roman Empire. Its superiority both in the field and during sieges is down to its perfect organization and strict discipline. The first Roman army was made up of citizens who served the state at certain times. It was from the second century BCE that it became a regular force of well-trained professional soldiers with an effective military strategy.

Organization

The infantry was the body of the legion and was made up of Roman citizens. At its peak, a legion could have 6,000 men organized into cohorts and these, in turn, into centuries. During the expansion of the empire, auxiliary cohorts (such as archers and slingers) were added, recruited from barbarian peoples without Roman citizenship, and cavalry squadrons who covered the flanks.

ATTACK FORMATION
In the fourth century BCE, combat training in three lines of infantry was established, with each line divided into blocks called "maniples," arranged in a checkerboard formation. Later, this arrangement was replaced by the ten cohorts in four lines. Legionaries, covered by their shields, advanced to within 50 ft/15 m of the enemy. Then they threw their javelins and continued to advance, sword in hand. On the centurion's command, the second line replaced the first, and so on.

Structure of the Legion

Legion ▸ 107 cohorts

Cohort ▸ 6 centuries

Century ▸ 10 conturbenia, commanded by the centurion

Conturbernium ▸ 8 men who shared a tent or barracks and ate together

Differences The superiority of the legions was not so much due to their equipment and weapons, which were similar to those of their enemies, but their strong discipline and the way they applied military tactics.

THE ORDERS
The centurion, promoted on merit, was in command of the century. Above him the officers were members of the ruling classes, whose function and number varied as the army expanded and became more professional.

Legate
Commanded the legion.

Tribune
Six per legion, responsible for choosing the soldiers.

Centurion
Commanded each century of the infantry.

Decurion
Commanded each unit of the cavalry.

Professionalism

Around 107 BCE, consul Gaius Marius reformed the army, opening the doors of the legion to the lower classes and equipping all legionaries with the same equipment and pay. Thus, the Roman army was transformed into a professional force.

Centurion Stood at the front of the century and managed the battle and daily life in the encampment.

Standard Carried by the *signifer*, with the symbol of the legion (each legion had its own symbol), it was used to indicate the position of the commander in the battlefield.

Signum Each century had its own standard, which was carried by a junior officer and used as a reference point for soldiers in battle.

Trumpet
Played by a *cornicen*, or junior officer, it served to communicate simple orders.

The Legionaries

The legionaries were Roman citizens, usually volunteers, who joined the army around the age of twenty in exchange for modest pay and a certain future. They enlisted for a period of 25 years, the last five as reserves. At the end of this long period of service they usually received a plot of land. Subject to tough training and instructed in strict discipline, they were the backbone of Roman military might.

Pilum This javelin had a metal rod with a pyramid-shaped tip that could pierce the shield and armor of an opponent.

Helmet This is a model from the imperial era. They wore protection for the cheeks (jawbone) and neck, and a shoulder pad at the front to protect against a vertical impact from a sword.

CIVIL AND MILITARY WORKS
The legionaries carried out many civil as well as military works. On campaigns, they built walls, strongholds, and forts surrounded by ditches and palisades. They built numerous public structures such as bridges, roads, and aqueducts over the length and breadth of the empire.

Sandals They wore leather sandals, called *caligae*, that were very strong. In cold climates they wore *udones*, a type of sock made from hide.

Belt The leather and bronze protection for the pelvis identified them as soldiers.

Gladius Short sword of about 23 inches/60 cm, designed for rapid thrust attacks in hand-to-hand combat.

LIFE IN THE ENCAMPMENT
In imperial times, the legionaries spent much of the time in the encampment, where they trained daily and carried out everyday tasks. They also patrolled and guarded areas at risk.

Tunic The tunic was made of wool and was similar to that used by civilians, but a little shorter.

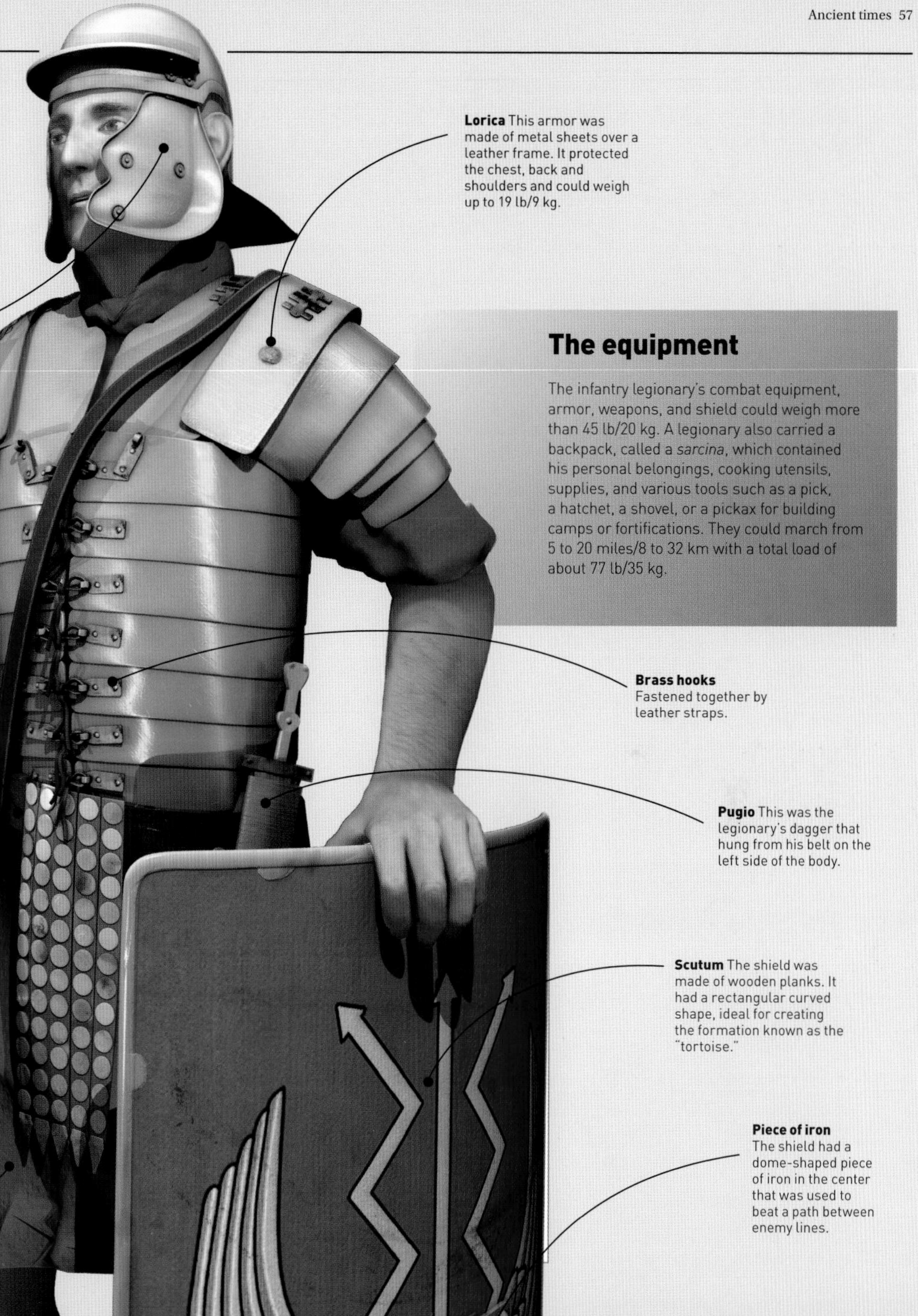
Lorica This armor was made of metal sheets over a leather frame. It protected the chest, back and shoulders and could weigh up to 19 lb/9 kg.
Brass hooks Fastened together by leather straps.
Pugio This was the legionary's dagger that hung from his belt on the left side of the body.
Scutum The shield was made of wooden planks. It had a rectangular curved shape, ideal for creating the formation known as the "tortoise."
Piece of iron The shield had a dome-shaped piece of iron in the center that was used to beat a path between enemy lines.

The equipment

The infantry legionary's combat equipment, armor, weapons, and shield could weigh more than 45 lb/20 kg. A legionary also carried a backpack, called a *sarcina*, which contained his personal belongings, cooking utensils, supplies, and various tools such as a pick, a hatchet, a shovel, or a pickax for building camps or fortifications. They could march from 5 to 20 miles/8 to 32 km with a total load of about 77 lb/35 kg.

The Battle of Cannae

This is one of the most famous battles in history. It took place during the Punic Wars, which pitted Rome against Carthage for control of the western Mediterranean. In 216 BCE, near the Apulian town of Cannae, one of the greatest military disasters in the history of Rome was played out. An army, much greater in number, was annihilated by a multiethnic force commanded by General Hannibal Barca. The strategy deployed by the Carthaginian leader is still studied in military academies.

The Italian campaign

In anticipation of the Roman plan to invade Hispania, Hannibal decided to attack the Romans on their own turf. He left Hispania, traveled through Gaul and crossed the Alps with 70,000 troops. Despite attempts to stop them from Rome, the Carthaginians enjoyed victory after victory. With a view to putting an end, once and for all, to the Carthaginian army, Rome recruited a powerful force of eight legions and took the battle to Cannae.

HANNIBAL'S TACTICS

At Cannae, Hannibal implemented a double encirclement tactic that destroyed the Roman army. This maneuver, also called the "pinch," consisted of a coordinated quadruple attack from the front, both sides, and the rear.

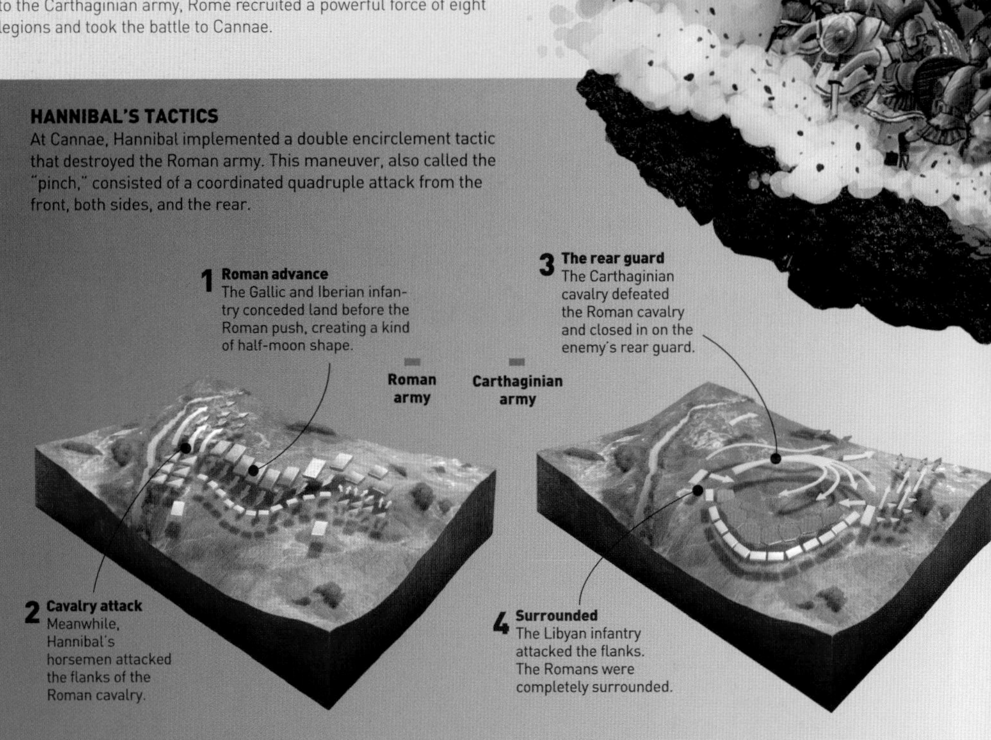

1 Roman advance
The Gallic and Iberian infantry conceded land before the Roman push, creating a kind of half-moon shape.
2 Cavalry attack
Meanwhile, Hannibal's horsemen attacked the flanks of the Roman cavalry.
3 The rear guard
The Carthaginian cavalry defeated the Roman cavalry and closed in on the enemy's rear guard.
4 Surrounded
The Libyan infantry attacked the flanks. The Romans were completely surrounded.
Roman army
Carthaginian army

Deadly phalanx The Libyan infantry of the Carthaginian army, arranged in a phalanx, crushed the Romans from both sides.

Nowhere to go The Romans were trapped without enough space even to use their weapons.

Mounted attack The Carthaginian cavalry emerged from the rear, preventing the legions from withdrawing.

THE PARTICIPANTS

Led by consuls Gaius Terentius Varro and Lucius Aemilius Paullus, the Romans had some 86,400 troops; 80,000 Roman and Italian infantrymen and 6,400 cavalrymen. Hannibal's troops comprised 50,000 Libyan, Gallic, Gaetulian, and Balearic infantrymen and 10,000 Numidian, Gallic, and Iberian cavalrymen. Hannibal lost just 8,000 men compared with around 50,000 Roman casualties.

ROMAN COUNTERATTACK

After the defeat at Cannae, the Romans avoided confronting Hannibal in the open field. They rearmed themselves and moved the conflict to Hispania and the African territories under Carthaginian domination. This forced Hannibal to return to Africa. The Roman victory at the Battle of Zama signified the end of Carthage as a power, although it was not completely annihilated until 146 BCE at the end of the Third Punic War.

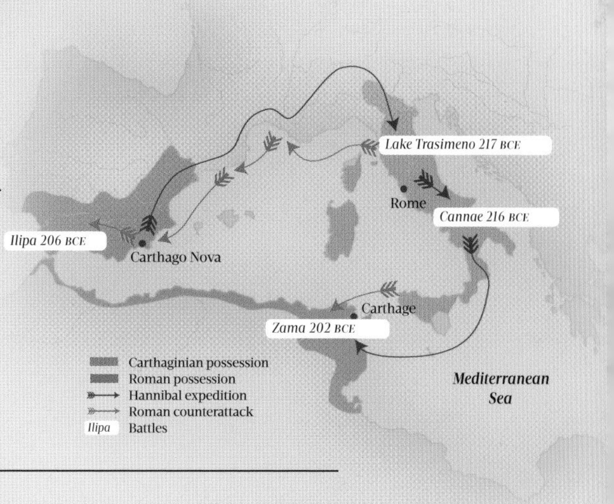

Lake Trasimeno 217 BCE
Rome
Cannae 216 BCE
Ilipa 206 BCE
Carthago Nova
Carthage
Zama 202 BCE
Mediterranean Sea

Carthaginian possession
Roman possession
Hannibal expedition
Roman counterattack
Ilipa Battles

The Battle of Alesia

In 58 BCE, Julius Caesar was named proconsul of the Gauls. His campaign there was successful: Helvetii, Germans, and Belgians submitted, and he carried out an invasion of the southeast of Britain. In 54 BCE, he faced an uprising of the Gallic tribes led by Vercingetorix. Vercingetorix was completely defeated at the Battle of Alesia in 52 BCE, in which some 180,000 Gauls were overcome by a force of around 60,000 legionaries. Alesia conclusively sealed Rome's conquest of Gaul.

The siege perimeter

In September 52 BCE, Vercingetorix, pursued by Caesar, took refuge with about 60,000 soldiers in the walled city of Alesia, to await the arrival of reinforcements. Caesar besieged the city by building an inner and an outer wall—a marvel of military engineering. The Gauls, trapped in the city, made four attempts to leave, but failed, while the external reinforcements also failed to break the Roman defensive lines.

Palisades The walls built by the Romans included palisades, towers, and ditches.
Defensive towers These defenses were used by archers and legionaries equipped with missiles.

CAESAR'S TACTICS

While the Romans were building the inner wall, a group of Gallic cavalrymen managed to escape in order to look for reinforcements. Caesar then built another, external wall to detain the reinforcements. When they arrived, the Romans were attacked on two fronts, but their cavalry were able to force the external reinforcements to retreat, and Vercingetorix had to surrender.

Roman troops

Gallic attack

Roman attack

1 Reinforcements External Gallic reinforcements arrived in the third month of the siege.

3 Roman attack In a desperate measure, 6,000 Roman horsemen left the walls and attacked the Gauls at the rear, who eventually fled.

Internal wall

External wall

2 Internal attack The Gauls who had taken refuge in Alesia launched attacks that were coordinated with those outside.

Fire and death The Gauls tried to breach the palisade by setting it on fire.

The Gauls The brave soldiers in their cavalry were their strongest asset.

MASTER STROKE

The inner wall was 13 ft/4 m high and had towers located every 400 ft/120 m. Then there was a V-shaped ditch, 19 ft/6 m wide by 19 ft/6 m deep, then another, 14 ft/4.5 m wide, filled with water, followed by a series of ditches with sharpened stakes, and finally a series of hidden pits with iron tips inside.

The Siege of Masada

The period between 66 and 73 CE saw the first of three Jewish revolts against Roman rule. After the fall of Jerusalem in 72 CE, some survivors took refuge in the fortress of Masada, next to the Dead Sea. The Romans, under the command of General Flavius Silva, set out to end this source of rebellion and began a siege and assault on the fortress in 73 CE. The besieged fortress resisted for two years and tested the ingenuity of the Roman legions in siege and assault tactics.

Roman tactics

To prepare for the siege and resist a possible ambush, the Romans surrounded the hilltop with encampments, walls, and towers. However, Masada had sufficient resources to resist for years. So the Romans went on the offensive. They built a ramp 1,950 ft/600 m long up to the walls of the fortress, and moved a siege tower onto it with a battering ram that penetrated the walls of the city. By the time they entered, most of the 960 inhabitants of Masada had already committed suicide. They found only two women and two children hidden in a water pipe.

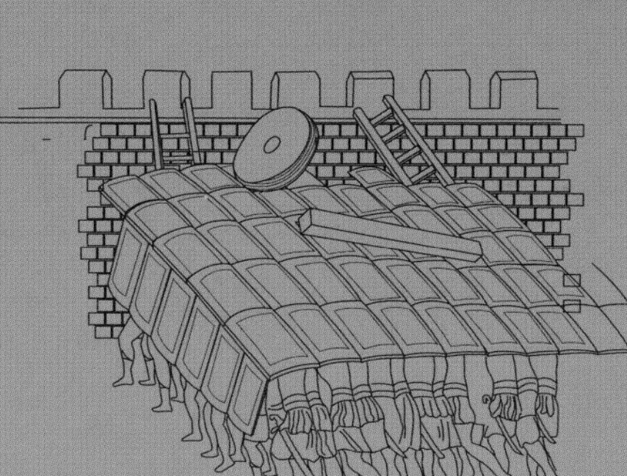

THE TORTOISE FORMATION
For the assault on the fortifications, the legionaries adopted the *testudo*, or tortoise formation, in which they overlapped their shields forming a compact protective barrier. Thus, as they approached the walls, they could withstand the hail of stones and arrows that were launched at them by the besieged occupants from the walls and towers of the fortress.

SIEGE MACHINES

The ballista
The smallest ballista fired arrows or javelins. The larger ones could launch stones nearly 1,640 ft/0.5 km.

The onager
This catapult launched rocks weighing some 176 lb/80 kg and flaming bitumen into the besieged city.

The scorpion
Could fire iron projectiles up to 1,300 ft/400 m.

The fortress Situated on a hill 650 ft/200 m high, it had two palaces, an aqueduct and was surrounded by walls 16 ft/5 m high with 37 towers, from which the inhabitants constantly harassed the Roman besiegers.

The siege tower The catapults were not powerful enough to knock down walls. To do this, the legionaries had to get closer to the walls and use the battering rams.

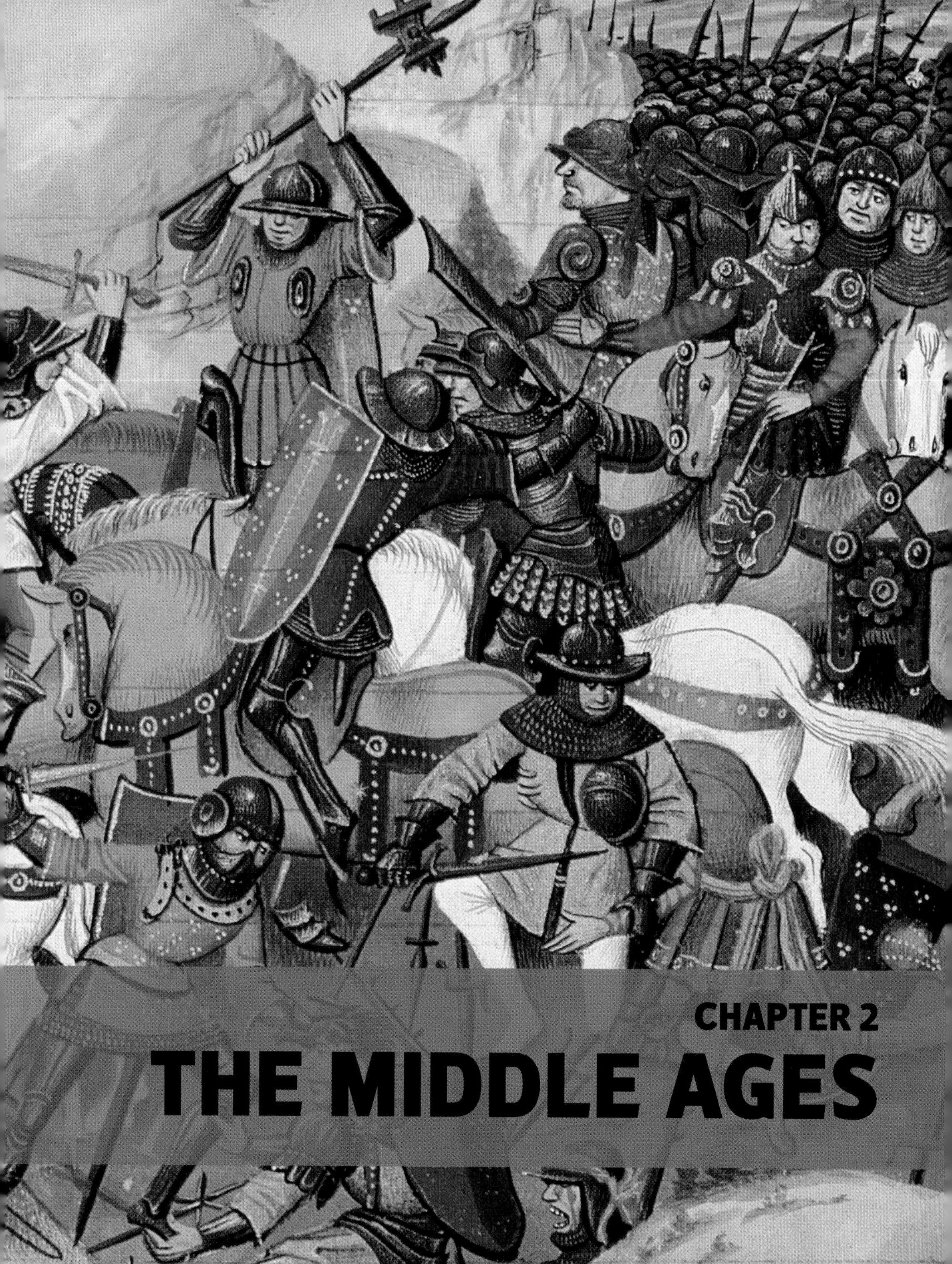

CHAPTER 2

THE MIDDLE AGES

ROMAN LEGACY

The essential aspects of the organization, strategy, and military tactics in the Middle Ages (which is divided into two periods: the Early Middle Ages, between the fifth and tenth centuries, and the Late Middle Ages, between the eleventh and fifteenth centuries) show that until the discovery of gunpowder and firearms in the fourteenth century, there was a surprising continuity with the times of the Roman Empire. In part, this is because the infrastructure that the Romans built in the West—walled cities, forts, ports, and roads—were still in a good condition up until the fifteenth century and later. The Middle Ages were a time of castles and fortifications, in which the siege system, liberation, and battle characterized the Western practice of war.

In the early centuries, civilians were frequently called upon to form armies. Nobles and kings of Roman-Germanic states conducted military crusades among their vassals so that they participated in military operations, something that was widespread throughout Europe for centuries.

In the Byzantine Empire, as in the Early Roman Empire, the size of armies was much greater than in the time of Julius Caesar or Augustus. In 300 CE, Diocletian commanded more than 435,000 men, and in 430, the Eastern and Western divisions may have had as many as 645,000. Byzantium, which in 503 had 52,000 troops in the war of Emperor Anastasius against Persia, had 170,000 men in the time of Justinian (527–565).

Between the seventh and tenth centuries, three cultures simultaneously dominated different parts of Europe. From the north, Scandinavian Vikings carried out a large number of raids throughout western Europe. They were fearsome warriors and excellent navigators, with fast and versatile ships. Their tactics consisted of a surprise attack, followed by looting and then fleeing. They dominated Iceland, Norway, Sweden, and Denmark and established themselves in Britain and Normandy. They fought using spears, swords, and axes and were protected by coats of mail and iron helmets. Their strategy consisted of a frontal assault in a formation known as *svinfylking*, or "boar-snout formation," where 20 to 30 warriors charged the enemy and were arranged in the shape of an arrow tip.

In modern-day France, after the fall of the Roman Empire, the Franks were able to take control of land from the northeast of Spain to Denmark, including the north of Italy. Under the rule of Pepin the Short and his son Charlemagne, between 774 and 843, the Carolingian Empire based its conquests on a heavily armed cavalry, who charged with spears at the ready. The army recruited some 150,000 men, of whom 35,000 were cavalry. The strategy was to keep their cities, conquer those of their neighbors, and equip their strongholds with permanent garrisons. The generals therefore had to minimize the destruction caused by their military actions.

From the Middle East, which saw the first Muslim state emerge in 620, a new society expanded rapidly in the Mediterranean and to the east, until it gained control of Asia. In 661, with the Omeya Caliphate in Damascus, the Arabs dominated all of Egypt, Persia, Syria, and Palestine, and in one century managed to conquer the entire Mediterranean coast of Africa and the Iberian Peninsula and reach the center of France. A new form of war, the *jihad*, or "holy war," an organized administration (they used camels to transport provisions and equipment), and a huge capacity for learning (they copied and improved Byzantine military techniques) enabled them to wage war with considerable success. Although the main bodies of their armies, particularly from the ninth century, were made up of slaves, their cavalry was fearsome and their archers skilled.

From the ninth century, naval warfare became hugely important. Alfred the Great of Wessex (849–899), King of the Anglo-Saxons, built special ships with 60 oars to defeat the Vikings, and the Byzantine armada was determined to keep its grip on the empire. Christian naval powers, such as Byzantium and Genoa, also equipped an army of 60,000 men who, between 1096 and 1099, went to the Middle East on the First Crusade, probably the most difficult and complex campaign waged by a Western army in the Middle Ages.

In China, the Tang Dynasty (618–907) organized a system of local militias for rural areas who served for one month in every five if they were 155 miles/250 km from the capital and two for every eighteen if they lived more than 620 miles/1,000 km away. There had already been a perfect organization of units of 1,200 men (Zhechongfu), 300 (Tuan) and 10 (Huo), who also worked on the land and were self-sufficient, although this system was abandoned in the eighth century in favor of full-time units. This was the system in the Sung Dynasty (960–1279), the army of which consisted of two infantry units—the *jinjun* (palace guard) and *xiangju* (border troops)—among which the Sheng Chuan (elite force) is particularly notable. The figure amounted to 1.26 million in 1041; and by this time many new weapons, such as the crossbow and several models of heavy and light catapults, in addition to explosives and incendiary weapons, had been invented. The first written mention of gunpowder was in China in 1044, in a document that mentioned grenades of smoke, incendiary grenades, and *pili huoqiu* (explosive grenades). The Sung first explored the incendiary potential of this material, then

its explosive capability and, ultimately, its use as a force to propel missiles from bamboo tubes, from which they launched lead bullets or bundles of arrows. They also established a significant navy, composed of hundreds of vessels, some of which were battleships. The Sung Dynasty ended with the conquest of China by the Mongol leader, Kublai Khan (1215–1294), who proclaimed himself first emperor of China of the Yuan Dynasty.

Kublai was the grandson of Genghis Khan (1162–1227), who united all the Mongol tribes in 1206 and created one of the largest empires in history, ranging from Korea to the Danube at its peak. He also formed the best army in the world between the twelfth and thirteenth centuries.

In Japan from the Heian period (794–1185), a warrior class known as the "samurai," who were heavily armed and sought individual combat, flourished. They used the *katana*, a sword that was considered to be the "spirit of the Samurai." Lightly curved and manufactured using many layers of iron and steel, it had a perfect blade and could cut a man in two. The samurai were superb horsemen and expert archers (they described their military vocation as "the way of the horse and bow"), and their sense of honor and high degree of preparation were legendary.

At the end of the European Middle Ages, the Hundred Years' War (1337–1435), the conquest by England and the defense and assertion by France, would open new avenues in the art of war. Major battles were fought (Sluys, Crécy, Calais, Poitiers, Agincourt, and Orléans), although the main tactic of the English was the cavalry raid carried out by armies of two or three thousand men, not against another army, but against the population, the economy, and the social structure. Fleets of warships and artillery also played a major role, although the bulk of the army was made up of paid soldiers, mainly foot archers and pikemen.

Chronology and Principle Battles

Throughout the Middle Ages, armies passed from the idea of the classic battle, a chivalrous confrontation between armies, to a war of conquest in which the destruction of the population was a key objective. Improvements in the design and manufacture of ships, weapons, and armor, and the invention of siege machines, crossbows, gunpowder, and firearms, changed the practice of war and geopolitics forever.

507 Victory of the Franks of Clovis over the Visigoths in Vouillé

555 Byzantine people destroy the kingdom of Theodoric and recover Sicily and Italy

568 Italy falls into the hands of the Lombards

614 The Persians occupy Jerusalem

642 Unification of China under the Tang

711 The end of the Visigoth Empire and the beginning of the Islamic conquest of the Iberian Peninsula

732 The Franks, with their king Charles Martel at the front, defeat the Arabs, Tariq and Musa, in Poitiers

768 Charlemagne, King of the Franks

778 Battle of Roncevaux Pass. The Basques defeat Carolingian troops

790 Viking raids in the British Isles

911 The Franks concede Normandy to Rollo, the king of the Vikings

929 Abd al-Rahman III is proclaimed the Caliph of Córdoba

1055 The Seleucids take Baghdad and control almost all the Middle East

1066 Battle of Hastings. The Normans are victorious over the Anglo-Saxons

500

1000

527 Justinian, Emperor of Byzantium

537 The Ostrogoths besiege Rome for more than a year

570 Muhammad is born

591 Byzantines conquer Armenia

630 Conquest of Mecca by followers of Muhammad

656 Split of Islam after naming Alí bin Abu Talib, a cousin and son-in-law of Muhammad, as Caliph

756 Abd al-Rahman proclaims Al-Andalus Caliphate independent of Bagdad

800 Charlemagne proclaims himself Emperor of the West

845 The Vikings head up the River Seine

960 End of the Tang Dynasty in China, beginning of the Sung Dynasty

996 The caliph Al-Hakim establishes Cairo

1000 The Vikings arrive in Newfoundland

Monument to Leif Ericson, discoverer of Newfoundland, erected in 1853.

THE ARMY THAT RECONQUERED GRANADA
On the Iberian Peninsula, the army that seized Granada from the Nasrid king, Boabdil, in January 1492 had one cavalry soldier for every three or four infantrymen.

The surrender of Granada

A YEAR OF SIEGE
Granada was besieged in 1491, but fell thanks to the skill of King Ferdinand, who sowed the seeds of discord between the Nasrids.

Genghis Khan and his family

1071
The Battle of Manzikert between the Seleucids and Byzantines, who are defeated

1095
Pope Urban II calls the First Crusade against the Turks

1099
The Crusaders take Jerusalem and establish several Christian kingdoms

1128
The pope approves the order of the Knights Templar

1147
Pope Eugene III organizes the Second Crusade

1180
Genpei wars between clans in Japan

1187
Battle of Hattin. Saladin reconquers Jerusalem and defeats the Crusaders

1192
The Minamoto clan establishes the Shogunate of Japan

1206
Genghis Khan unites the Mongols. The Mongol Empire begins

1241
Battle of Mohi. Mongol victory over the Hungarians

1258
Siege of Baghdad by Hulagu, grandson of Genghis Khan, and the end of the Abbasid Caliphate

1279
Kublai Khan, grandson of Genghis Khan, initiates the Yuan Dynasty in China

1280
Foundation of the Ottoman Empire by Osman I

1291
The Muslims take Acre, the last stronghold of the Crusaders

1304
First Arabic firearms

1314
Battle of Bannockburn. Scottish victory over the English

1339
The Hundred Years' War begins

1346
Battle of Crécy, in which the English defeat the French

1350
Firearms arrive in Europe

1368
Red Turban Rebellion in China against the Mongols. Start of the Ming Dynasty

1380
The Mongol leader Timur conquers Persia

1396
Battle of Nicopolis. Defeat of the Christian coalition by the Ottomans

1400
The European cavalry use full armor

1415
Battle of Agincourt. The English defeat the French again

1429
Joan of Arc defeats the English at Orléans

1453
Constantinople falls before the Turks

1488
Great Wall of China reinforced by Hongzhi

1492
Columbus travels to America. Conquest of Granada by the Catholic kings, ending the Islamic presence on the Iberian Peninsula

1500

The crusades in Jerusalem.

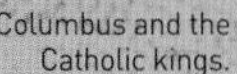

Columbus and the Catholic kings.

Famous Military Men

They fought in a time when armor had reached a high degree of sophistication and castles played a fundamental role in armed conflict, the primary object of which, in addition to the settling of scores between feudal lords or monarchs, was usually to acquire more wealth. In the Middle Ages, many kingdoms expanded their frontiers through military campaigns and became empires. Their leaders would enter history as great conquerors.

483–565

JUSTINIAN I THE GREAT
Byzantine emperor from 527, he took back the empire of Theodosius from the hands of the Barbarians. He put Belisarius in command of his armies, who occupied Naples and Rome. He reintegrated Italy through the Pragmatic Sanction of 554, making the bishops the civil authority of Rome.

747–814

CHARLES THE GREAT, CHARLEMAGNE
King of the Franks (768) and emperor of the West (800), he extended Frankish dominion over Europe. He conquered Italy, subdued the Saxons, and the Alans and Agilolfings of Bavaria. He fought the Slavs beyond the Elbe and won.

950–1003

ERIK THORVALDSSON, ERIK THE RED
Viking explorer, trader, and sailor, he reached the coast of Greenland in 982. In 985, Viking settlers arrived but conflicts with the Inuit and pirates and the distance from their country forced them to leave.

1138–1193

SALAH AL-DIN YUSUF, SALADIN
Symbol of refinement and chivalry, he recaptured Jerusalem from the Crusaders after his victory in the Battle of Hattin. Defender of Sunni Islam, unified the Near East, conquering Egypt, Syria, and Mesopotamia.

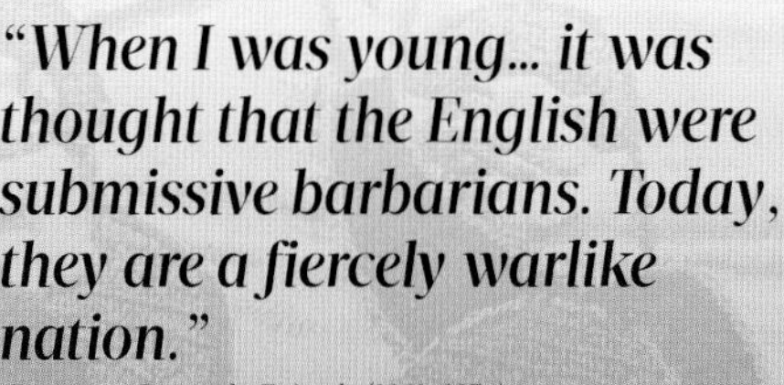

"When I was young... it was thought that the English were submissive barbarians. Today, they are a fiercely warlike nation."

Francesco Petrarch, Epistole (1361–1374).

NOT A SINGLE BUILDING LEFT STANDING

In the same text Petrarch wrote: "[the English] have reduced the entire kingdom of France with fire and the sword to such condition that [...] I thought I wasn't in the same country. Outside the city walls not a single building is left standing."

1154–1184

MINAMOTO NO YOSHINAKA

Japanese general from the Heian period and member of the Minamoto samurai clan, he rebelled against the Taira clan starting the Genpei Wars. He defeated the Taira army in the Battle of Kurikara and began the march on Kyoto. He was assassinated in Awazu by his cousins.

1157–1199

RICHARD I OF ENGLAND

Called Richard the Lionheart, he rebelled against his father along with the French in order to crown his brother Henry king, and failed. He left for the Crusades and, on his return, was named King of England (1189). He faced numerous rebellions, which he suppressed with an iron fist.

1162–1227

TEMÜJÍN, GENGHIS KHAN

Founder of the Mongol Empire, he united the nomadic peoples of northern Asia and begana series of conquests toward Europe and the Pacific. He controlled all of China, and to the West overcame the Khwarazmian Empire and reached Persia and Afghanistan.

1371–1433

ZHENG HE

Muslim eunuch under the orders of the emperor of China, Emperor Yongle of the Ming Dynasty. He commanded one of the largest fleets in history, the "Treasure Fleet," which transported 30,000 people on each trip. The "Treasure Ships" measured 400 ft/120 m long and 160 ft/50 m wide.

Medieval Weapons

In the battlefields of the Middle Ages, increasingly perfected forms of spears, maces, axes, and bows and arrows were used, and from the twelfth century the crossbow, a fearsome weapon, appeared. The sword, the weapon of choice of the cavalry who were protected with heavy armor, was also a symbol of prestige. Although the first firearms appeared in the fourteenth century, it wasn't until the following century that they played a significant role in war.

Swords

The sword was a weapon par excellence for the cavalry and a valuable possession for medieval warriors. In the early periods they were heavy and blunt, but with the continual improvements to weaponry, the sword became longer and sharper. Its manufacture was a real art in the manipulation of metals that conferred a distinctive status and standing.

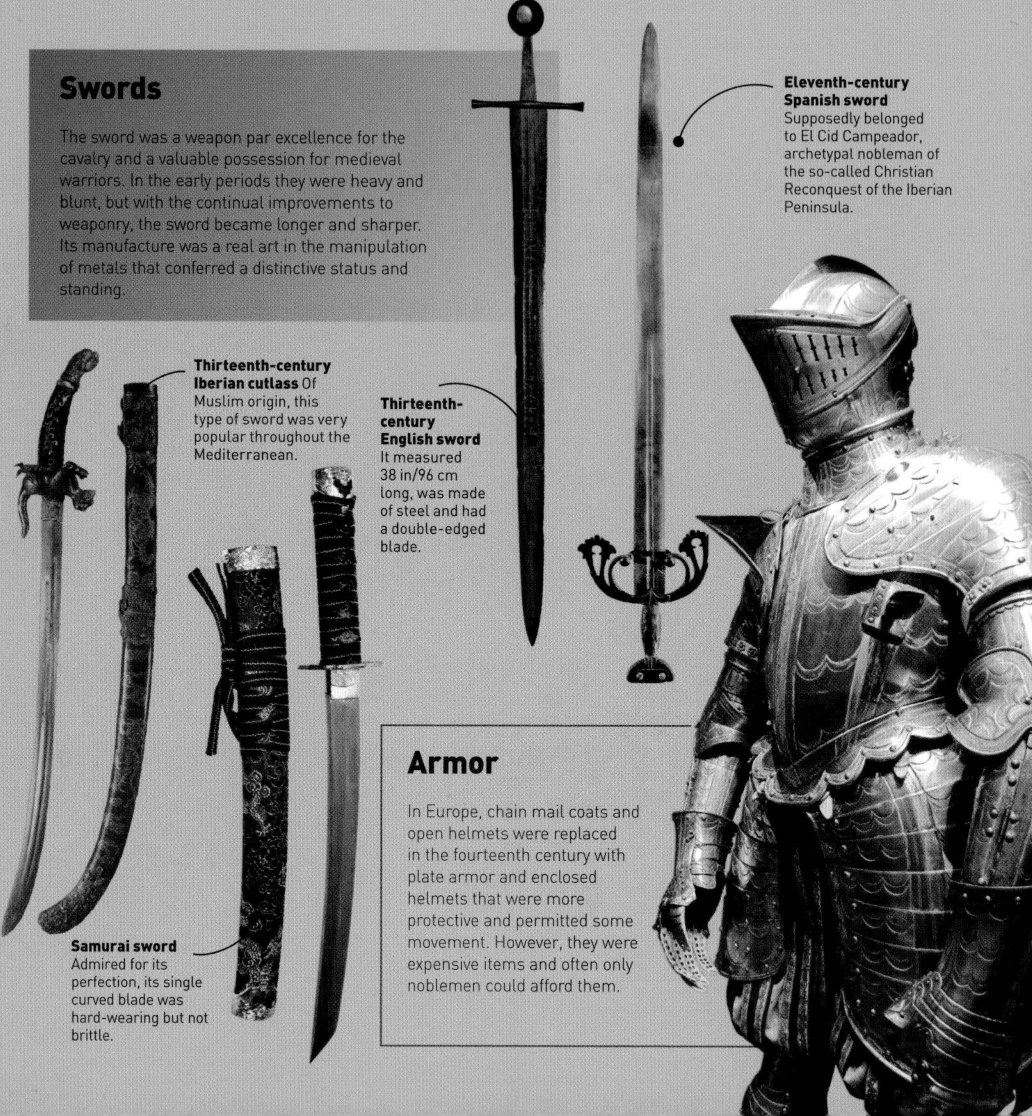

Eleventh-century Spanish sword Supposedly belonged to El Cid Campeador, archetypal nobleman of the so-called Christian Reconquest of the Iberian Peninsula.

Thirteenth-century Iberian cutlass Of Muslim origin, this type of sword was very popular throughout the Mediterranean.

Thirteenth-century English sword It measured 38 in/96 cm long, was made of steel and had a double-edged blade.

Samurai sword Admired for its perfection, its single curved blade was hard-wearing but not brittle.

Armor

In Europe, chain mail coats and open helmets were replaced in the fourteenth century with plate armor and enclosed helmets that were more protective and permitted some movement. However, they were expensive items and often only noblemen could afford them.

Crossbows, bows, and arrows

Crossbows, originating in China, quickly spread west from the twelfth century and became a key weapon in battle and in the defense of fortresses. The archers, either on horseback or on foot, were a key part of the medieval army, firing accurate projectiles or destroying the enemy with a hail of arrows.

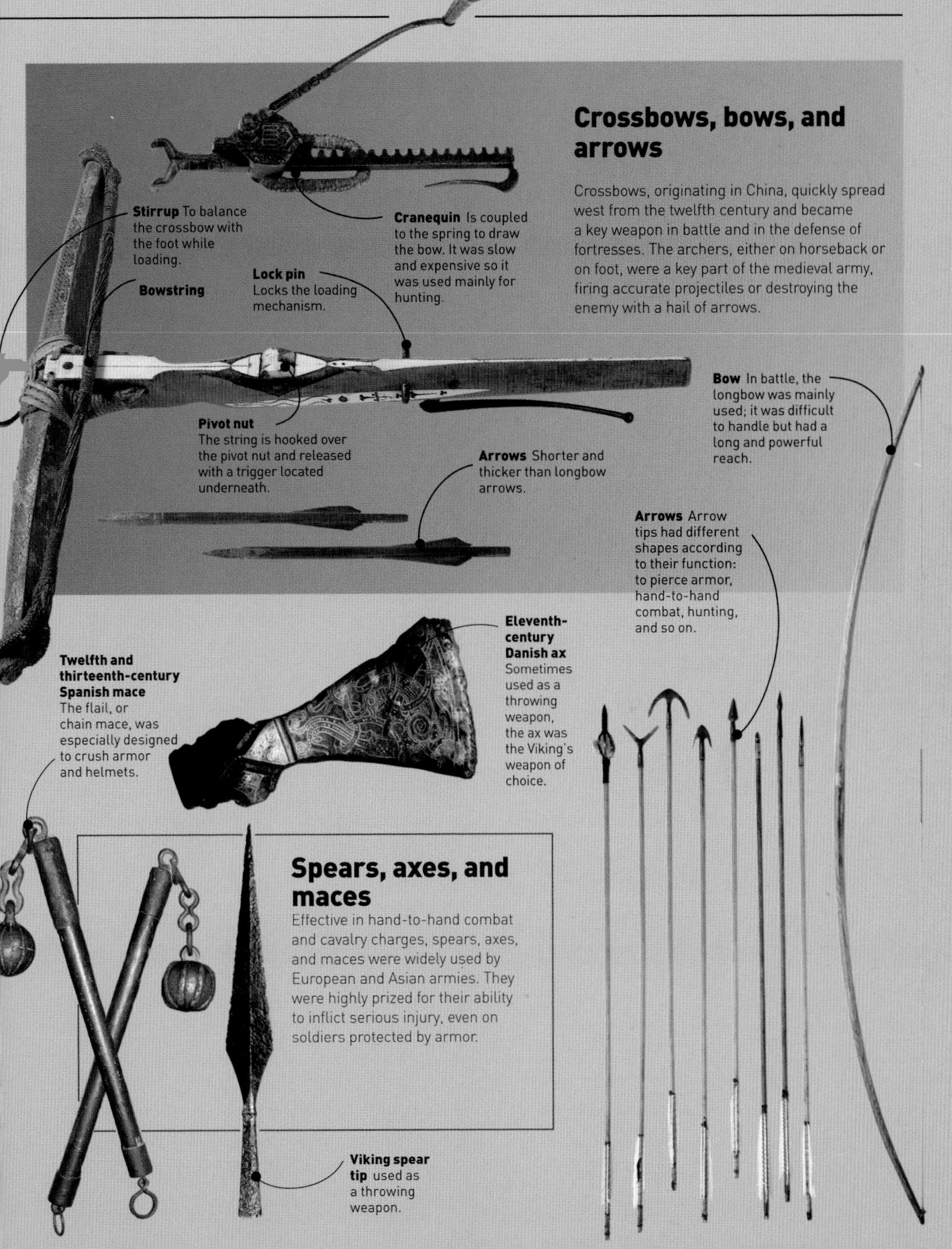
Stirrup To balance the crossbow with the foot while loading.
Bowstring
Lock pin Locks the loading mechanism.
Cranequin Is coupled to the spring to draw the bow. It was slow and expensive so it was used mainly for hunting.
Pivot nut The string is hooked over the pivot nut and released with a trigger located underneath.
Arrows Shorter and thicker than longbow arrows.
Bow In battle, the longbow was mainly used; it was difficult to handle but had a long and powerful reach.
Arrows Arrow tips had different shapes according to their function: to pierce armor, hand-to-hand combat, hunting, and so on.
Eleventh-century Danish ax Sometimes used as a throwing weapon, the ax was the Viking's weapon of choice.
Twelfth and thirteenth-century Spanish mace The flail, or chain mace, was especially designed to crush armor and helmets.
Viking spear tip used as a throwing weapon.

Spears, axes, and maces

Effective in hand-to-hand combat and cavalry charges, spears, axes, and maces were widely used by European and Asian armies. They were highly prized for their ability to inflict serious injury, even on soldiers protected by armor.

The Castle

Castles were the fortified residences of kings, noblemen, and lords. They were usually built on high ground as a strategic measure to control and contain external threats and attacks. The castle also served as a refuge for the peasants of the manor in the event of armed aggression and prolonged sieges. From the thirteenth century, the progress of offensive weapons used by the besiegers forced the structure of the interior of the castles to be changed and their defense systems improved.

The keep This was the main tower and served as the residence for the lord and his family. Their riches were stored in the lower section.
Wall The entire enclosure was surrounded by a high, thick wall. Its towers and battlements had holes from which to shoot at the enemy.
Drawbridge Often the castle was surrounded by a moat to prevent access by the enemy, and could only be entered via a drawbridge.
Circular towers The floors were accessed by a spiral staircase that descended to the basement. Many towers had their own well in order not to depend on the outside.

MANTLETS

The gaps in the battlements left soldiers on the walkway exposed. This problem was resolved during the thirteenth century with the creation of shutters or mantlets—barriers usually made of wood or metal that could be fixed or removable.

Fixed wooden mantlet
Iron, detachable
Wood, detachable
Walkway Narrow walkway on top of the wall. Allowed sentinels to keep watch over the outside and to organize themselves in the event of an attack.
Parade ground Central space of the castle from where the rest of the rooms were accessed—among which were the chapel and the stables or armory.
Bread oven Located within the castle to ensure there was a supply of bread in the event of attack.

English Archers

The Middle Ages was a time of knights armed to the teeth and protected by armor that could weigh up to 66 lb/30 kg. Although they appeared to be invincible, there was one weapon, identified with the lower classes, that could dismantle the pride of an aristocratic knight—the longbow. It was used for the first time as a weapon of war by the Welsh at the end of the twelfth century. In the following century it became part of English army weaponry, and in the fourteenth century it became the national weapon of the British Isles.

Rain of death

The day before combat, the archers set up reference posts that enabled them to calibrate distances on the battlefield. The head of the line had a spear with notches in it indicating the angle of shot required in order to reach the posts. When the enemy reached the first mark, the head of the line used his spear to place his bow at the correct angle and gave the order to fire. In this way, they unleashed a rain of arrows with deadly effectiveness. First, they tried to reach the horses, since the fallen rider was immobilized by the weight of his armor and became easy prey.

HISTORICAL VICTORIES
During the Hundred Years' War, English archers defeated enormous armies of French knights in the battles of Crécy (1346), Poitiers (1365), and Agincourt (1415). However, by the sixteenth century, the archers had practically disappeared from the battlefield, coinciding with the spread of firearms.

GENERAL CHARACTERISTICS

The archers' effect during battle was devastating. Jean Froissart, chronicler of the Battle of Crécy, described it thus: "They fired so many arrows and so many together that it looked as if it was snowing."

The St. George's Cross flag of England.

The colours of the French crown in the Battle of Crécy.

Campaign divisions ▸ 1

Number per division ▸ Between 5,000 and 7,000

Firing speed ▸ An expert archer could fire 12 arrows per minute

In combat ▸ They preferred to be at the sides to have a greater shooting range, or on uneven ground so that better-protected opponents could not reach them.

ARROW TIPS
Arrows with long tips penetrated the knights' armor, while barbed tips were used against infantry and at smaller distances.

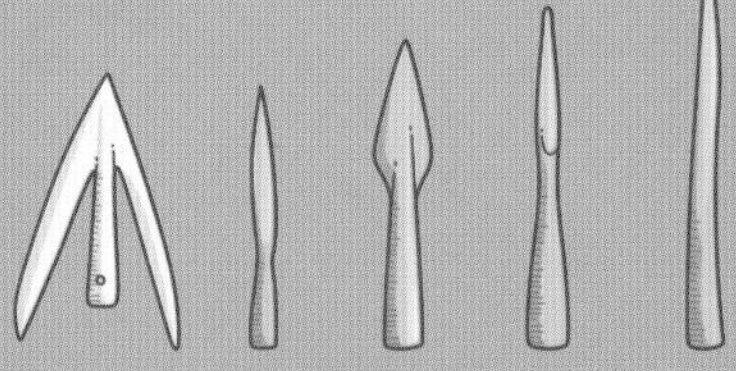

Longbow Measured 6 ft 6 in/2 m long and was made of a single piece of yew wood.
Finger tab Protected the archer's fingers from string friction.
Wrist guard Prevented the string from hitting the arm when releasing.
Buckle The hand shield with which they protected themselves.
Gambeson A kind of padded protection with multiple layers of fabric.
Helmet The models used were the *capeline*, the *bascinet*, and the *sallet*.
Sword The main weapon in hand-to-hand combat.
Dagger This dagger finished off the fallen knights.
Coin purse Carried their meager possessions.
Arrows Stuck into the ground in front of them to help them to shoot faster.
Posts Placed before the archers to stop the advance of the cavalry.
Quiver Each archer had an allowance of 24 to 36 arrows, in clusters of 12.

The Battle of Hastings

In October 1066, William the Conqueror, Duke of Normandy, invaded England to claim the throne. He took it after his victory at the Battle of Hastings, where his troops faced Saxon king Harold II. With cunning, William divided his army into groups (archers, infantry, and cavalry) to attack the Saxon troops made up only of infantry. The battle, which lasted all day and caused thousands of deaths, demonstrated the importance of the cavalry.

Tactics

William tried throughout the day to break the lines established by Harold. Frontal attacks were unsuccessful. However, he achieved his goal by using two tactics: fake withdrawal and a rain of arrows.

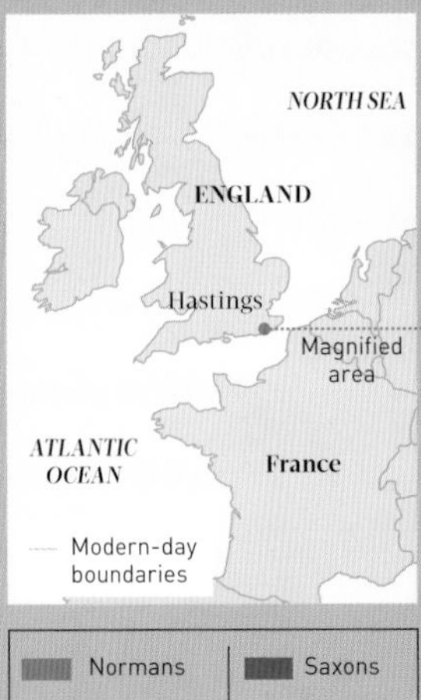
NORTH SEA
ENGLAND
Hastings
Magnified area
ATLANTIC OCEAN
France
Modern-day boundaries

Normans | Saxons
Norman advance | Saxon advance
Norman withdrawal

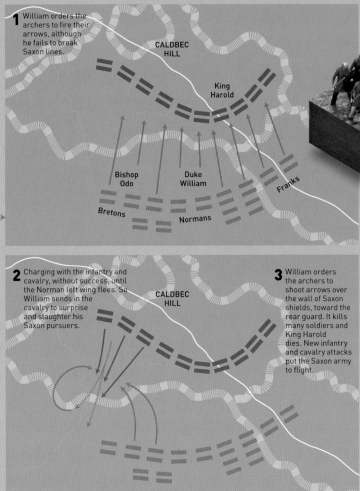

1 William orders the archers to fire their arrows, although he fails to break Saxon lines.

CALDBEC HILL
King Harold
Bishop Odo
Duke William
Bretons
Normans
Franks

2 Charging with the infantry and cavalry, without success, until the Norman left wing flees. So William sends in the cavalry to surprise and slaughter his Saxon pursuers.

CALDBEC HILL

3 William orders the archers to shoot arrows over the wall of Saxon shields, toward the rear guard. It kills many soldiers and King Harold dies. New infantry and cavalry attacks put the Saxon army to flight.

Balance of power

SAXONS ▸ Around 9,000 soldiers between militia and *huscarls* (elite forces)

NORMANS ▸ Between 7,000 and 15,000 soldiers with archers, infantry, and cavalry.

Uphill battle

The battle took place on a hill. At the top were the Saxons in a closed shield formation. The Normans had to attack uphill.

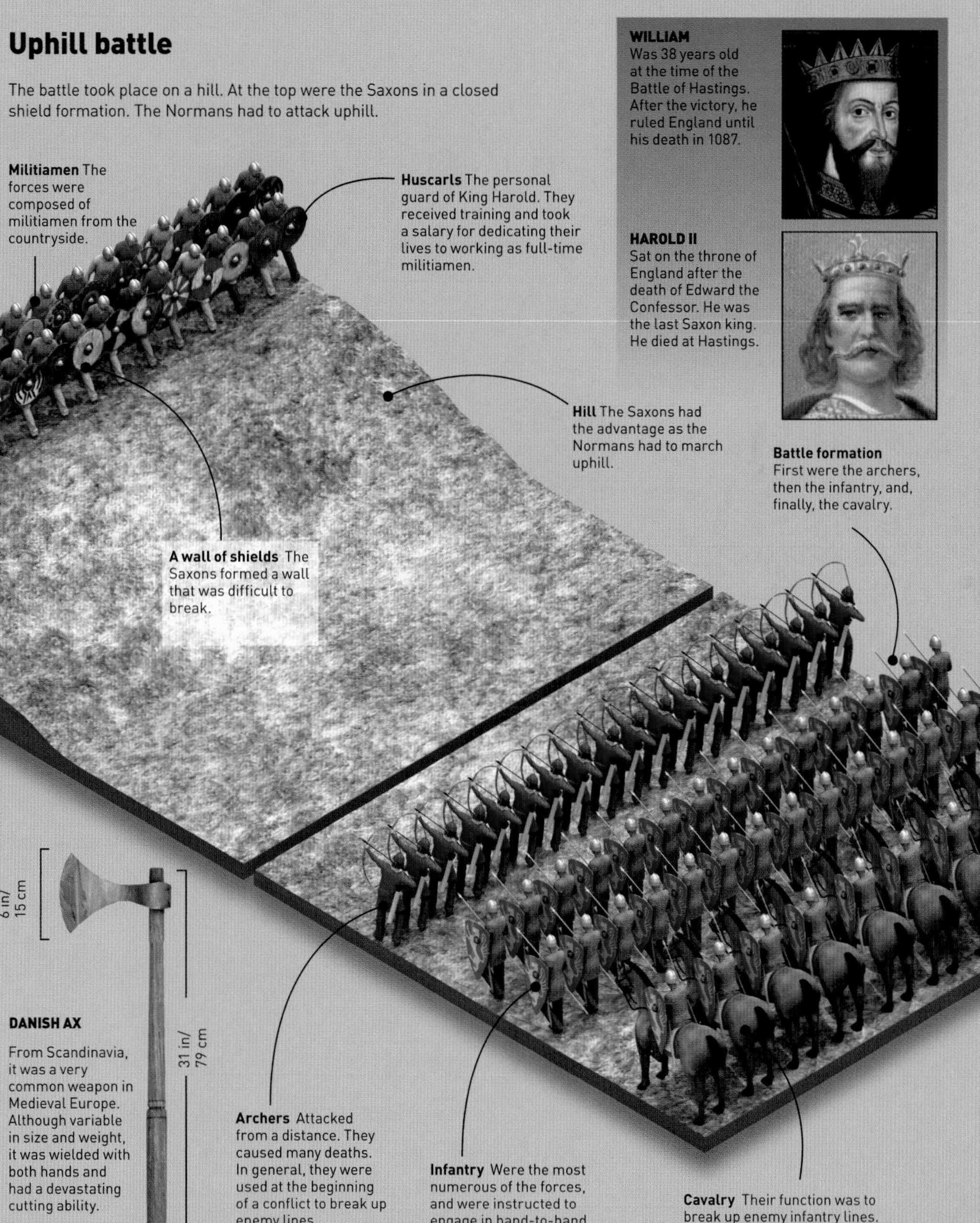
Militiamen The forces were composed of militiamen from the countryside.
Huscarls The personal guard of King Harold. They received training and took a salary for dedicating their lives to working as full-time militiamen.
WILLIAM Was 38 years old at the time of the Battle of Hastings. After the victory, he ruled England until his death in 1087.
HAROLD II Sat on the throne of England after the death of Edward the Confessor. He was the last Saxon king. He died at Hastings.
Hill The Saxons had the advantage as the Normans had to march uphill.
Battle formation First were the archers, then the infantry, and, finally, the cavalry.
A wall of shields The Saxons formed a wall that was difficult to break.
6 in/ 15 cm
31 in/ 79 cm
DANISH AX From Scandinavia, it was a very common weapon in Medieval Europe. Although variable in size and weight, it was wielded with both hands and had a devastating cutting ability.
Archers Attacked from a distance. They caused many deaths. In general, they were used at the beginning of a conflict to break up enemy lines.
Infantry Were the most numerous of the forces, and were instructed to engage in hand-to-hand combat.
Cavalry Their function was to break up enemy infantry lines. They were the equivalent of modern-day tanks.

Viking Warriors

At the end of the eighth century, on board ships in the shape of dragons, the Vikings emerged from the frozen seas of the North to strike terror in Europe. They were explorers, traders, and settlers who reached locations as far away as Scandinavia and Russia, the Middle East, and America. They were ferocious, astute, and ruthless warriors who overlooked nothing in their pillaging. Because of this, they were considered devils and from this idea arose the myth that their helmets had horns.

Permanent militia

The Vikings did not have a professional army; they were farmers, traders, carpenters, blacksmiths, and so on, who took up arms in combat when the occasion demanded it. They familiarized themselves with the use of weapons from adolescence, by hunting, fighting, and playing sport. Many of the main weapons used were derived from their working tools such as the hatchet and the hammer. However, they had tremendous discipline and great courage, based on the belief that Paradise (Valhalla) was waiting for those who fell in combat.

THE DEVILS OF THE NORTH
The Vikings only created armies of several thousand men when they fought each other. During the looting raids their numbers did not exceed a hundred. The Viking warrior's forte was in individual combat, where he could take advantage of his physical strength, and his skill in handling weapons.

Flag The majority of Viking warriors used it. It is thought to represent Odin, the god of war.

FIRST DOCUMENTED RAID
On June 8, 793, the Vikings landed on the coast close to Lindisfarne Monastery, on an island off the northern coast of England. They ransacked it and put the monks to the sword. It was the first Viking raid ever recorded in history and a demonstration of the effectiveness of their lightning-quick surprise attacks.

REPRESENTATION
Ninth-century rune stone on which two fighting warriors are depicted on the Viking journey to Valhalla.

VIKING SAGAS
They narrated the exploits of the heroes—some of them mythical, others real. In this wood carving from the twelfth century, Sigurd kills Regin.

Helmet Contrary to legend, they did not have horns. They were made of iron and were conical.
Byrnie This is what they called the coat of mail. They wore it with sleeves and short skirts.
Ax Was their favorite weapon. They used one or both hands to wield it.
Tunic Made of wool, decorated with knots on the neck. It gave them freedom of movement.
Protection Under the coat of chain mail, they usually wore a padded skin.
Coat of mail Small metallic rings that were hammered to flatten them out.
Sword They used it to knock down their enemies and then stab them—a simple design with a double-edged blade.
Shield Made of wood and riveted. In the center, it had a metal protector covering the handle, and was decorated with a family rune.
Dagger Was double edged and was 8–20 in/20–50 cm long.
Kyrtill Was a type of tunic with a skirt and full sleeves.
Ax handle Could be 3 ft/1 m long, which gave more force to the blow.
Cape Made of thick wool, it kept them warm and offered protection from knives.

The Viking Ship

The Vikings were expert navigators who dominated the maritime routes and rivers of northeast Europe between the eighth and ninth centuries. They also reached certain places on the Mediterranean coast. For raiding and looting they used a long, narrow and lightweight boat called the *drakkar*, while for commercial activity they used a broader, flatter vessel, especially designed for the transport of timber, wool, hides, wheat, and even slaves.

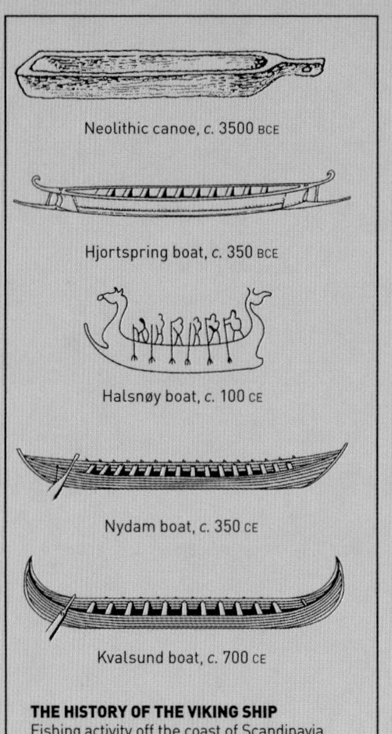

Neolithic canoe, *c.* 3500 BCE

Hjortspring boat, *c.* 350 BCE

Halsnøy boat, *c.* 100 CE

Nydam boat, *c.* 350 CE

Kvalsund boat, *c.* 700 CE

THE HISTORY OF THE VIKING SHIP
Fishing activity off the coast of Scandinavia fostered the construction of boats. How they are made, which is shown here, is known thanks to the different archaeological discoveries of boat remains as well as sketches and reliefs on flat stones.

The Gokstad ship

The discovery in 1880 of the Gokstad ship in southern Norway advanced our current knowledge of the Vikings. This *drakkar* dating from around 900, measures more than 75 ft/23 m in length and weighs, including the rigging, around 20 tons.

Figurehead
Skilled craftsmen, the Vikings carved a symbolic animal on wood. It was a combination of a dragon and a snake wrapped around itself.

Cargo Being a warship, the *drakkar* had little space for cargo. In contrast, the *knarr* were merchant ships dedicated to trade and could even carry livestock on the deck.

The keel Made of a single piece of oak over 80 ft/25 m long, the keel provided great strength and allowed the ship to be navigated in just 3 ft/1 m of water.

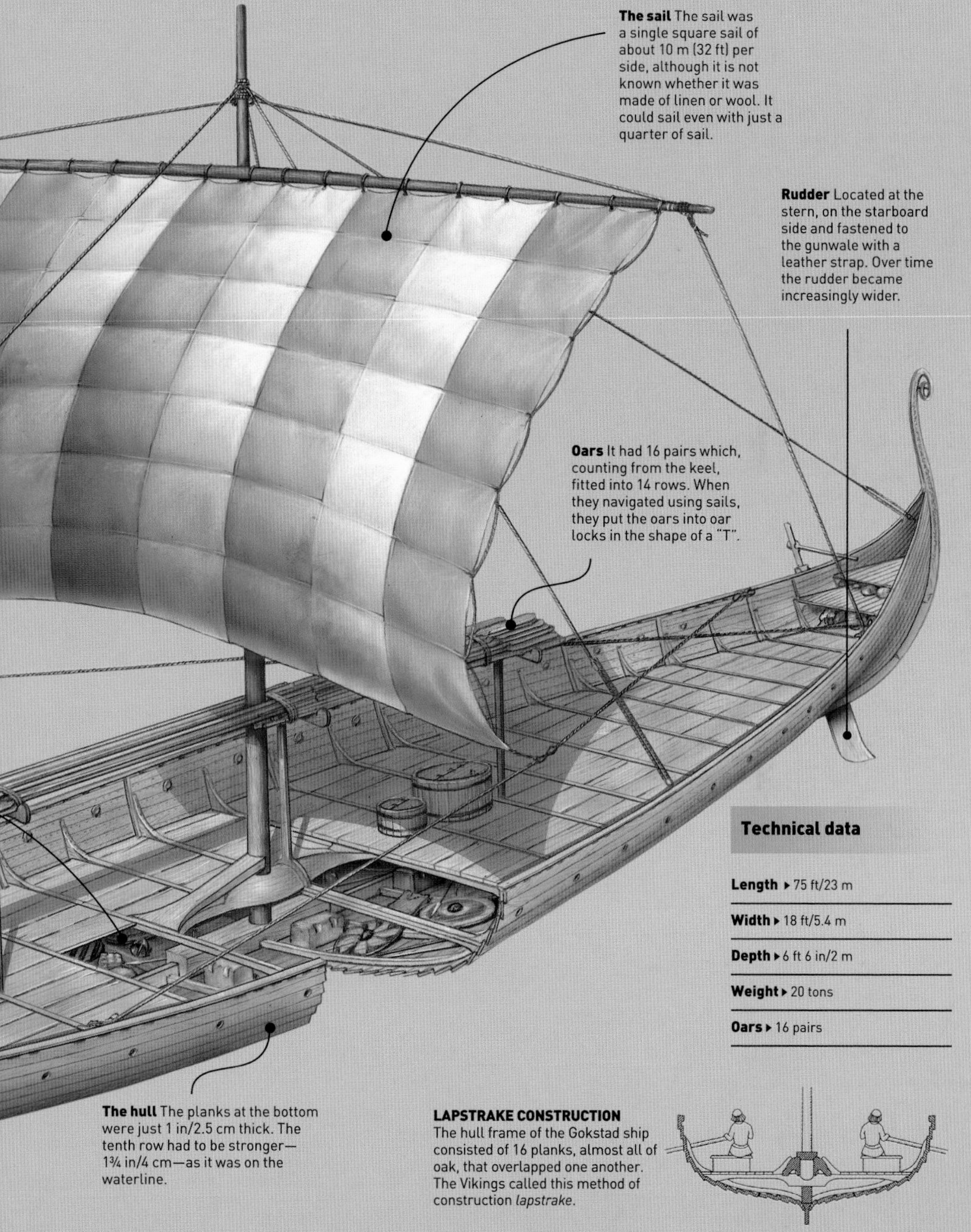
The sail The sail was a single square sail of about 10 m (32 ft) per side, although it is not known whether it was made of linen or wool. It could sail even with just a quarter of sail.
Rudder Located at the stern, on the starboard side and fastened to the gunwale with a leather strap. Over time the rudder became increasingly wider.
Oars It had 16 pairs which, counting from the keel, fitted into 14 rows. When they navigated using sails, they put the oars into oar locks in the shape of a "T".
The hull The planks at the bottom were just 1 in/2.5 cm thick. The tenth row had to be stronger—1¾ in/4 cm—as it was on the waterline.

Technical data

Length	▸ 75 ft/23 m
Width	▸ 18 ft/5.4 m
Depth	▸ 6 ft 6 in/2 m
Weight	▸ 20 tons
Oars	▸ 16 pairs

LAPSTRAKE CONSTRUCTION
The hull frame of the Gokstad ship consisted of 16 planks, almost all of oak, that overlapped one another. The Vikings called this method of construction *lapstrake*.

The Armies of the East

In the Middle Ages, Asia witnessed the rise of great empires and the fall of others, the creation of federations of kingdoms and the emergence of feudal states. They all had armies of a diverse nature that often ended up confronting each other. From the massive regiments of the Chinese dynasties to brave Korean warriors, from the elite Japanese samurai to the fearsome Mongol retinues, all were formidable armies.

China: from Sung to Ming

The Sung Dynasty (960–1279) organized a large permanent army to quell nomadic invasions, where crossbow archers were the most prized force. They also developed gunpowder for creating all types of weapons (e.g. the fire arrow and the flame thrower.) Despite its great military power, the Chinese Empire could not repel the invading force of another great Asian empire, the Mongols, who ruled China from 1279 to 1368, when the Ming Dynasty regained control.

In command
In his final years, Kublai Khan, who suffered from gout, led his army from a high domed pavilion erected on several elephants.

THE MING DYNASTY
The Ming Dynasty (1368–1644) equipped China with an extensive fleet and an enormous permanent army; and they also reinforced and extended the Great Wall to protect themselves from further nomadic invasions.

Mongol might

After unifying the tribes of northern Asia in 1206, Genghis Khan began a wave of conquests creating a great empire that culminated in his grandson, Kublai Khan, subduing the Sung Dynasty of China. The terrible Mongol army was almost exclusively cavalry, with the bow being the most favored weapon. Over time they assimilated Chinese war techniques and weapons (e.g. siege engines and gunpowder.)

The Korean kingdom of Goguryeo

Goguryeo was one of the Three Kingdoms that arose in Korea between 57 and 668. It occupied the south of modern Manchuria, the north and center of the Korean Peninsula, and the south of Primorye, part of modern-day Russia. It was one of the most powerful states in eastern Asia and its expansionist policies led to confrontations with China over different periods.

KOREAN SOLDIERS
In addition to its infantry and archers, the Goguryeo was distinguished by its excellent cavalry.

Infantryman Archer Horseman

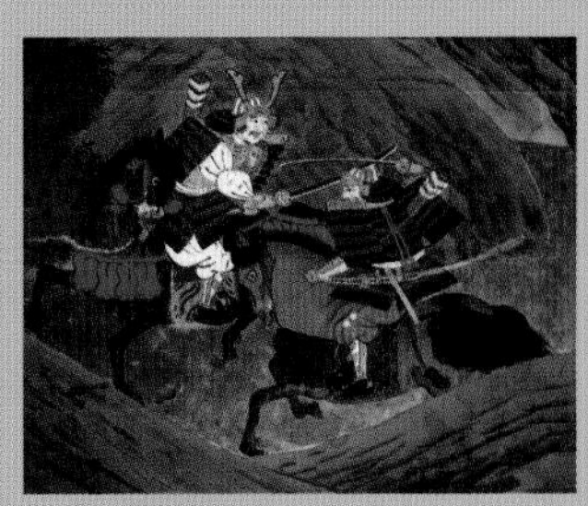

FEUDAL JAPAN
During the Middle Ages, Japan experienced a turbulent period marked by a weak central government and an ongoing civil war. A feudal state existed in which the samurai (elite warriors) formed powerful clans that ended up fighting each other. At the end of the twelfth century, the Minamoto clan defeated the rest and established the Shogunate, a military dictatorship that had to face the Mongol invasion.

The Battle of Salsu

In 612, the Chinese emperor Yangdi, of the Sui Dynasty, invaded Goguryeo with an army of 1,133,800 men. However, some of these troops were ambushed in the River Salsu by Goguryeo soldiers. When the Chinese crossed the semidry riverbed, Korean General Eulji Mundeok ordered the destruction of the dam that was holding back the waters.

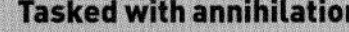

Tasked with annihilation
The Goguryeo army cavalry ambushed the survivors on the banks. Only 2,700 of the 300,000 Chinese escaped.

Drowned
Thousands of Chinese were drowned in the waters of Salsu without even seeing combat.

The Fleet of Zheng He

Six centuries ago, the Indian Ocean was witness to the passing of one of the most formidable squadrons in history. More than 300 vessels and almost 30,000 men were sent by the emperor of China, under the command of the legendary Admiral Zheng He, to explore, trade among, and conquer the coastal towns. Between 1405 and 1433, the fleet made seven journeys that took it to places as far as East Africa.

The treasure ships

They were the most luxurious ships of Zheng He's fleet. They measured perhaps more than 330 ft/100 m in length and more than 165 ft/50 m wide. But there are very few remains of their existence.

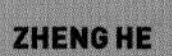

The treasure ship
–*Santa Maria*
330 ft/100 m

Size comparison between the treasure ship of Zheng He and Christopher Columbus's *Santa Maria*.

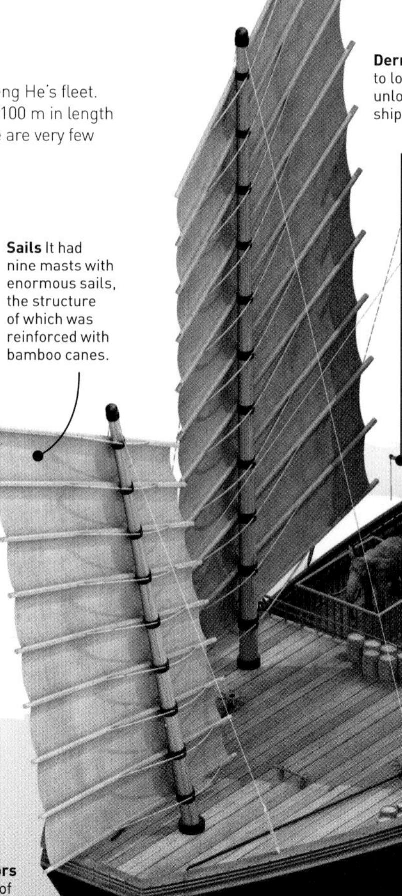

Derrick Used to load and unload the ship.
Sails It had nine masts with enormous sails, the structure of which was reinforced with bamboo canes.
Anchors Made of iron, they measured more than 6 ft 6 in/2 m and were located at the stern.

ZHENG HE
The great Chinese admiral was a eunuch of Muslim origin who made seven journeys over 28 years in the service of the Ming Dynasty.

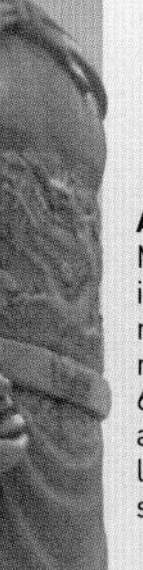

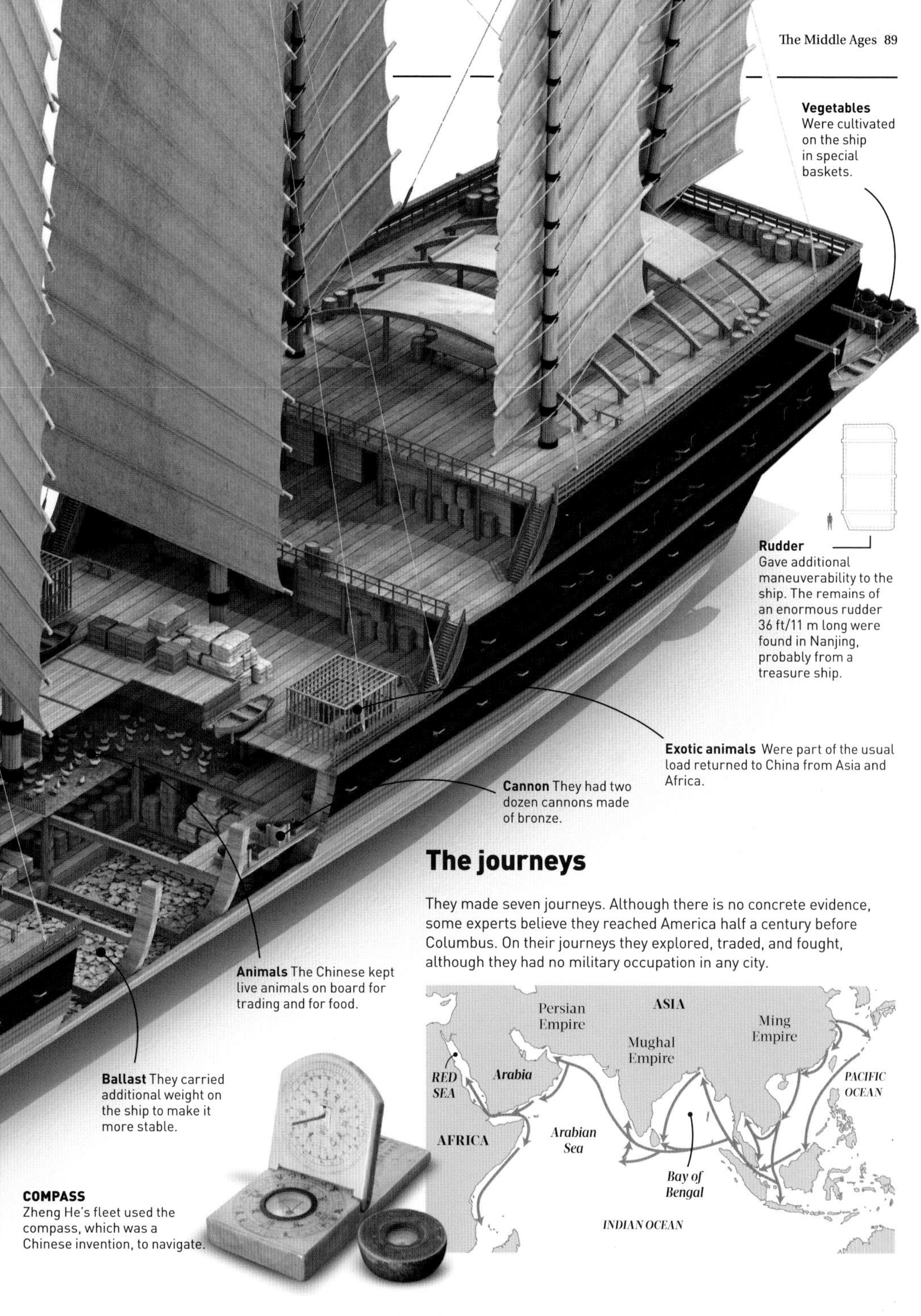

Vegetables
Were cultivated on the ship in special baskets.
Rudder
Gave additional maneuverability to the ship. The remains of an enormous rudder 36 ft/11 m long were found in Nanjing, probably from a treasure ship.
Exotic animals Were part of the usual load returned to China from Asia and Africa.
Cannon They had two dozen cannons made of bronze.
Animals The Chinese kept live animals on board for trading and for food.
Ballast They carried additional weight on the ship to make it more stable.

The journeys

They made seven journeys. Although there is no concrete evidence, some experts believe they reached America half a century before Columbus. On their journeys they explored, traded, and fought, although they had no military occupation in any city.

Persian Empire
ASIA
Ming Empire
Mughal Empire
RED SEA
Arabia
PACIFIC OCEAN
AFRICA
Arabian Sea
Bay of Bengal
INDIAN OCEAN

COMPASS
Zheng He's fleet used the compass, which was a Chinese invention, to navigate.

The Samurai

The samurai emerged around the tenth century in the court of Kyoto. This caste of professional warriors gained prominence during the civil wars that rocked Japan in the Middle Ages until it became a powerful social class that ended up controlling the country through a military regime. Initially expert archers on horseback, the samurai became masters in the art of the sword and hand-to-hand combat.

The Bushido Code

The samurai followed a strict code of conduct called *bushido* (the way of the warrior), in which the concepts of "loyalty" and "honor" were above everything, and they scorned the material side of life. If a warrior lost his honor, the only way he could recover it was through *seppuku*, or *harakiri*, a suicide ritual. According to their philosophy of life, the goal of the samurai was to reach a high level of physical and mental perfection. To achieve this they practiced Zen meditation and underwent tough training in different martial arts.

GREAT ARCHERS
Originally, samurai warriors were expert horsemen and very skilled with the bow and arrow. This weapon predominated in Japanese battles until the twelfth century, when the samurai developed great skill in handling the sword (*katana*).

Technique They needed only a third of the length of their bow to fire arrows with precision while they rode.

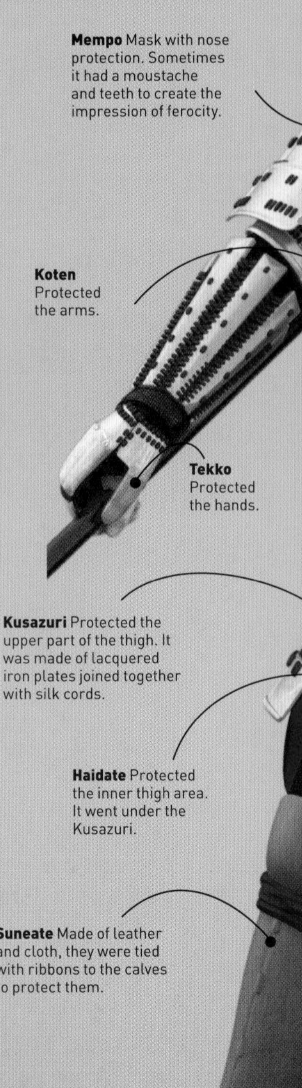

Mempo Mask with nose protection. Sometimes it had a moustache and teeth to create the impression of ferocity.

Koten Protected the arms.

Tekko Protected the hands.

Kusazuri Protected the upper part of the thigh. It was made of lacquered iron plates joined together with silk cords.

Haidate Protected the inner thigh area. It went under the Kusazuri.

Suneate Made of leather and cloth, they were tied with ribbons to the calves to protect them.

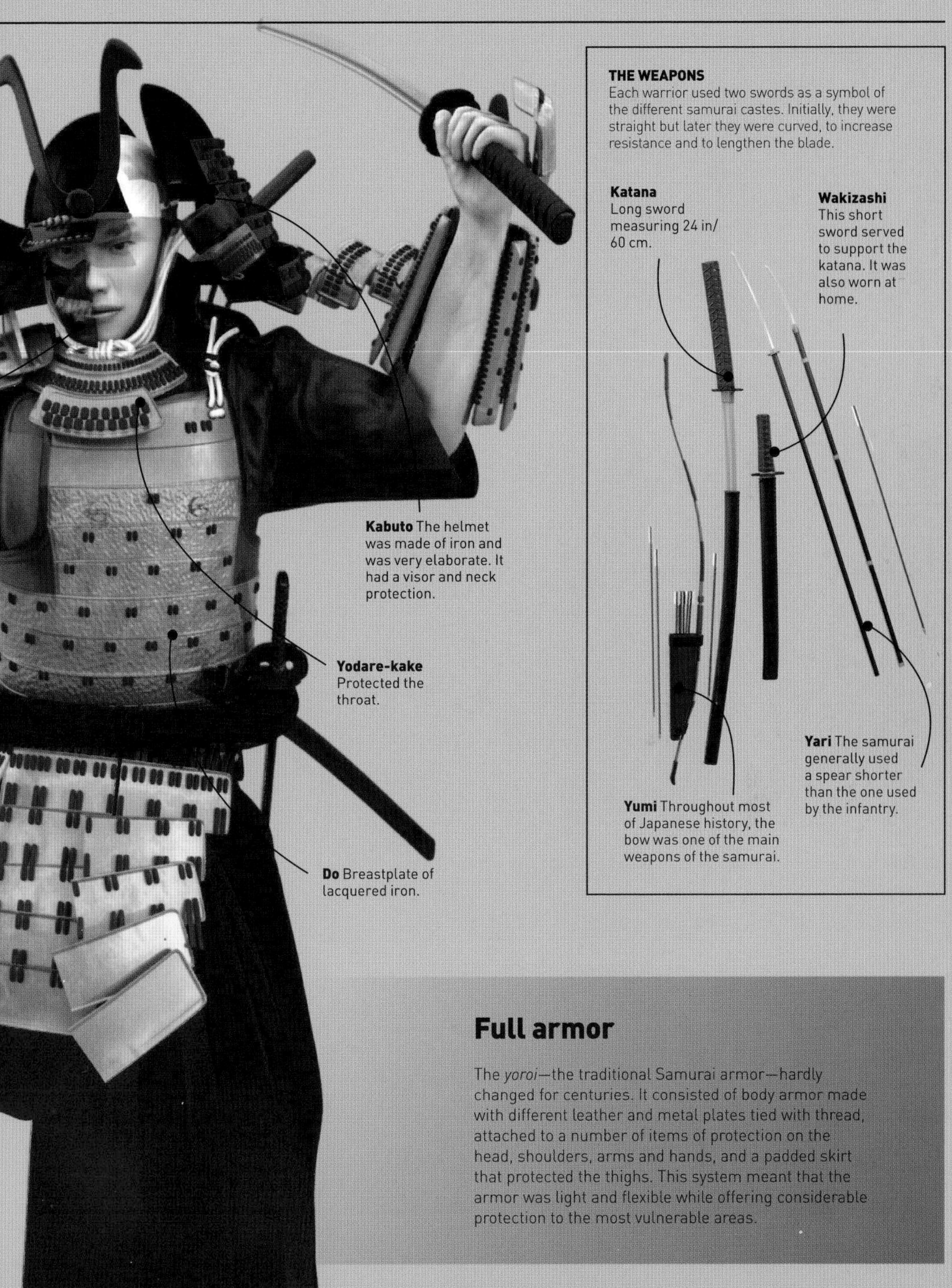
Kabuto The helmet was made of iron and was very elaborate. It had a visor and neck protection.
Yodare-kake Protected the throat.
Do Breastplate of lacquered iron.

THE WEAPONS
Each warrior used two swords as a symbol of the different samurai castes. Initially, they were straight but later they were curved, to increase resistance and to lengthen the blade.

Katana Long sword measuring 24 in/ 60 cm.

Wakizashi This short sword served to support the katana. It was also worn at home.

Yumi Throughout most of Japanese history, the bow was one of the main weapons of the samurai.

Yari The samurai generally used a spear shorter than the one used by the infantry.

Full armor

The *yoroi*—the traditional Samurai armor—hardly changed for centuries. It consisted of body armor made with different leather and metal plates tied with thread, attached to a number of items of protection on the head, shoulders, arms and hands, and a padded skirt that protected the thighs. This system meant that the armor was light and flexible while offering considerable protection to the most vulnerable areas.

GUARDIANS OF THE FAITH

After the conquest of Jerusalem in 1071 by the Seljuq Turks of Syria and Palestine, the idea of taking the Holy City for Christianity took root in the papacy. On November 27, 1095, the last day of the council held at Clermont-Ferrand in France, Urban II called for the "holy war." Shouting "God willing" he ceremonially allocated crosses to those who would undertake the journey to Jerusalem to "rescue" the city from the unfaithful. To do this, he decreed full forgiveness for the Crusaders' sins, to protect their families and property, and offered immunity, declaring those who died in the campaign as martyrs.

Urban II managed to launch an army of some 60,000 men recruited from southern Italy to Lombardy, from Aquitaine to Normandy, Flanders and the Netherlands, Germany, the Rhineland, the North Sea region, and Denmark. Under the leadership of a charismatic preacher, Peter the Hermit, a diverse group of men set off eastward following the course of the Danube. They reached Constantinople, conquered Nicaea in 1097 and arrived in Syria the same year, where the Christian army remained until January 1099. They reached Jerusalem in June, and in July, with terrible slaughter, they carried out a successful assault on the city. There were also many casualties among the Crusaders. It is estimated that no fewer than 14,000 men arrived in the holy city, the vast majority of whom returned to the West. In 1100, barely 300 men remained in Palestine. Four Christian states were then created in Palestine, one of which—the county of Edessa—was taken by the Turks in 1144, prompting Pope Eugene III to announce a new crusade—the Second—which was a failure. The Crusaders were defeated in October 1147 in Anatolia and again in Damascus in July 1148.

The financial weakness of the Christian kingdoms overseas and the lack of Western support and of an heir to the throne of Jerusalem worsened the situation until, in 1187, Saladin annihilated the Christian army at the Battle of Hattin and took Jerusalem in October of that year. Again, this provoked a massive reaction in the West, which armed the Third Crusade that would unite the kings of Germany, France, and England. This time, dominion over the sea was decisive, and although Acre was taken in 1191, Jerusalem could not be rescued in 1192. After this, support for the reconstituted kingdom of Jerusalem (which would last a further hundred years, although the city only fell back into the hands of the Christians between 1229 and 1244), arrived by sea. There was a Fourth Crusade, between 1201 and 1204, a Fifth between 1213 and 1229 and, according to some historians, up to eight, although only one important one reached the Eastern Mediterranean—that of Louis IX of France (1248–1254), before the permanent loss of the last Christian strongholds in Syria and Palestine, in 1291.

Medieval Knights

In Europe in the Middle Ages, kings were dependent on the small armies of feudal lords to protect their power. As part of those armies, the knights, elite horseback warriors, were particularly noteworthy and their prestige quickly grew. The majority were young men from the nobility, who served their lords in the pursuit of glory, honor, titles, land, and money. The Crusades gave them a new motivation and religion, while the Hundred Years' War saw the end of their dominance.

Heavy armory

The armor and methods of combat of medieval knights did not evolve significantly through the entire medieval period. Their equipment was fundamentally made up of their horse, armor, helmet, shield, spear, and sword. Their typical strategy of combat was to charge. Feudal armies comprised three sections—vanguard, center, and rear guard—which launched charges sequentially, in waves. Knights lunged with their spear and, if it broke, used their sword or mace.

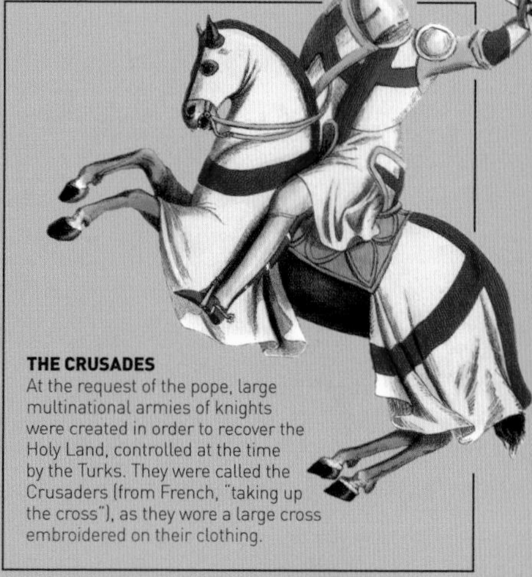

THE CRUSADES
At the request of the pope, large multinational armies of knights were created in order to recover the Holy Land, controlled at the time by the Turks. They were called the Crusaders (from French, "taking up the cross"), as they wore a large cross embroidered on their clothing.

The art of taking up arms

Putting on armor, involving dozens of separate parts and a considerable weight, was a cumbersome task, with which knights needed assistance. To this end, they used a squire.

FABRIC CLOTHING
The squire assisted the knight in putting on his armor over his clothing.

COAT OF MAIL
This was the first item that a knight had to put on. He dressed from his feet up.

GORGET
This item was placed over the coat of mail, with the cuirass and brassard.

FASTENING
The parts were fastened together using straps, hooks, nuts, and studs.

The armor

Between the tenth and twelfth centuries, knights used only a coat of mail, a helmet, and a shield. Toward the end of the twelfth century, metal plates were incorporated to protect certain parts of their body. By the fourteenth century, knights wore full armor. The subsequent invention of gunpowder and firearms rendered them obsolete.

Helmets
Those made of a single piece were known as a Corinthian helmet. There were also other types of helmet with a hinged visor to enhance face protection. They often also had some level of internal protection.

Gorget and bevor
The gorget covered the knight's neck, throat and thorax; the bevor protected his jaw and mouth.

Very heavy
The armor had up to 250 metal parts and weighed up to 110 lb/50 kg. A fully armored knight weighed so much that it was difficult to move and if he were to fall from his horse, he would be left defenseless.

Complete protection
Large spaulders covered the shoulders; brassards, the upper arm; couters, the elbows; and vambraces, the arms and forearms.

SWORD
Used for close combat, as its tip could pierce almost all armor used during the period. It had a straight, double-edged blade and was made from hardened steel.

Coat of mail
Comprising a mesh of small metal rings.

Large size
The sword measured between 30 and 33 in/75 and 85 cm, and weighed between 2.9 and 3.3 lb/ 1.3 and 1.5 kg.

Cuisse They served to protect the thighs; the greaves were worn on the lower part of the leg, while full greaves also offered calf protection.

The Templars

In just two centuries, following its appearance after the First Crusade in 1119 until its disappearance in 1312, the Order of the Poor Knights of Christ, more commonly known as the Order of the Temple, went from being a small, defensive Christian military unit (its mission was to protect pilgrims visiting Jerusalem) to a hugely powerful organization with significant political, economic, and military interests spread across Europe and the Near East.

Territorial organization

The main administrative unit of the Knights Templar was the trust—a type of medieval fief that was generally established from donations. Trusts were divided into "bailiwicks," which in turn were divided into "provinces," The commander was responsible for governing and administering these fiefs, sending the profits to the headquarters of the Order, in addition to the religious head.

HEADQUARTERS
The Temple of Solomon in Jerusalem (see left) served as the Templars' headquarters until Saladin took the city. Thereafter, it moved to Acre (1191–1291) in northern Israel and finally, Cyprus (1291–1312).

TRUST
There were both rural and urban trusts. Generally, a trust comprised a castle, a chapel, and different households.

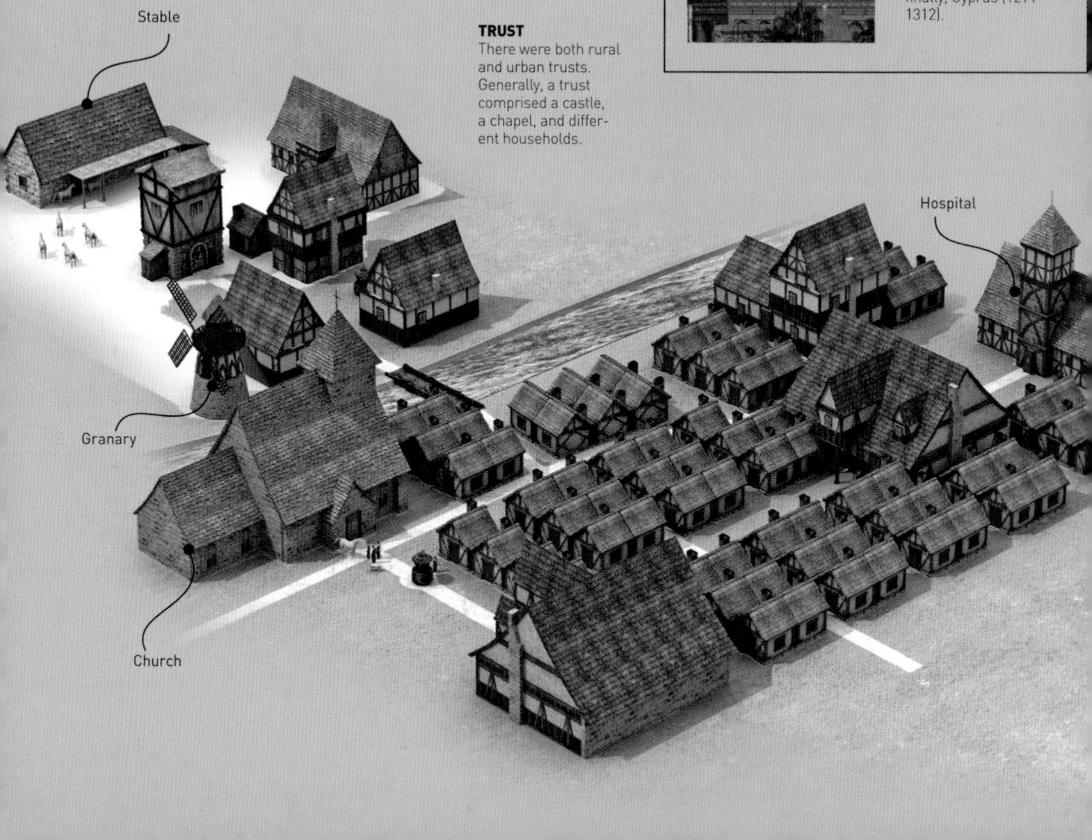

Stable

Hospital

Granary

Church

Members of the Order

Depending on their role and social status, members of the Order of the Temple were divided into four main groups: knights, sergeants and squires, priests, and those known as "brethren of the Order," who were occupied with domestic chores and who did not participate in convent life.

TURCOPOLES
They did not belong to the Order. They were mercenary soldiers (horseback archers) from the Byzantine region.

SQUIRES
They were responsible for maintaining and transporting the knights' weaponry. They were not warriors.

PRIESTS
Entrusted with religious matters, but also performed administrative tasks.

SERGEANTS
Warriors of humble origins. They occupied secondary positions in the Order and were assigned a horse and a squire.

KNIGHTS
From the nobility, they had at least one squire and three horses. On the trust, they fulfilled monastic vows; however, on the battlefield, they were fierce warriors.

Decision-making: the Chapters

The Chapters were colleges that wielded the effective power of the Order. There were three types: the general chapter, responsible for taking important decisions, presided over by the Grand Master and comprising thirteen Templar Knights (eight knights, four sergeants, and one priest, of different nationalities where possible); provincial chapters, responsible for addressing local issues; and the ordinary chapters, where those responsible for each trust would meet to discuss domestic issues.

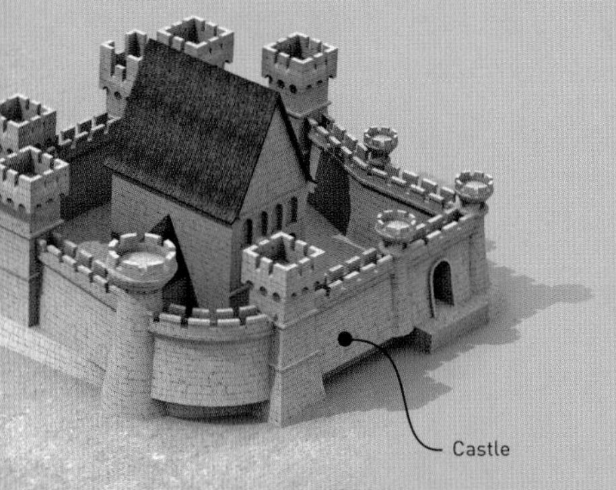
Castle

Distinctive
The knights were the only members of the Order allowed to wear the white cape and mantle with the red cross.

TEMPLAR HIERARCHY
The absolute head of the Order was the Grand Master. He lived in Jerusalem and was answerable only to the pope, although he was also accountable to the general chapter. The seneschal was his right-hand man. Other key figures were the marshal, responsible for the military, and the treasurer, who controlled finances. The different commanders followed in the hierarchy.

The Battle of Hattin

Also known as the Horns of Hattin, this battle was a prelude to the Christian loss of the Kingdom of Jerusalem, the city having been conquered almost a century before. In July 1187, coming to the rescue of the city of Tiberias, the Christian army clashed with the Muslim army, led by Saladin. The lack of water, the suffocating heat of the desert and the adept strategy employed by the Muslim leader annihilated the thirsty Christian forces led by Guy de Lusignan.

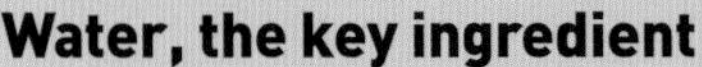

Water, the key ingredient

Saladin sought to prevent the Christians from reaching Tiberias, where they would have had access to water. To this end, he led his forces to an extinct twin-peaked volcano known as "the Horns of Hattin," to head them off.

1 After a day marching with no access to water and harassed by enemy attacks, the Christian troops decided to camp before changing route to retrieve water from the fountains of Hattin.

2 Muslim forces cut off their route to Hattin with a cavalry unit. The cavalry of the Christian army charged. The Muslims allowed them to pass, but later surrounded the Christians, ensuring their defeat.

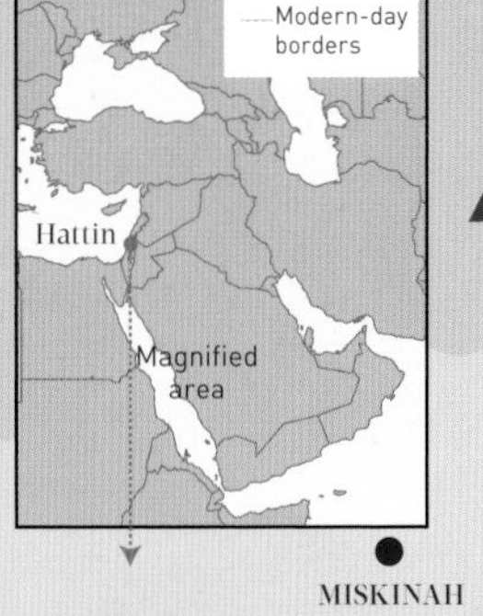

Modern-day borders
Hattin
Magnified area

Muttawiya volunteers Poorly trained and inadequately armed militia.

MISKINAH

Taqi al-Din Light cavalry, with no archers, commanded by Saladin's nephew.

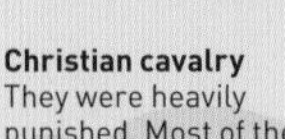

Christian cavalry They were heavily punished. Most of the horsemen were left to fight on foot after their horses were killed.

Christian army Commanded by Guy de Lusignan, King of Jerusalem, and split into three divisions, including infantry, heavy cavalry, and Turcopoles (mounted archers, with Turkish-style weaponry).

Turkomans Highly skilled mounted archers.

Saladin (bulk of the army) Arab and Turkish infantry with heavy cavalry. Around 70 camels provided water from Lake Tiberias.

To Tzippori

The True Cross A relic with the remnants of the cross on which Christ died, which was placed on the front line of battle. Muslim forces captured it at Hattin and it was lost forever.

The final assault

The battle was won following an attack by the bulk of the Muslim army on a thirsty and depleted Christian army at the foot of the Horns of Hattin.

BALANCE OF POWER

CHRISTIANS ▸ 15,000 infantrymen and 2,000 horsemen, including 500 Turcopoles

MUSLIMS ▸ Around 30,000 to 40,000 troops, including infantrymen and the cavalry

To Tiberíades

▲ Christians
▲▲▲▲ Muslims
Water source
Combats

SARADIN

SALADIN
The Sultan of Egypt and Syria, the great Muslim general, unified his people and reconquered Jerusalem, which was in Christian hands at the time.

GUY DE LUSIGNAN
French knight who became the king of Jerusalem in 1186 following his marriage to Princess Sibylla. He was captured at Hattin and released shortly afterward.

HATTIN

3 The Christians advanced toward the Horns. Taking advantage of a westerly wind, the Muslims set fire to the land. The smoke confused and scattered the Christians, who were surrounded and attacked by the bulk of Muslim troops.

Muslim troops
In addition to a size advantage, they were well rested and more agile than their Christian counterparts.

THE CRUSADES

Coat of mail
This item served to protect the knights' bodies. Made from leather, into which rings or metal plates were inserted.

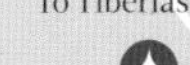
To Tiberias

Templar shield
Made using wooden boards, covered in iron. Worn on the knight's left arm.

Extra weight The full attire of a Templar Knight weighed around 88 lb/40 kg, with which they had to move powerfully and quickly.

Fire The Muslims ignited the dry pastures, using the smoke and heat to confuse their enemies.

Siege of Jerusalem

Although in Hebrew its name means "city of peace," Jerusalem has been the front line of battle on numerous occasions. In the Middle Ages, the city fell into Byzantine and Arab hands, but was conquered in 1099 by the Christians, who founded the Kingdom of Jerusalem. In 1187, the Muslim leader Saladin took control of the holy city and, with the exception of a period of Christian occupation between 1228 and 1244, the Crusaders would not return to Jerusalem again. Following the Mamluk period, the Ottoman Turks definitively assumed control of the region in 1517.

Widespread killing

Based on the grounds that the Via Dolorosa, the Church of the Holy Sepulchre and other sites sacred to the Christian faith were located in Jerusalem, the Church of Rome made taking Jerusalem the objective of the Crusades. In June 1099, Godfrey of Bouillon, one of the leaders of the First Crusade, arrived there for the first time. The explosion of the expeditionary force into the city resulted in widespread killing of Muslims and Jews, with women, children, and the elderly given no reprieve.

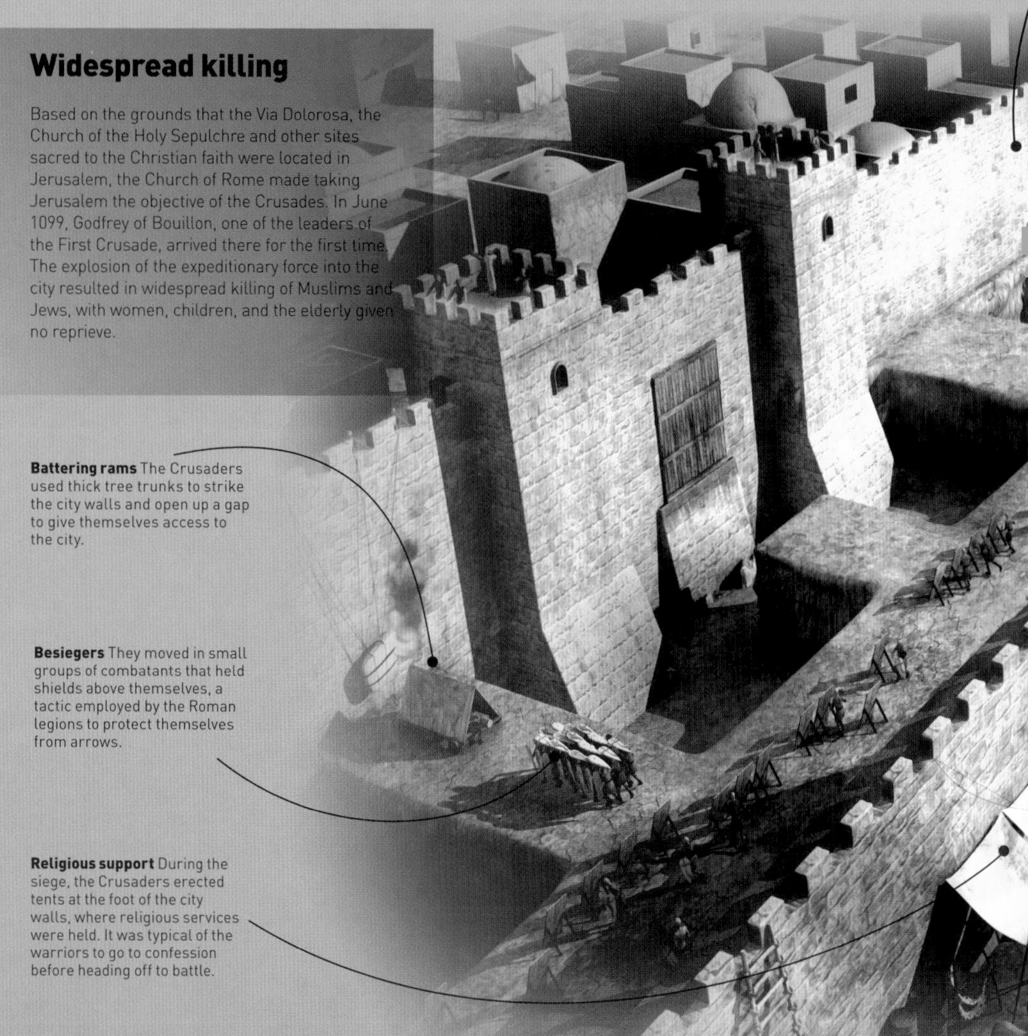

Battering rams The Crusaders used thick tree trunks to strike the city walls and open up a gap to give themselves access to the city.

Besiegers They moved in small groups of combatants that held shields above themselves, a tactic employed by the Roman legions to protect themselves from arrows.

Religious support During the siege, the Crusaders erected tents at the foot of the city walls, where religious services were held. It was typical of the warriors to go to confession before heading off to battle.

The city walls Along its 2.8-mile/4.5-km perimeter, there were 43 watchtowers and 11 gates, of which only eight remain. They measured between 16 and 50 ft/5 and 15 m high.

Catapults The Crusaders' catapults launched stones and flammable material into the city. However, as they were made of wood, they could also be ignited by those repelling the attack from within.

Mobile siege towers The Crusaders sought to get closer to the city walls using wooden towers, of a similar height, mounted on wheels; by doing so, they were able to force themselves into the city.

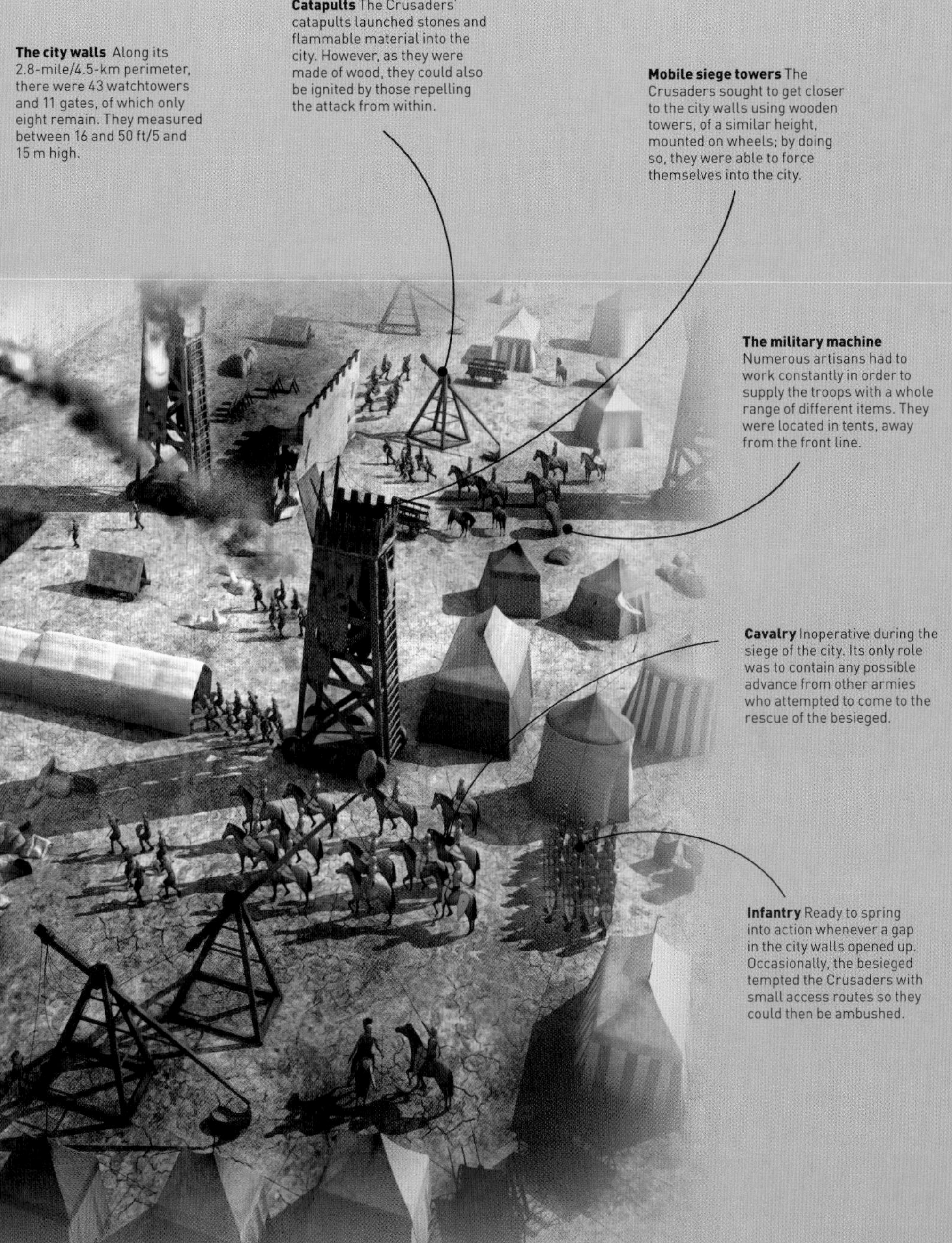

The military machine Numerous artisans had to work constantly in order to supply the troops with a whole range of different items. They were located in tents, away from the front line.

Cavalry Inoperative during the siege of the city. Its only role was to contain any possible advance from other armies who attempted to come to the rescue of the besieged.

Infantry Ready to spring into action whenever a gap in the city walls opened up. Occasionally, the besieged tempted the Crusaders with small access routes so they could then be ambushed.

JUSTINIAN'S LEGACY

The Byzantine army, after decades of imperial decline, began to rally under Justinian I (483–565), when the emperor obtained the financial resources to maintain it, delegating his power to two magnificent generals: Belisarius and Narses. Previously, under Diocletian (284–305) and Constantine the Great (306–337), the empire, despite at its peak having numbered hundreds of thousands of men, had no significant network of reserves or mobile troops. Nonetheless, gradually the number of foot archers increased, as did the strength of its cavalry, whose members adopted more comprehensive armor which protected both rider and mount, and were known as cataphracts. Under Theodosius (379–395), the army also incorporated Barbarian riders, known as *foederati*, although his successors, Leo I (457–474) and Zeno the Isaurian (474–491) reduced the number of these mercenaries, resulting in problems between local troops. Both limited themselves to securing the borders of an empire that was only resuscitated under Justinian, who referred to himself as "he who never sleeps."

Justinian established three categories among his troops: the *numeri*, normal heavy infantry soldiers equipped with a spear and shield; the foederati, or soldiers of fortune, and the *bucellarii*, the household troops of noblemen. Under the emperor, the heavy cavalry, armed with spears and swords, and the mounted archers, who did not wear full-length armor, became the main weapons in battle.

During the seventh century, at the time of the Muslim conquests, Constantinople had around 25,000 men spread around the city and the armies had an average of 20,000 soldiers, although the total number of men at the service of the empire was significantly greater. The Byzantine army attached great importance to its armor, and was also able to transport horses long distances by sea, which were ready for combat upon disembarkation. Furthermore, the Byzantines were the first to construct boats with frames, and their conventional vessels, the *dromon*, were equipped with two benches of oarsmen. Over 100 men fought from each boat, performing tasks such as launching the so-called "Greek fire" (an inflammable liquid, the composition of which remains unknown) at their enemies, in addition to launching catapults.

However, despite these advances and their victories against the Vandals in the Battle of Tricamarum in 535, against the Ostrogoths in 552 at the Battle of Taginae, and the fall of the Persian Empire in 628, the Byzantine Empire, significantly weakened by a century of war on both the eastern and western fronts, lost a large amount of its eastern territory during the seventh and eighth centuries: Syria, the Holy Land, Egypt, North Africa, and most of Italy soon fell into enemy hands.

Byzantine Cataphracts

The cataphracts, bodies of heavy cavalry horses with both riders and horses covered in armor, were an elite force in the Byzantine army. Their contribution to the Byzantine victories were decisive for centuries until, after the defeat before the Turks in Manzikert (1071) they all but disappeared.

Armored riders

The Byzantine cataphracts were practically impenetrable and had devastating power. They were disciplined and, unlike medieval knights, they comprised a combat unit under a joint military command. They also had greater maneuverability and tactical variants that included frontal assaults as well as enveloping actions, double-flanking, wedging, and harassment, among others.

Horse They were also covered in full armor and had a chamfron for the face.

Crest The horses wore a crest in the color that identified their tagma.

PERIODS OF SPLENDOR
In the sixth century, they were the elite troops with which General Belisarius expanded the frontiers of the empire in the Western Mediterranean. In the tenth century, Emperor Nikephorus II designed new tactics to harness the power and mobility of the cataphracts in their successful campaigns.

BYZANTINES VERSUS ARABS
Battle of the year 842; one of the chronicles of the eleventh century Byzantine historian, John Skylitzes.

GENERAL CHARACTERISTICS

In the tenth century, the tactical unit of the cavalry was the *tagma*, which in turn was grouped into *moirai* (made up of between two and five tagma). Three moirai formed a *turmai*, or regiment.

Insignia
The double-headed eagle with the *sympilema* (dynastic cipher) of Palaiologos in the center, was the symbol of the Byzantine Empire.

COMMAND ▸ Strategies

TAGMATA ON CAMPAIGN ▸ 15

SOLDIERS PER TAGMA ▸ 300

IMPENETRABLE
The armor was so effective that the Emperor Alexios I Komnenos ended the battle with numerous spearheads embedded in his, but none of them had touched his body.

Helmet Conical-type helmet, could be attached to the head covering, protecting the entire head without restricting mobility.
Head covering Attached to the helmet and made of three layers, leaving only the eyes visible.
Epiloricon A padded coat; unlike European knights, the Byzantines wore it over their armor.
Armor plating Called *klibania*, this was the distinctive hallmark of the cataphracts.
Chain mail Worn under the epiloricon.
Shield Although it was not always used, the most common in the tenth century was round and small and generally carried on the back.
Paramerion A short cavalry sword with a curved edge and a single blade on the inside.
Bardoukion The mace was the preferred weapon for close combat.
Kontos The spear was 11.5 ft/3.5 m long. It was used for charging rather than as a throwing weapon.
Spathion A straight, double-edged, large sword. Each cataphract carried two swords.

The Battle of Manzikert

In August 1071, to the east of modern-day Turkey, the Byzantine army of Romanos IV Diogenes was defeated by the Seljuq Turks led by Alp Arslan. The improvised nature of command and the numerous desertions among Byzantine ranks at the height of battle caused chaos that led to resounding defeat. Manzikert marked the start of the decline of the Byzantine Empire and opened the door to Turkish dominance in Anatolia.

Combat

Byzantine emperor Romanos IV Diogenes led a vast army to the eastern front of the empire to put an end to the Seljuq incursions in Anatolia. In Manzikert, they would face the troops of the Sultan, Alp Arslan.

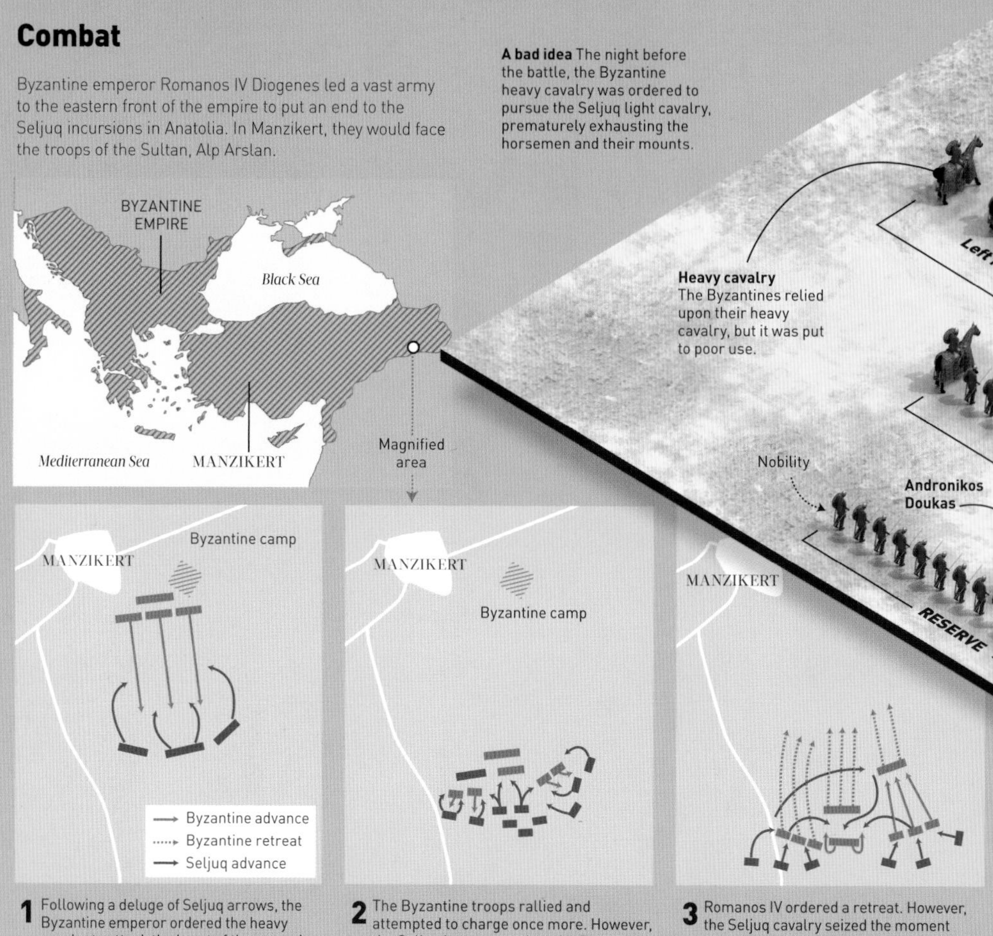

A bad idea The night before the battle, the Byzantine heavy cavalry was ordered to pursue the Seljuq light cavalry, prematurely exhausting the horsemen and their mounts.
BYZANTINE EMPIRE
Black Sea
Mediterranean Sea
MANZIKERT
Magnified area
Heavy cavalry The Byzantines relied upon their heavy cavalry, but it was put to poor use.
Nobility
Andronikos Doukas
RESERVE
MANZIKERT
Byzantine camp
Byzantine advance
Byzantine retreat
Seljuq advance

1 Following a deluge of Seljuq arrows, the Byzantine emperor ordered the heavy cavalry to attack the heart of the enemy's ranks. The latter avoided all-out combat and retreated while the flanks advanced, trapping both the Byzantine flanks and rear guard with a shower of arrows.

2 The Byzantine troops rallied and attempted to charge once more. However, the Seljuq barrage against the Byzantine flanks persisted and opened a gap between the flanks and the center of the army.

3 Romanos IV ordered a retreat. However, the Seljuq cavalry seized the moment to attack. The right Byzantine flank absconded. The left flank and the reserves were attacked by the Seljuqs, and fled as a result. The imperial center of the Byzantine army was surrounded. The overwhelming Byzantine defeat was confirmed.

Duel between cavalries

The Battle of Manzikert was a strategic duel between two cavalries: the Byzantine heavy cavalry and the Seljuq light cavalry, with the latter emerging victorious.

BALANCE OF POWER

BYZANTINES ▸ Between 40,000 and 60,000 men, comprising natives and mercenaries.

SELJUQS ▸ Around 30,000 men, most light cavalry horsemen.

Turkomans

Right flank

Seljuqs

Light cavalry The Seljuqs were supported by their light cavalry, armed with bows and arrows; they were more vulnerable, but also more maneuverable.

Macedonians, Thracians, Thessalians, Uzos, Slavs, and Pechenegs.

Nikephoros Bryennios

Imperial center At the heart of the formation, the Byzantine emperor himself commanded his troops. Romanos IV was taken prisoner following his defeat.

Taranges

Center

Turkomans and Seljuqs

Scolas, Optimates, Hikanators, and Excubitors (elite corps).

Cappadocians, Armenians, Georgians, Pechenegs, and Uzos.

Center

VANGUARD

Left flank

Theodore

REAR GUARD

Right flank

Foreigners Both armies comprised a large number of allied forces. Only a small number were native Byzantines or Seljuqs.

Varangian Guard, Russians, and the numeri.

Normans, Franks, and the elderly.

Desertions The Normans and the rear guard retreated from battle, abandoning the emperor.

ROMANOS IV DIOGENES A military Byzantine emperor, who ruled for just three years. He was deposed and assassinated following the defeat at Manzikert.

◂ **ALP ARSLAN** The second Seljuq sultan and celebrated warrior, he died just a year after Manzikert at the hands of a prisoner.

NOMADIC SOLDIERS

Under Genghis Khan (1162–1227), the Mongol army became one of the most efficient and disciplined in the world. Made up of elements taken from a variety of different tribes and cultures, it nonetheless displayed an enviable level of cohesion and professionalism; historians have attributed this to principles of religious tolerance and the pragmatism promoted by its leader, who also implemented a decimal system to enhance its organization. Thus, an *arban* comprised ten men; a *zagún* one hundred men; a *mingam* a thousand men; and a *tumen* ten thousand men. Each arban included soldiers from different ethnicities and origins, thus promoting the development of a sense of brotherhood between them. Officers, who were responsible for taking decisions on the battlefield, were selected based on merit, and not depending upon their origins or family ties. The troops, not including infantry, were very fast and soon earned a reputation as being terrifying and extremely destructive. All the troops had at least four mounts, which they would ride in turn to facilitate mobility. In fact, they could travel up to 250 miles/400 km in just three days, which at the time represented an enormous advantage over their enemies. Furthermore, the relationship between horsemen and their mounts, both accustomed to a nomadic style of life, started during childhood, and the bond between a soldier and his horse was absolute. They never transported tools that were not strictly necessary, and they fed their animals conscientiously, using the best pastures they could find on their travels. The soldiers were also expert hunters, and the army employed hunting as a form of military training. They hunted animals until they trapped them in a circle of horsemen, and they only sacrificed those required for sustenance; soldiers had to kill animals with a single blow in order to maintain the utmost respect.

The efficiency of the army allowed the Mongol Empire to expand its territories quickly. As a result, they had to implement a communications system by which a message could be transmitted from one side of the empire to the other. To this end, they established a category of especially quick horsemen–the yam (or *Ortoo* in Mongolian)–and a network of posts, each around 22 miles/35 km apart, where messengers could obtain water and food, provided by local families. Soldiers were outfitted only with absolutely essential equipment: a compound bow and a quiver for arrows, a short sword and a dagger, a wicker shield and a javelin, in addition to a waterproof leather pack with which they could wade along the rivers. Among Genghis Khan's successors, in the thirteenth and fourteenth centuries, the use of helmets was introduced to army officers, occasionally adorned with plumes or well-worked steel plate armor laid on top of leather.

Mongol Horsemen

The army created by Genghis Khan was almost exclusively made up of cavalrymen, divided into heavy and light cavalry. Its power lay in its extraordinary mobility, the effectiveness of its specifically created tactics and that it was a highly qualified army for the type of war it fought. Mongol warriors were not only magnificent horsemen and archers, they also demonstrated a surprising toughness, hardened by the harsh conditions of life on the Eurasian steppes.

Born to fight

In Mongol society, all men between the ages of 16 and 60 who were physically fit to fight were warriors. Some 60 percent of the Mongol cavalry was light and 40 percent heavy, although they complemented each other tactically, combining the shock power of the latter with the rain of arrows of the former. The riders were so skilled with the bow and arrow that they could load and fire while at a gallop with almost infallible precision.

CRUEL BESIEGERS

Although they preferred to fight in open country where they could use their horsemen effectively, Mongols learned the art of laying siege to a city, to which they added large doses of cruelty. They could set fire to a whole city and, once captured, indiscriminately execute men, women, and children.

The Mongols, under the command of Hulagu Khan, laid siege to and took the city of Bagdad in 1258.

GENERAL CHARACTERISTICS

Each warrior was responsible for his own food and equipment and had at least three reserve horses. By constantly changing their mount, they traveled enormous distances in a very short time.

Insignia
The Black Standard, or Khar Sulde. Made from horsehair, it was used only for war.

ARMIES IN CAMPAIGN ▸ Between 5 and 8 (150,000 to 240,000 men)

TUMEN PER ARMY ▸ 3 (30,000 soldiers)

HISTORIC VICTORIES ▸ Battle of Indus (1221), Battle of the Kalka River (1233), Battle of Köse Dag (1243)

SHOOTING AN ARROW

Each bow, depending on its use and characteristics, has a distinct way of firing. The Mongols had their own technique for firing arrows.

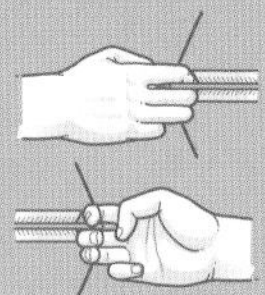

Mediterranean
The arrow is held with the index finger, without using the fingertip. The string is pulled using the middle and ring fingers.

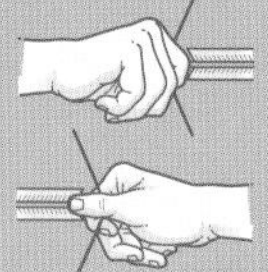

The pinch
The end of the arrow is gripped with the index finger and thumb. The string is pulled using the middle and ring fingers.

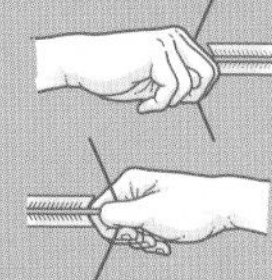

Mongol
The thumb, the strongest digit, pulls the string. The index and ring fingers strengthen the grip around the back and the thumb.

Helmet In combat, the traditional wool hat was substituted for a helmet of leather or iron.
Armor Under the leather armor they wore a silk shirt, capable of reducing the impact of an arrow.
Bow Two types were used: one for short distance, the other for long distance. The long-distance bow could shoot more than 1,000 ft/ 300 m.
Whistling arrows Used as a signaling technique, the whistle was caused by the air passing through the holes made in the end.
Protection Sometimes their protection was reinforced with leather shoulder pads and wrist guards.
Saber Instead of swords, they used sabers, a cavalry weapon. They were curved, short and light.
Horses They belonged to the Przewalski subgroup, small, strong, fast, and tough.
Saddle Under it they carried their ration of raw meat, which became tenderized over time.
Shield They often went without a shield. If they did use one it was small, made of wicker and wrapped in leather.
Stirrups They were short, which allowed them to be more secure in order to shoot their arrows.
Quiver They carried two, which contained at least 60 arrows of different types.

The Battle of Mohi

Under the reign of Ögedei, son of Genghis Khan, the Mongols continued their expansion westward, with successful campaigns in Poland and Hungary. The resounding Mongol victory against the Hungarian Army at Mohi, on April 11, 1241, made the threat of a Mongol invasion of Western Europe a real prospect. The battle claimed thousands of victims, resulted in the destruction of Hungary, and opened the doors of the Old Continent to the invaders from the steppes. Only the death of the Mongol emperor stopped his armies from continuing in their quest for the rest of Europe.

Battle at the bridge

The stone bridge over the River Sajó played an important role in the Battle of Mohi. However, the Mongol strategy of surrounding the Hungarian troops was vital in deciding its outcome.

BALANCE OF POWER

HUNGARIANS ▸ 25,000 men, including Hungarians, Templar Knights, Teutonic Knights, and Cumans.

MONGOLS ▸ Around 30,000

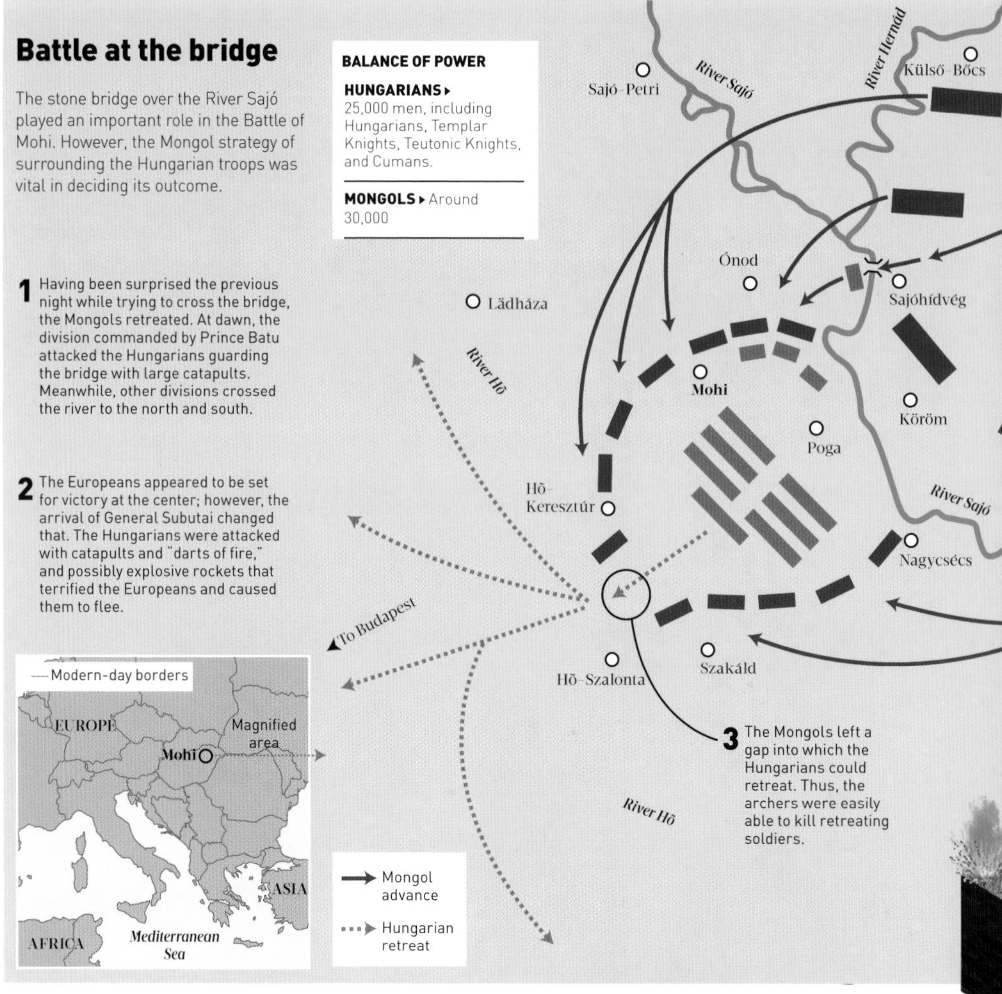
Sajó-Petri
River Sajó
River Hernád
Külső-Bőcs
Ónod
Lädháza
Sajóhídvég
River Hő
Mohi
Köröm
Poga
Hő-Keresztúr
River Sajó
Nagycsécs
To Budapest
Hő-Szalonta
Szakáld
River Hő
Modern-day borders
EUROPE
Magnified area
Mohi
ASIA
AFRICA
Mediterranean Sea
Mongol advance
Hungarian retreat

1 Having been surprised the previous night while trying to cross the bridge, the Mongols retreated. At dawn, the division commanded by Prince Batu attacked the Hungarians guarding the bridge with large catapults. Meanwhile, other divisions crossed the river to the north and south.

2 The Europeans appeared to be set for victory at the center; however, the arrival of General Subutai changed that. The Hungarians were attacked with catapults and "darts of fire," and possibly explosive rockets that terrified the Europeans and caused them to flee.

3 The Mongols left a gap into which the Hungarians could retreat. Thus, the archers were easily able to kill retreating soldiers.

The power of fire

It is likely that during the Battle of Mohi, the Mongols used gunpowder brought from China for the first time. History books mention "darts of fire," although it is not clear exactly what they were.

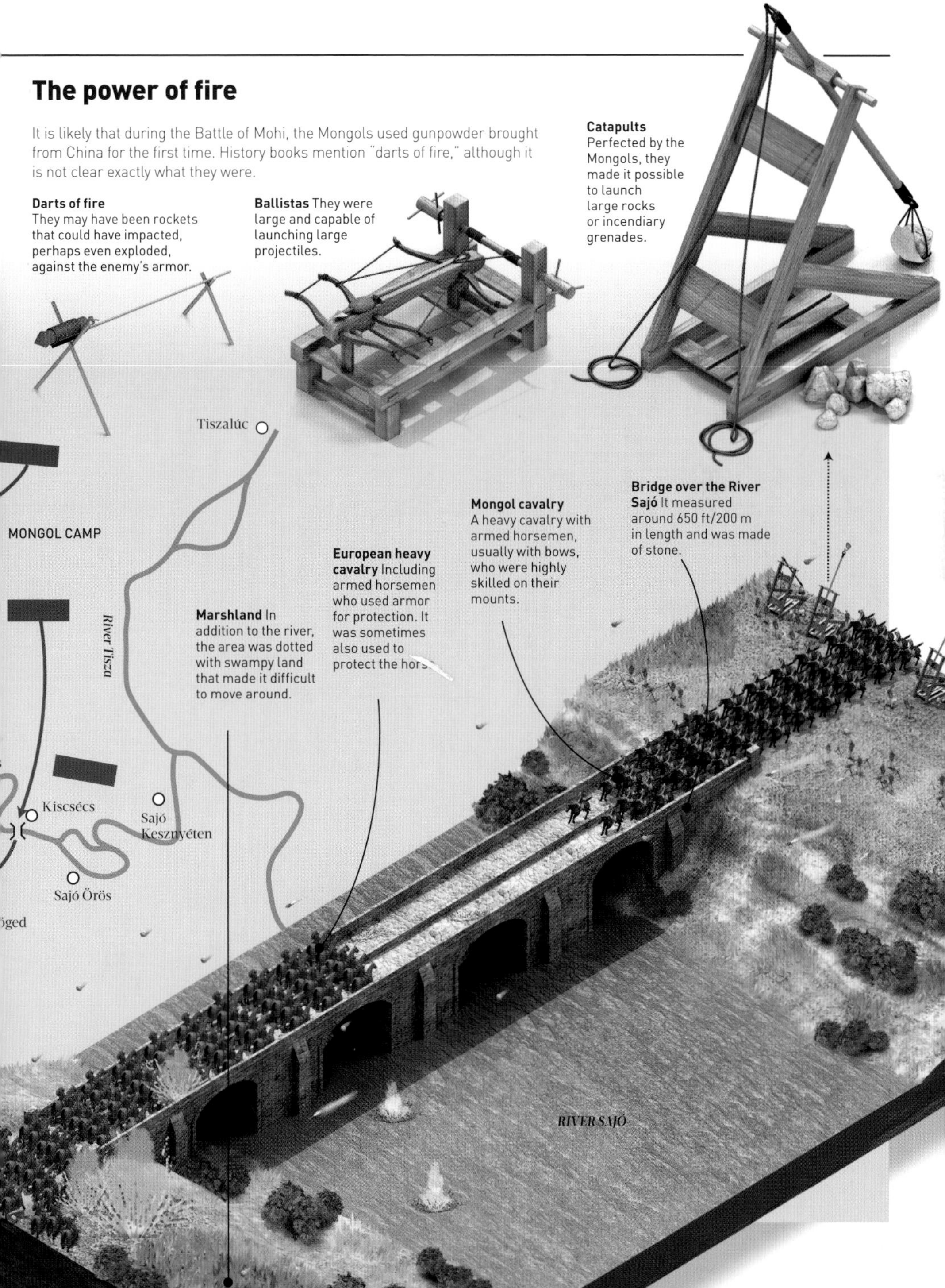

Darts of fire
They may have been rockets that could have impacted, perhaps even exploded, against the enemy's armor.
Ballistas They were large and capable of launching large projectiles.
Catapults
Perfected by the Mongols, they made it possible to launch large rocks or incendiary grenades.
Tiszalúc
MONGOL CAMP
River Tisza
Kiscsécs
Sajó Kesznyéten
Sajó Örös
Marshland In addition to the river, the area was dotted with swampy land that made it difficult to move around.
European heavy cavalry Including armed horsemen who used armor for protection. It was sometimes also used to protect the hors
Mongol cavalry
A heavy cavalry with armed horsemen, usually with bows, who were highly skilled on their mounts.
Bridge over the River Sajó It measured around 650 ft/200 m in length and was made of stone.
RIVER SAJÓ

CHAPTER 3

THE MODERN AGE

3 **INTRODUCTION**

THE AGE OF GUNPOWDER

The Modern Age, between the sixteenth and nineteenth centuries, was an era of great European maritime empires in which technological advances were crucial in the manufacture and use of weapons and military strategy and tactics. Armies were modernized and became professional, revolutions took place that changed the world, and European nations were formed almost as we know them today.

In the sixteenth century, the Mediterranean Sea was the battleground between Christians from the North and West, and Muslims from the South and East. It was a time of guns and sails. Warships replaced the ram at the bow with a platform for artillery, which by 1530 was using metal projectiles. The Spanish monarch Philip II assembled nearly 200 galleys; boats that carried up to 400 men and had a large central cannon, with two to four heavy and several light pieces of weaponry. These were the protagonists of the great battles, which were usually frontal assaults on fortifications or took place near major anchorages, such as Preveza (1538), Djerba (1560), Malta (1565), Lepanto (1571), and Tunisia (1573). The sixteenth century was also the Golden Age of the conquistadors. Interestingly, when the Ottomans threatened Europe by land, there was an unprecedented expansion by sea among the European kingdoms. The Spanish completely dominated the Atlantic, the Mediterranean, and the Pacific, and the Portuguese, British, and Dutch were forces in the Indian Ocean and the China Sea.

On land, three elements characterized these centuries: the revolution in the design of forts; the evolution and improvement of firearms; and the increase in the number of men making up the armies whose objectives, in principle, were not enemy armies but fortified cities. Sieges outnumbered battles in the sixteenth and seventeenth centuries, in which there were more warlike activities than in any other war period in European history. Emperor Charles V provided his legions with uniforms, music, permanent regiments, chaplains, doctors, and a better supply of weapons, which in the time of Fernando Álvarez de Toledo (3rd Duke of Alba) included muskets with support pins capable of penetrating armor plating from 590 ft/180 m away.

During the sixteenth century, when most of the fighting was for dynastic rights, Spain and France were constantly at war. The Ottoman Empire, the Habsburgs, and Sweden fought every two out of three years. Spain fought three out of four, and Poland and Russia, four out of five. In two hundred years there were only ten years of complete peace on the entire continent of Europe.

The seventeenth century, in which they fought for control of territories and for religious reasons, was "the century of soldiers." There were between ten and twelve million Europeans, but the lack of funds resulted in a lack of discipline, desertion, and mutinies in all armies, which eventually incorporated mercenaries. In the Thirty Years' War (1618–48), more than 300 Swiss and German "entrepreneurs" hired complete armies and put them at the service of one or another faction. They also changed strategies and inline formations appeared, in which three rows of musketeers were rotated, thus creating a constant barrage of fire. The first military academy in Europe was created in 1616 by Count John of Nassau, who also wrote the first instruction manual.

After its victory against Spain in 1659, France created a new model for a permanent army which would be imitated by the Prussians and Russians. Under Louis XIV (1643–1715), 350,000 men were added, and he created a Ministry for War (1675), the first hierarchy in which seniority of rank prevailed. In 1699, the flintlock musket appeared, which was faster than the matchlock. In 1703, France enlisted troops with bayonets and prepared an order for battle with two or three lines of infantry in the center, cavalry on the flanks (the dragoons, which fought on horseback and on foot), and artillery across the width at the front. Ambitious kings and statesmen promoted clashes between countries. In Western Europe, England, Spain and the Netherlands fought France, while to the east it was Austria, France, Sweden and Russia. After the War of the League of Augsburg (1688–97) and the War of Spanish Succession (1701–14), the death of Louis XIV in 1715 marked the end of an era for France and the beginning of Prussian supremacy.

In Austria, King Frederick William (1713–40) brought together an army of 80,000 men and created the Prussian officer corps; the most professional army in Europe. He also elevated its officers to the highest places in the social hierarchy. Frederick the Great (1740–86) would turn the country into a great military power in a state that was, in reality, created to support his army. Then the Seven Years' War (1756–63) broke out. It was a conflict of global dimensions that was fought in Europe, North America, and South Asia and opened a new era in which military requirements would shape governments and determine the fate of the European states.

As the English consolidated their hold on the sea and created their own army in India supported by the sepoys (Indian soldiers hired and trained in the European style), in Europe, new weapons and new ideas for combat were put into practice. After 1750, European armies incorporated light infantry, formed into lines and columns during battle, and improved their cannon, which was cast in one piece and then pierced, greatly improving projection. In addition, as was the case in France, cadet schools were created and officers became professionals.

Between 1763 and 1815 war, and the world, changed completely. By 1775, with the War of American Independence, marauders and snipers came onto the scene, and a "people's army" was established. After 1783, with the Treaty of Paris, which recognized the independence of the United States, and after the French Revolution of 1789, nothing would ever be the same again. After the dissolution of the French army of the "old regime," the citizen–soldier would emerge. In 1790, France was a nation in arms that enlisted a million politically educated soldiers. Effective tactics and mobile cannon gave them their first victories in 1792, although the strategic greed of Napoleon Bonaparte, the looting carried out by his troops, as well as improvements in his enemies' armies, such as those of the English and Prussians (who created a War Academy to train state officers) would soon put an end to French supremacy in Europe. In 1815, after 25 years of war between the European powers, the English, who were masters of the sea and world trade, outstripped them all, especially after the naval battle of Trafalgar, in which Admiral Horatio Nelson, the inspiration for "dogfight tactics" (boat against boat, breaking the enemy formation), died.

The Crimean War in 1853, in which the Russians invaded the territory of a very weak Ottoman Empire, is considered the last war of the modern age which, for many historians, ended in 1864 with the signing of the First Geneva Convention–the first international treaty for the protection of victims of armed conflict. The American Civil War (1861–65) would then introduce the military practices of the twentieth century.

Chronology and Main Battles

Between the sixteenth and nineteenth centuries, warships were the protagonists of many military actions in a race, in which all the European powers participated, to acquire the latest weapons. Most ships had more artillery than many of the forts on land, and fleets, like armies, required enormous financial resources. The growing professional troops increased their firearms capacity exponentially.

1498
Vasco de Gama rounds the Cape of Good Hope

1501
Isabella I of Castile authorizes the use of black slaves in America

1522
Magellan sails around the world

1525
French defeat in Pavia, Italy

1526
The Turkish army of Suleiman I defeats the Hungarians at the Battle of Mohács

1545
The Council of Trent meets, and lays the foundations for the Counter-reformation

1571
John of Austria, with the help of Venice and the papacy, defeats the Ottomans at the Battle of Lepanto

1588
Defeat of the invincible Spanish Armada by the English

1600
Creation of the British East India Company

1618
The Thirty Years' War begins

1654
Russia and Poland fight for control of Ukraine

1660
The monarchy is restored in England

1701–1714
War of Spanish Succession

1703
Founding of St. Petersburg

1500 — **1700**

1514
The Ottoman army defeats the Safid army in the Battle of Chaldiran

1517
Luther criticizes Catholic practices leading to the Protestant Reformation

1519
Hernán Cortés begins the conquest of Mexico

1533
Pizarro conquers Cuzco. End of the Incan Empire

1558
Death of Charles V, Emperor of the Holy Roman Empire and King of Spain

1562
First Religious War in France between Protestants (Huguenots) and Catholics

1592
First Japanese invasion of Korea

1598
The eighth French Religious War ends

1642–51
English Civil War

1689
Peter the Great, Tsar of Russia

1700–21
Great Northern War between Russia and Sweden

E T . H E S P E R I Æ

Standards with the arms of Aragon, Leon, and Castile during the funeral rites for the death of Charles V.

THE TAKING OF TENOCHTITLÁN
In May 1521, Hernán Cortés, commanding some 1,000 Spanish, lay siege to Tenochtitlán, the Aztec capital. He conquered it on August 13. In less than three months, 100,000 Aztecs died.

One island, 13 boats
Cortés had 13 small boats built, each with a cannon on the bow to conquer the city, located in the middle of a large lake.

Proclamation by Abraham Lincoln, in which the President of the United States of America announces the liberation of the slaves.

1721
Introduction of rifles in America

1769
Invention of the steam engine

1775–83
War of American Independence

1793
King Louis XVI is executed. France declares war on Great Britain, the Netherlands, Spain, and the Italian territories

1799
Napoleon carries out a coup d'état, defeats the Directorate and establishes the Consulate

1805
Napoleon's army defeats Russia and Austria at the Battle of Austerlitz

The English fleet defeats the Franco-Spanish fleet at the Battle of Trafalgar

1808
The Napoleonic invasion of the Iberian Peninsula meets with resistance from Spanish guerrillas

1835
Texas becomes independent from Mexico

1839–42
Opium wars in China

1861–65
American Civil War

1862
The United States Federal Congress abolishes slavery

1863
Unionist victory at the Battle of Gettysburg (American Civil War).

1864
First Geneva Convention

1884
Conference in Berlin divides up Africa between the European powers

1900

1732
Prussia creates compulsory military service

1756
Prussia invades Saxony. Beginning of the Seven Years' War

1783
Russia annexes Crimea

1789
French Revolution

1803
The British defeat the Marathas at Assaye (India)

1804
Napoleon is crowned Emperor of the French

1815
Battle of Waterloo. Napoleon is defeated by an alliance between the English, Dutch, and Prussians

1818
Shaka occupies the Zulu throne and begins the expansion of this African kingdom

1853–56
Crimean War between Russia and the Ottoman Empire, supported by France and England

1857
Mutiny against British rule in India

1876
Battle of Little Big Horn. Sioux and Cheyenne Indians annihilate the U.S. Cavalry

1878
The Zulus defeat the British in Isandlwana

The storming of the Bastille.

Zulu warriors in a nineteenth-century engraving.

Famous Leaders

They ruled empires, colonized new worlds, established trade routes worldwide, and benefited from the technological advances of their era to arm their immense armies which, over time, ended up as almost completely professional units. During the Modern Age, emperors, kings, and statesmen were at war almost constantly for nearly three centuries, with the tactics and strategies employed during these wars reaching high levels of specialization.

1494-1566

SULEIMAN KANUNI
Known as "the Magnificent," he developed science and the arts. An Ottoman Sultan between 1520 and 1566, he personally led his army during the conquest of Belgrade, Rhodes, Hungary, and the siege of Vienna in 1529. His empire continued to expand after his death.

1500-1558

CHARLES OF AUSTRIA
He governed an extremely vast empire as Holy Roman Emperor Charles V and King Charles I of Spain. A fierce defender of Catholicism, he tried to slow down Lutheran reform and the constant threat from the Turks. He died in retirement at Yuste Monastery.

1672-1725

PETER I THE GREAT
Crowned Czar of Russia in 1682. He decided to westernize his country, modernizing the tools used in the countryside; he also created a permanent army and transformed Russia into a great power. He was constantly at war with the Turks and founded St. Petersburg.

1712-1786

FREDERICK II THE GREAT
King of Prussia, he reformed and professionalized the army, making it one of the best of his time. Thanks to him, and as a result of his military successes during the Seven Years' War, Prussia expanded its territories and created a gap between the large European powers.

"At sea we fight at a distance, as if from walls or fortresses, and we seldom come close enough to fight hand to hand."

Fernando Oliveira, *The Art of the War at Sea* (1555).

THOUSANDS OF MEN ABOARD

It was the Scots who were first to arm the so-called "first-rate ships." In 1688, the Dutch fleet comprised 102 warships, the French fleet 221, and the English fleet 173. The latter was carrying 45,000 men when it defeated Spain in 1690.

1758-1805

HORATIO NELSON

He enrolled in the English army at age twelve, and was captain by twenty. He fought in America against the Thirteen Colonies, and was named admiral during the successful wars against Napoleonic France, winning the decisive Battle of Trafalgar, in which he died.

1769-1821

NAPOLEON BONAPARTE

Strategist extraordinaire, he served as a brigadier during the French Revolution. In 1799, he took power during a *coup d'état*. He led a military campaign that saw him control almost all of Europe, before dying in exile on the island of St Helena after defeat at Waterloo.

1809-1865

ABRAHAM LINCOLN

Committed to abolishing slavery, he was elected President of the United States in 1860. His election hastened the secession of the southern states and the end of the American Civil War, during which he led the Union to victory. He was assassinated by a sympathizer of the South.

c1831-1890

SITTING BULL

Chief of the Sioux tribe, he led the rebellion of several Indian tribes against government forces that had occupied their land. He achieved a significant victory at the Battle of Little Bighorn, but was eventually confined to a reservation, where he was assassinated.

Weapons of the Modern Age

The spread of firearms led to a change in how war was waged in the Modern Age. The bow and crossbow gave way to the harquebus, musket, and rifle, while the appearance of mobile artillery led to cannons on the battlefields. However, the first firearms were heavy and slow. Therefore, pikes continued to be fundamental for the infantry well into the seventeenth century, as well as swords and sabers for the cavalry.

Muskets and rifles

The development of firearms led to an increase in fire power and accuracy. After the first harquebuses and matchlock muskets, the wheel lock followed in the middle of the sixteenth century. These faster and easier-to-use muskets became the weapon of choice of the armies of the time. At the same time cartridges appeared, incorporating gunpowder and the bullets required for a shot. Long-range rifles were introduced in the nineteenth century and reached their zenith with breech-loading rifles (where the cartridge is inserted into the chamber) with ridges or grooves in the barrel making them much more precise.

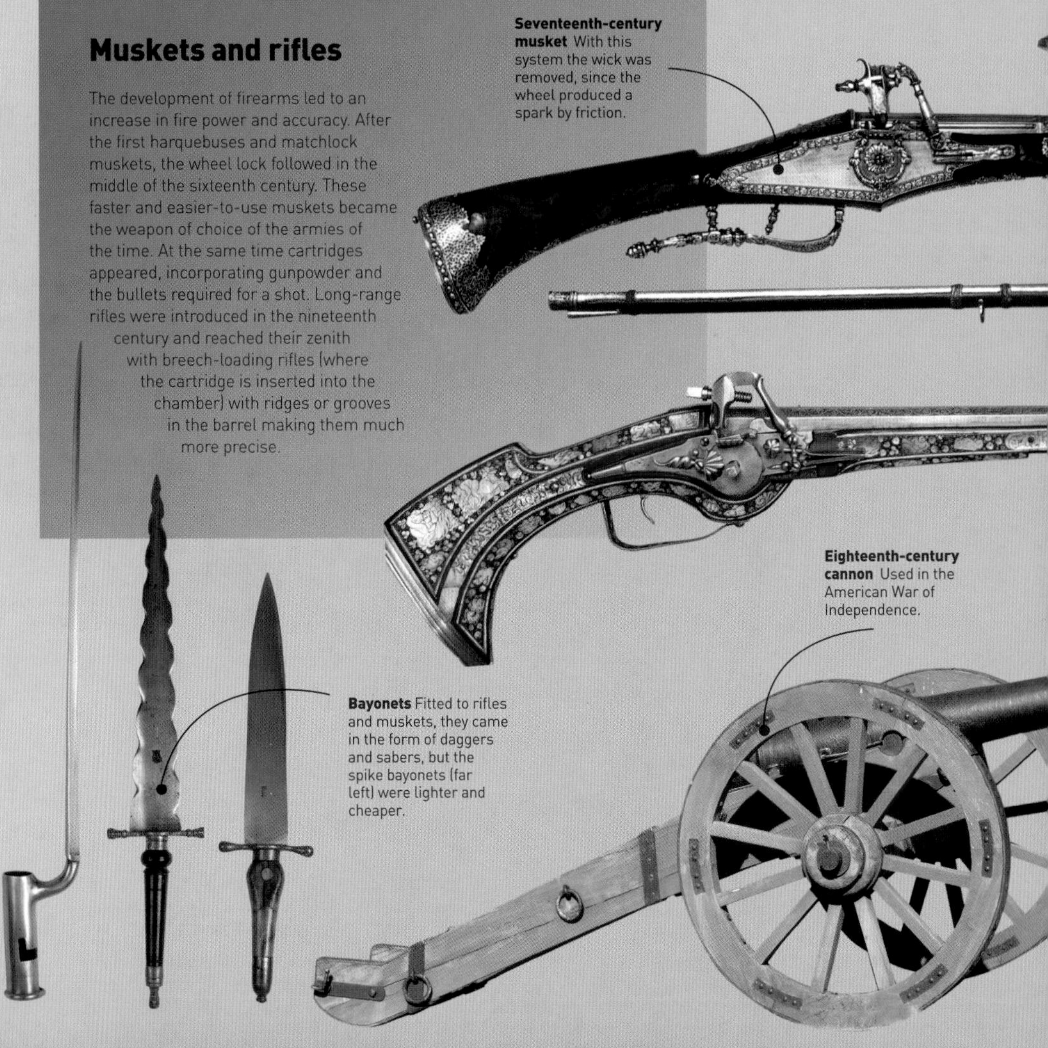

Seventeenth-century musket With this system the wick was removed, since the wheel produced a spark by friction.

Eighteenth-century cannon Used in the American War of Independence.

Bayonets Fitted to rifles and muskets, they came in the form of daggers and sabers, but the spike bayonets (far left) were lighter and cheaper.

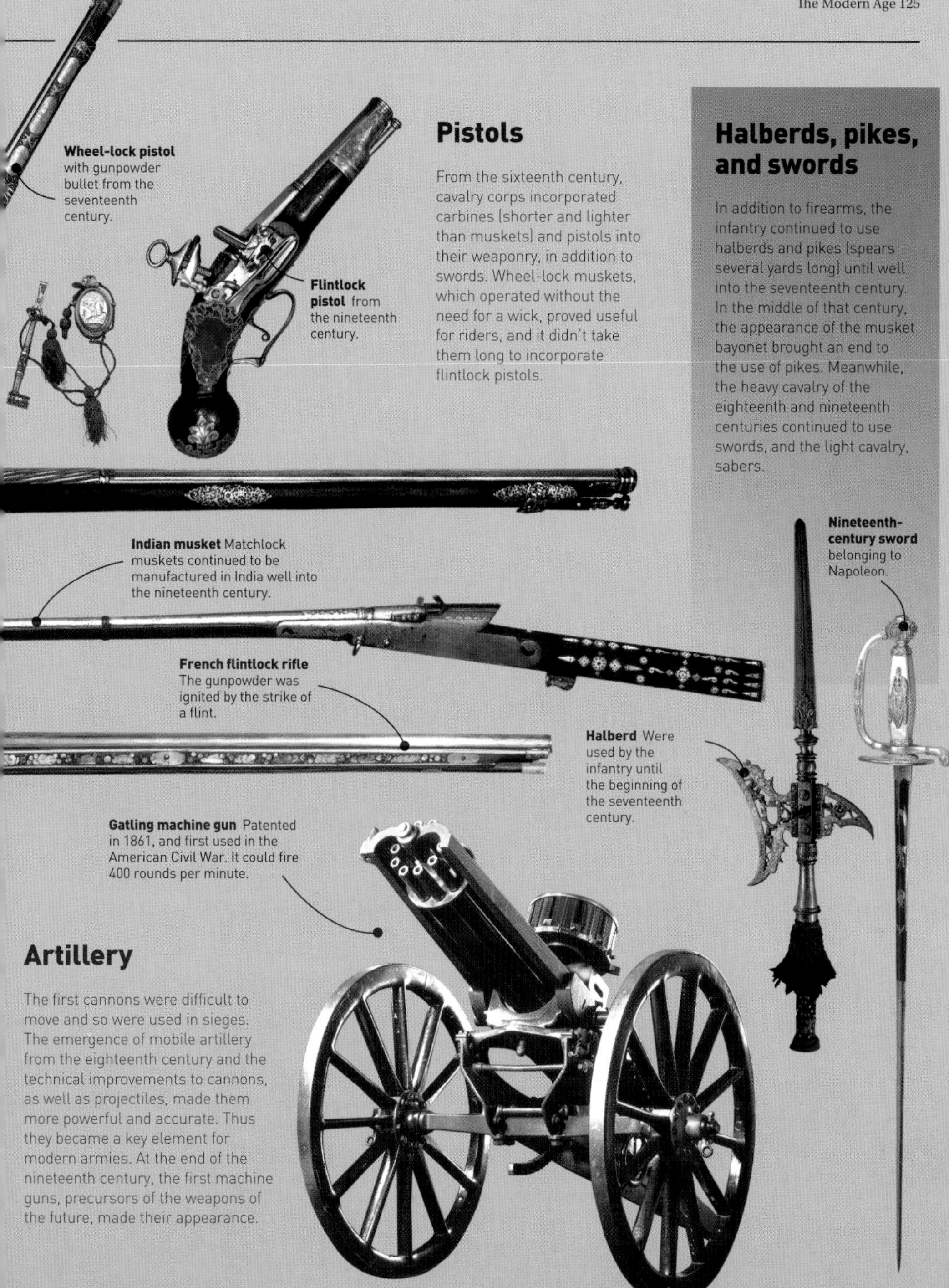

Wheel-lock pistol with gunpowder bullet from the seventeenth century.

Flintlock pistol from the nineteenth century.

Indian musket Matchlock muskets continued to be manufactured in India well into the nineteenth century.

French flintlock rifle The gunpowder was ignited by the strike of a flint.

Gatling machine gun Patented in 1861, and first used in the American Civil War. It could fire 400 rounds per minute.

Halberd Were used by the infantry until the beginning of the seventeenth century.

Nineteenth-century sword belonging to Napoleon.

Pistols

From the sixteenth century, cavalry corps incorporated carbines (shorter and lighter than muskets) and pistols into their weaponry, in addition to swords. Wheel-lock muskets, which operated without the need for a wick, proved useful for riders, and it didn't take them long to incorporate flintlock pistols.

Halberds, pikes, and swords

In addition to firearms, the infantry continued to use halberds and pikes (spears several yards long) until well into the seventeenth century. In the middle of that century, the appearance of the musket bayonet brought an end to the use of pikes. Meanwhile, the heavy cavalry of the eighteenth and nineteenth centuries continued to use swords, and the light cavalry, sabers.

Artillery

The first cannons were difficult to move and so were used in sieges. The emergence of mobile artillery from the eighteenth century and the technical improvements to cannons, as well as projectiles, made them more powerful and accurate. Thus they became a key element for modern armies. At the end of the nineteenth century, the first machine guns, precursors of the weapons of the future, made their appearance.

Sioux Warriors

The Sioux nation was one of the toughest of the many indigenous North American tribes against whom the white man battled. A people with a long fighting tradition, they believed in the glory of combat, through which tribal respect was earned. Between 1854 and 1890, they came up against the powerful U.S. Army in a series of armed conflicts known as the Sioux Wars.

Quick as lightning

The Sioux quickly employed horses, introduced by the Europeans, and made them an essential part of their tactics during combat. These tactics were based on speed and surprise. They were expert ambushers and excelled at hit-and-run attacks. During battleground combat, they attacked in waves, with large numbers of warriors repeatedly harrying the weak points of enemy lines until they were breached.

Horse The mustangs, wild horses that the Native Americans tamed, descended from those taken to America by the Spanish.

SITTING BULL

The Sioux had several chiefs, such as Red Cloud, Crazy Horse, and Sitting Bull, who was not just a leader in war, but also a spiritual leader. He was the most important leader between 1868 and 1876, commanding and inspiring the great Native American victory at Little Bighorn, where they beat the Seventh Cavalry led by George Custer.

Tatanka Iyotanka. This is how Sitting Bull was known to his people. An 1881 portrait of Sitting Bull in Bismark, Dakota Territory, nine years before his death.

USE OF THE RIFLE

During the mid-nineteenth century, the Native Americans started to obtain Winchester rifles and used them in battle. Nevertheless, they were always more adept with a bow, which they never stopped using.

HOW A LEVER-ACTION RIFLE WORKS

Often used by the Sioux, it is used manually and works with a repeating system. It allows the user to shoot several consecutive bullets without having to reload. When driving the lever downward and returning it to its original position, the mechanism sheds the used cartridge and introduces a new one into the chamber.

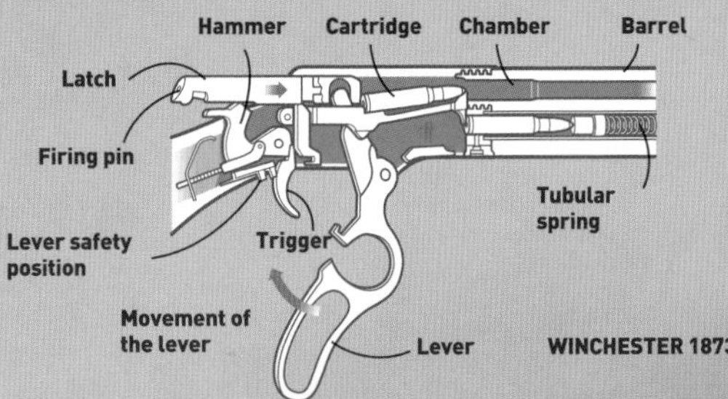
Hammer
Cartridge
Chamber
Barrel
Latch
Firing pin
Tubular spring
Lever safety position
Trigger
Movement of the lever
Lever
WINCHESTER 1873

Shield They typically used shields made from wood and skin; while useful against arrows, they offered no protection against rifle bullets.
Decoration Feathers often indicated how many men the holder had killed during battle.
Symbols War paint was used to depict symbols of protection and other symbols that represented the warrior's characteristics. A hand was used to show how many times he had been victorious in combat.
Mount They used a richly decorated blanket. Some, but not all, chose to use stirrups.
Each drawing and color had a special meaning. Red indicated war; green, resistance; yellow, a willingness to fight to the death; and black, a powerful warrior with experience on the battlefield.
Bear Courage and leadership.
Eagle Cunning, worth, and strength.
Peace, end of the war.
Arrowhead Warning.
Bow Each warrior made his bow from wood, and used dried animal tendons and intestines for the strings.
Tomahawk The ax was the favored hand weapon. They were able to throw it with great precision and accuracy.
Painting The tribes of the Great Plains also decorated their horses.
Gaiters A type of leather or suede trouser leg.
Head Originally fashioned from bone, but after contact with Europeans, metal became more customary.
Pipe Some tomahawks had a bored-out handle and holes, allowing them to be used as a pipe.
Moccasins

The Battle of Gettysburg

The election in 1860 of Abraham Lincoln as President of the United States of America and his opposition to slavery led to the secession from the Union of eleven southern states that formed the Confederacy. The war between the North and South broke out in 1861, lasting four years and costing around 600,000 lives. For many modern historians, the Battle of Gettysburg, Pennsylvania, fought July 1–3, 1863, was a landmark turning point that decided the American Civil War, with the Union finishing victorious.

Three days under fire

The battle was a succession of enormously violent clashes that involved around 150,000 men and left around 50,000 casualties in just three days.

COMPARISON OF FORCES

UNIONISTS ▸ 83,000 men	**CONFEDERATES** ▸ 75,000 men
CASUALTIES	**CASUALTIES**
dead ▸ 3,155	**dead** ▸ 4,708
injured ▸ 14,531	**injured** ▸ 12,693
captured or lost ▸ 5,369	**captured or lost** ▸ 5,830

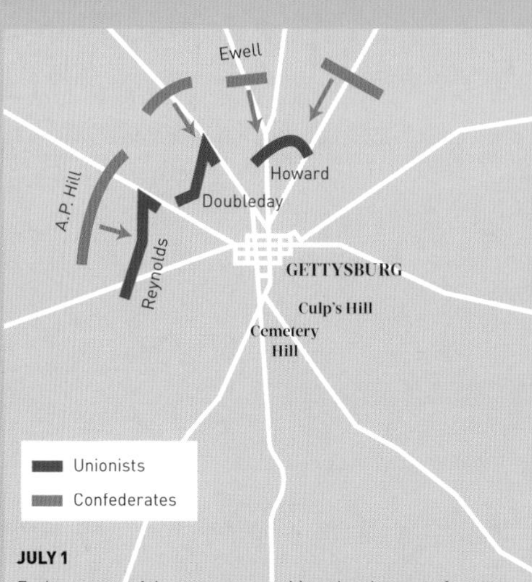

Ewell
Howard
Doubleday
A.P. Hill
Reynolds
GETTYSBURG
Culp's Hill
Cemetery Hill
Unionists
Confederates

JULY 1

Early on some of the troops are positioned to the west of Gettysburg. The fighting intensifies as more forces are added. By mid-afternoon, Union troops decide to withdraw toward Gettysburg. They regroup at the Cemetery Hill and Culp's Hill.

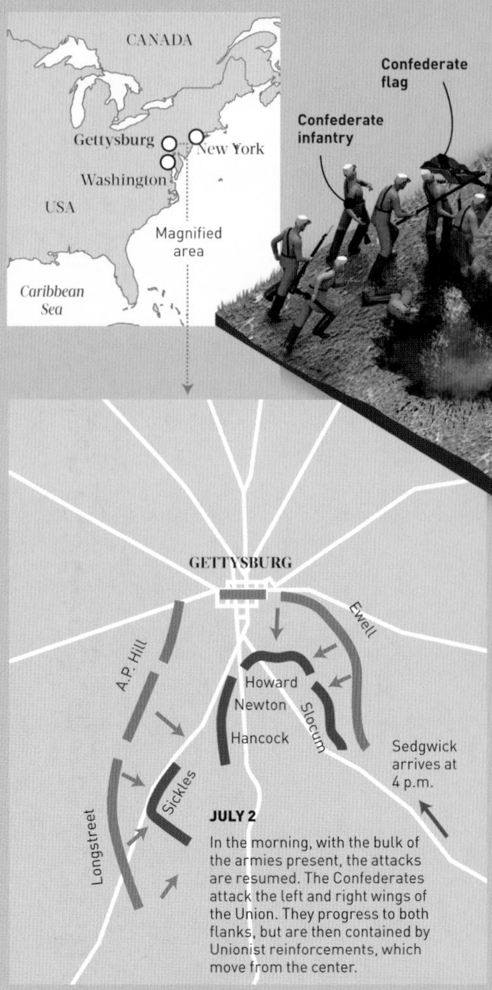

CANADA
Gettysburg
New York
Washington
USA
Magnified area
Caribbean Sea
Confederate flag
Confederate infantry
GETTYSBURG
Ewell
A.P. Hill
Howard
Newton
Slocum
Hancock
Sedgwick arrives at 4 p.m.
Sickles
Longstreet

JULY 2

In the morning, with the bulk of the armies present, the attacks are resumed. The Confederates attack the left and right wings of the Union. They progress to both flanks, but are then contained by Unionist reinforcements, which move from the center.

Frustrated Attack

One of the bloodiest moments of the battle was the brutal Confederate artillery attack, followed by a charge of the infantry, driven back by the Union's infantry and artillery.

Union flag

Union Infantry

Parrott cannon It was the most modern of its time. It was made by rifling and was able to fire projectiles of different calibers.

High ground The Unionists gained strength on the high ground, complicating the tactics of the Confederates.

Flint rifles They had very little aim and took several seconds to reload, but could cause very serious injuries.

GETTYSBURG

A.P. Hill

Ewell

Howard

Slocum

Hancock

Sickles

Sykes

Sedgwick

Longstreet

Kilpatrick Cavalry

JULY 3

Attacks to the right flank of the Union are resumed. The Confederates, after a heavy artillery attack, manage to break through the Unionist lines, but then are beaten back with heavy casualties. To the east of the town there is a clash of cavalry that leaves thousands dead. The Confederates decide to retreat.

ROBERT EDWARD LEE
The son of a hero of the War of Independence was chosen to command the Unionist forces. But he refused and crossed over to the southern side where he took charge of all the armies. He led the Confederates at Gettysburg.

GEORGE GORDON MEADE
He took command of the Unionist troops at Gettysburg, just three days before the battle. Although praised for his performance, he received some criticism for allowing the enemy to escape.

Zulu Warriors

Around 1878, the British Empire rapidly expanded into Africa, subjugating the peoples that it came up against. Located in modern-day South Africa, the Zulu kingdom was one of the last independent indigenous nations on the continent. Having emerged in the 1820s, it prospered and became one of the most powerful kingdoms in the region. Cetshwayo, crowned king in 1873, modernized its army. This decision was key, as it proclaimed war against the British in 1879.

Discipline and loyalty

The Zulus had no permanent army, but their troops were the personification of discipline. At age between 18 and 20, youths joined the warrior caste and were assigned a regiment. Instilled with a great sense of loyalty to the king and their colleagues, they undertook campaigns of no longer than three months in which they sought decisive victories and, once their mission was complete, they returned to their homes.

HEROES OF ISANDLWANA

In December 1878, the British authorities demanded that King Cetshwayo dissolve his kingdom. As he failed to respond, the English troops entered Zulu territory in January 1879, having every confidence in their weapons. On January 22, they were destroyed by the Zulus at Isandlwana. The total annihilation of one of its infantry battalions made the empire take its campaign against the Zulus seriously.

Isandlwana. The British regiment led by Lord Chelmsford tries to slow down the Zulu onslaught.

BUFFALO HORNS

The Zulus used this simple but lethal formation to trap their enemy. The most experienced warriors positioned themselves at the heart, with the youngest on the flanks (the "horns").

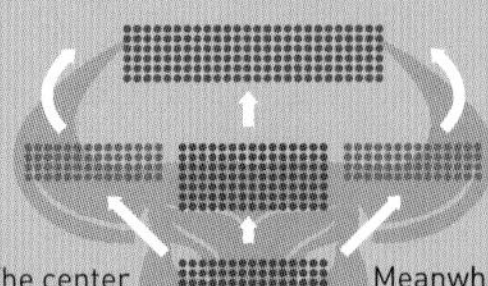

The center distracted the enemy, attacking head on.

Meanwhile, the "horns" attacked on both flanks, surrounding them.

Shield Made from animal skin, it was joined to a long wooden stick.

STRUCTURE OF THE TROOPS

The Zulu army, or *impi*, was structured in units known as *amabutho*, commanded by an experienced warrior (the *indhuna*).

The colors and design of a warrior's shield were a sign of which regiment he belonged to and his category.

High command ▸ The king

Amabuthos per impi ▸ 12

Personnel per impi ▸ 22,000

Historic victories ▸ Isandlwana, Intombe, Hlobane (all in 1879).

Iklwa A spear with a short pole but a large blade; it was practically a sword. It was used for close combat.
The full armory
Along with the spear and a wooden mace, they used javelins such as the *assegai* and the *isiJula*, which they threw in battle.
IsiJula spears
Mace
Iklwa
Feather headdress
Along with the shield, it identified the warrior's regiment.
Front
Made from leopardskin, it could only be worn by the most distinguished warriors.
Grip
Pole
IsiNene
A type of loincloth made using antelope or gazelle skin. It was tied around the wearer's waist.
Marks The white marks on a warrior's shield reflected his "status"; the more marks it bore, the more prestigious its carrier.
AmaShoba
These adornments were made using animal manes or fleeces tied to the wearer's legs and arms.

Korean Turtle Ship

In the late sixteenth century the Japanese attempted to conquer the Korean peninsula as a prelude to the invasion of China. However, they encountered fierce resistance and an efficient fleet of "turtle boats," the main deck of which was protected by armor plating, possibly metal, with large "pins" protruding from it. Although this cover was not useful for defending the ship from enemy arrows and cannon, its main function was to avoid being boarded.

Previous models

The Korean turtle ship probably came about from the restoration of other ships with a "shell," used around two centuries previously, the design of which is preserved in old illustrations.

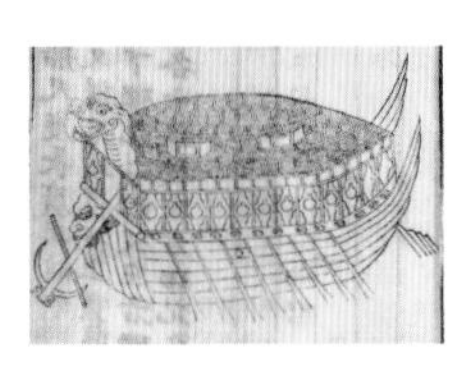

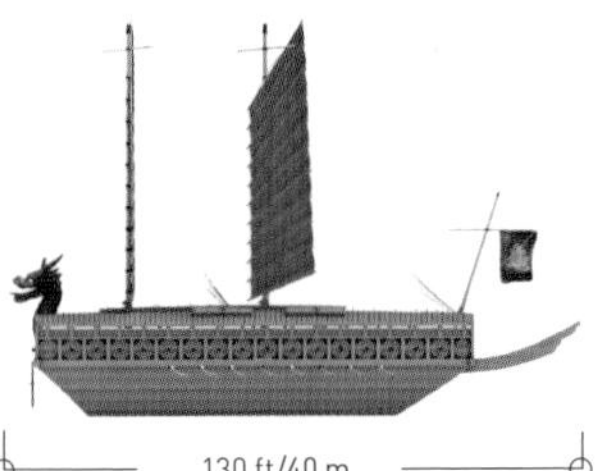
130 ft/40 m

Although there is no absolute certainty, it is likely they measured just under 130 ft/40 m in length.

YI SUN-SIN
Son of an admiral, he defended his nation against attacks from the powerful Japanese navy. His courage and cunning earned him recognition which endures to this day. He died in battle in 1598.

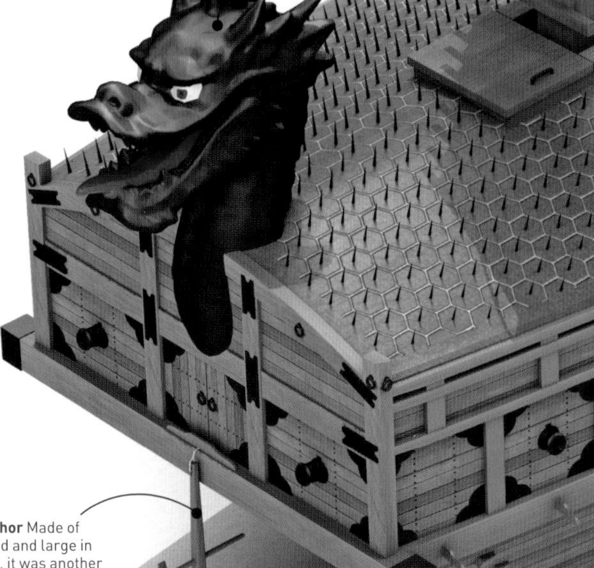

Head of a dragon It crowned the bow and it is highly likely that it contained a cannon inside, as well as flame throwers.

Anchor Made of wood and large in size, it was another distinctive feature of this type of ship.

Sails Were made from cloth reinforced with several rods that gave them great resistance.
Shell The most distinctive feature of the turtle ship. It is thought that it was made of iron studded with spikes, although it is also argued that it was made of wood.
Oars In addition to the sails, the driving force of the ship was a team of 80 oarsmen.
Ballast Provided additional weight to the ship, making it more stable.
Cannon Were of different types, with ranges of between 650 ft/200 m and perhaps 4,000 ft/1,200 m.

The Prussian Army

In the eighteenth century, the Prussian army was the most admired in Europe. Famous for its iron discipline and effectiveness, it was the power base of Prussia during the reign of King Frederick II, when the great European powers vied for supremacy on the battlefields. Frederick the Great created a highly professional army that was faster and more mobile than his contemporaries, earning him significant victories against armies often larger than his.

Mobility and efficiency

One of the aspects Frederick II insisted on was training the soldiers to make them real professionals. He also worked on the ability to maneuver. One of his main innovations was the creation of mobile artillery. These included light cannon that were transferred at a gallop to the area of the battlefield where their presence was more urgent, or located in a specific place following a particular strategy. To encourage his troops' autonomy of movement when they were on campaign, Frederick equipped his regiments with enough food and ammunition for nine days.

FREDERICK THE GREAT (1712-1786)
Barely one year after his coronation (1740) he began his first military campaign: the invasion of the Austrian province of Silesia. His biggest victory came on December 5, 1757 in Leuthen, during the Seven Years' War, which involved all of Europe. In Leuthen he fought some 80,000 Austrians with an army of just 36,000 men. After the war, in 1763, Prussia managed to become one of the major European powers.

The grenadiers They wore tall miters that distinguished them in the battlefield from riflemen, with small tricorns. In addition to the musket, the grenadier carried a saber and bags for bullets and grenades.

Uniforms and weapons

The image of the Prussian army was impeccable. Uniforms used colors and trimmings to differentiate between regiment and rank. The infantry usually wore a long dark blue coat with round red lapels.

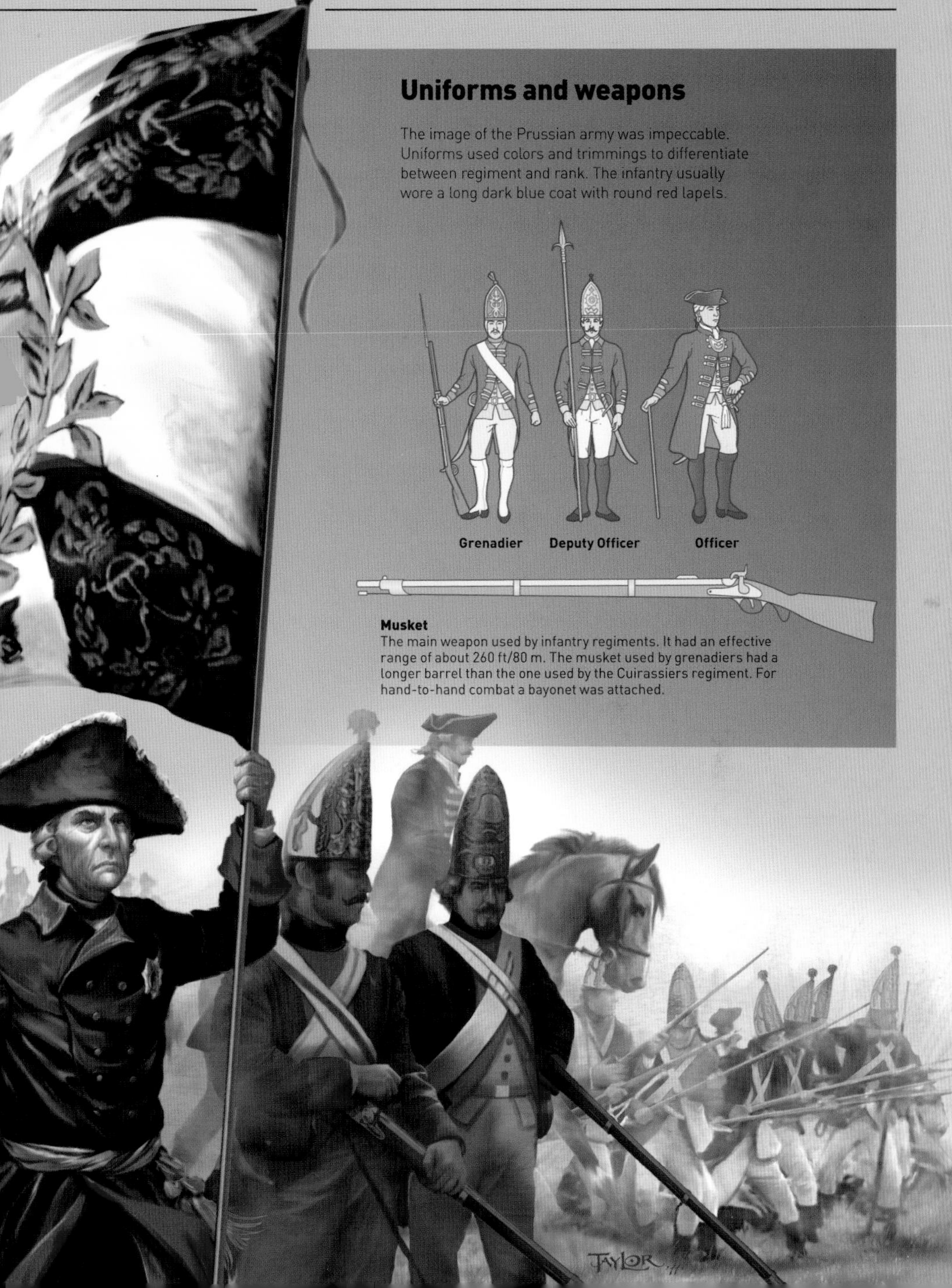
Grenadier
Deputy Officer
Officer
TAYLOR

Musket
The main weapon used by infantry regiments. It had an effective range of about 260 ft/80 m. The musket used by grenadiers had a longer barrel than the one used by the Cuirassiers regiment. For hand-to-hand combat a bayonet was attached.

THE OTTOMAN ARMY

THE SOLDIERS OF THE SULTAN

From the middle of the fifteenth century, almost until the end of the seventeenth century, the Ottoman Army was one of the most advanced in the world. Based on a system of recruitment and granting feudal territories and possessions in return for military support, its troops completely conquered Egypt, dominated the Mediterranean Sea in the sixteenth century, and fought for years against the Austrians over one of the borders of their empire and against the Persian Safavids on the other.

Using nomadic military tactics very similar to those used centuries before by the Mongols, they were among the first to use muskets and harquebuses, and on land were organized into bodies of infantry and light cavalry. In addition to squadrons of mercenaries, called *bashi-bazouk*, the bulk of the troops consisted of very well-trained infantry units, the Janissaries, who were the military elite. They were custodians of the sultan, and handled firearms, such as the blunderbuss and musket, with great skill, and used blades such as the feared daggers and swords with a curved blade that could cut off a head in a single swipe. The Janissaries were organized into various subgroups, such as the seventeenth-century *yerli*, integrated in the commercial and political life of the cities, or the *kapikulu*, troops sent to fight on the direct order of the sultan, loyalty to whom was unquestioning.

Among the cavalry corps were the *Akinci*, a division of light cavalry known for their courage, who were the first to enter battle, and the *Sipahi*, the elite troops whose status was equivalent to that of medieval European knights. In reality, they were owners of land that had been given to them directly by the sultan. Therefore, the gentlemen were entitled, in return for their military services, to all the income that these territories generated. They also drafted from among the farm workers, whom they recruited in times of war.

The Ottomans also had a formidable navy. Although war at sea was not part of their cultural tradition, by the twelfth century they had copied the naval construction techniques of their enemies. In fact, by the thirteenth century, they controlled the entire coast of Anatolia and were preparing to conquer Crete. In the fifteenth century the army had reached the Balkan and Italian coasts, and in the sixteenth century it was at its peak. It then defeated the Roman and Spanish fleets, and during its raids, reached the coast of the Iberian Peninsula and also Africa, although its defeat at the Battle of Lepanto, in 1571, was a definite turning point. After this episode, it would never regain control of the sea, and in the late seventeenth century, its decline as a military power was evident. The Battle of Zenta, fought against the Austrians in 1697 in an ambitious attempt to invade Hungary, was the final defeat of the Ottoman army.

The Janissaries

In 1330, Ottoman Sultan Murad I created an elite infantry corps by recruiting slaves and prisoners of war: the Janissaries. What began as a personal guard of the sultan would become the first permanent Ottoman army and the most feared regiment in the Ottoman Empire's greatest period of magnificence, between the sixteenth and seventeenth centuries.

Peak and decline

In the fourteenth century it had only around 1,000 troops, but by the end of the eighth century the figure had risen to 100,000. By then, the prestige gained in the empire through military exploits had been diluted. In 1826, Sultan Mahmud II decided to dissolve the unit, now militarily obsolete but with great political power. The Janissaries rebelled and Mahmud violently suppressed them, executing thousands (see right).

Uniform Unlike western knights, who used family colors and crests on their clothes, the Janissaries only used the colors of the sultan, as a sign of loyalty.

Kilij In hand-to-hand combat, they often used axes, or *kilij*, a type of saber—although the symbol of the regiment was the *yatagan*.

SUCCESS

The Janissaries took part in all of the Ottoman campaigns and were especially distinguished in the Battle of Mohács (1526) and the taking of Constantinople (1453) and Baghdad (1638).

Battle of Mohács against the Hungarians.

THEIR ADVERSARIES

Throughout its long history, the Ottoman Empire faced a diverse range of armies, from the Byzantines to the Mongols, from crusading Christians to Persian Safavids.

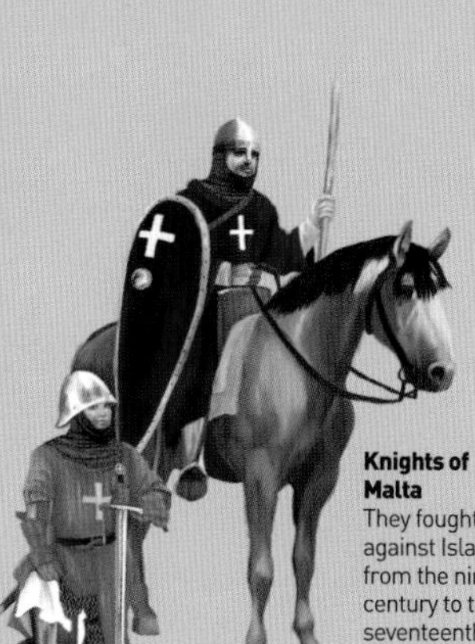

Knights of Malta They fought against Islam from the ninth century to the seventeenth century.

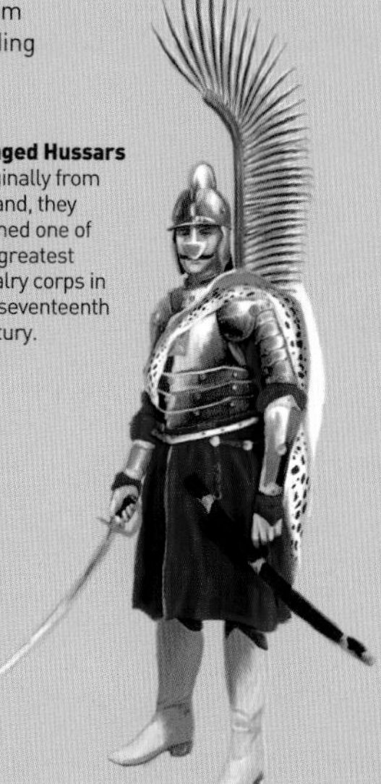

Winged Hussars Originally from Poland, they formed one of the greatest cavalry corps in the seventeenth century.

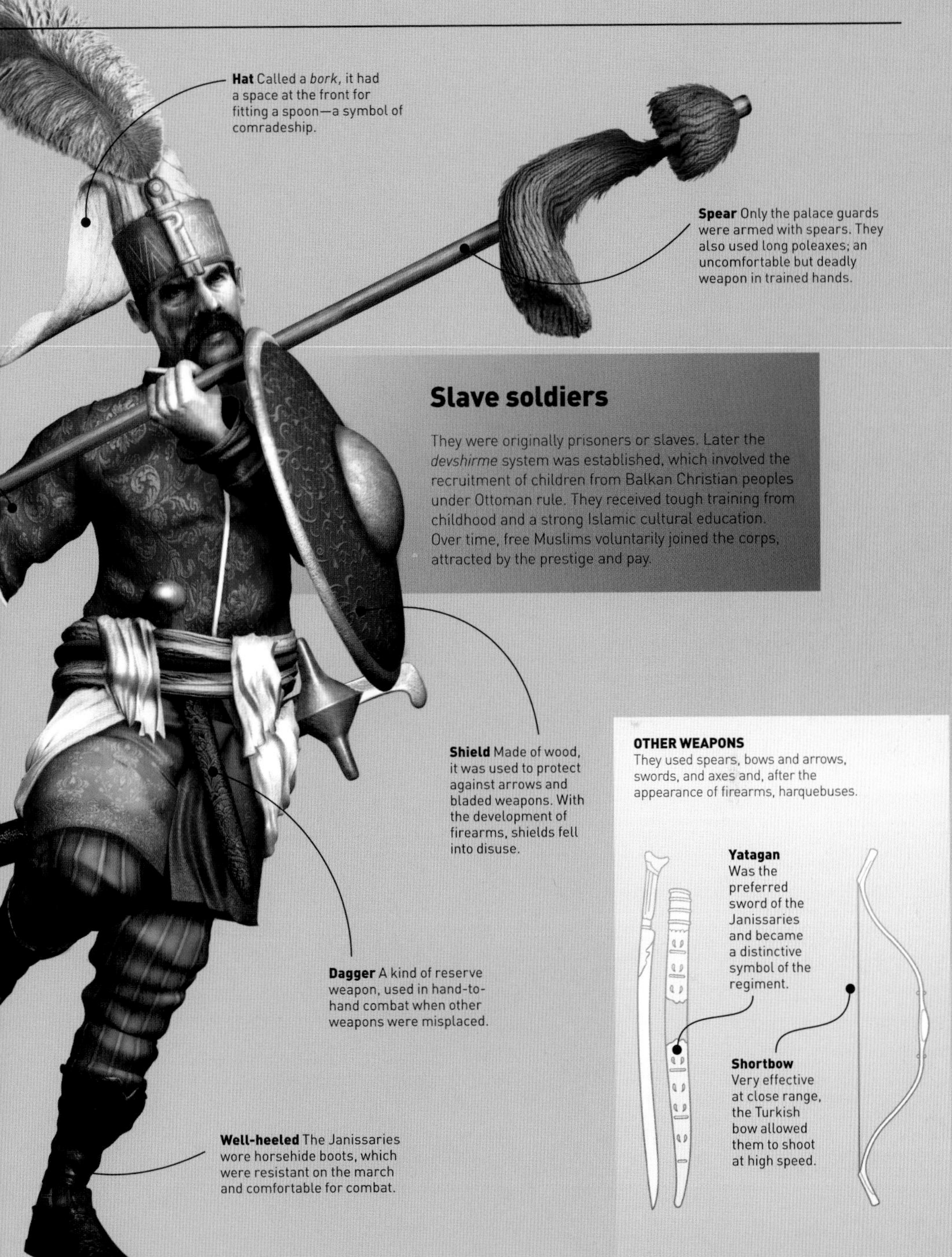
Hat Called a *bork*, it had a space at the front for fitting a spoon—a symbol of comradeship.
Spear Only the palace guards were armed with spears. They also used long poleaxes; an uncomfortable but deadly weapon in trained hands.
Shield Made of wood, it was used to protect against arrows and bladed weapons. With the development of firearms, shields fell into disuse.
Dagger A kind of reserve weapon, used in hand-to-hand combat when other weapons were misplaced.
Well-heeled The Janissaries wore horsehide boots, which were resistant on the march and comfortable for combat.

Slave soldiers

They were originally prisoners or slaves. Later the *devshirme* system was established, which involved the recruitment of children from Balkan Christian peoples under Ottoman rule. They received tough training from childhood and a strong Islamic cultural education. Over time, free Muslims voluntarily joined the corps, attracted by the prestige and pay.

OTHER WEAPONS

They used spears, bows and arrows, swords, and axes and, after the appearance of firearms, harquebuses.

Yatagan Was the preferred sword of the Janissaries and became a distinctive symbol of the regiment.

Shortbow Very effective at close range, the Turkish bow allowed them to shoot at high speed.

The Ottoman Cavalry

The powerful cavalry of the Turkish army was divided into two main gro ups: the *Akinci*, the light cavalry; and the *Sipahi*, the heavy cavalry. The former, comprising young recruited warriors, were the first to enter combat. The second were landowners, *timar*, whose land was directly conceded by the sultan in return for military service.

The Sipahi

The Sipahi took shape under the mandate of Sultan Mehmed II (1451–1481) and, over time, it became the best and biggest of the six cavalry divisions of the Ottoman army. Whenever the sultan required their participation in a campaign, the Sipahi had to respond with a certain number of men ready for battle; this varied depending on their rank within the unit and the size of their fiefs.

COMPLETE ARMOR

The Sipahi wore highly flexible full-body armor that offered excellent protection. It comprised a coat of mail and a series of metal plates that were joined by straps and buckles.

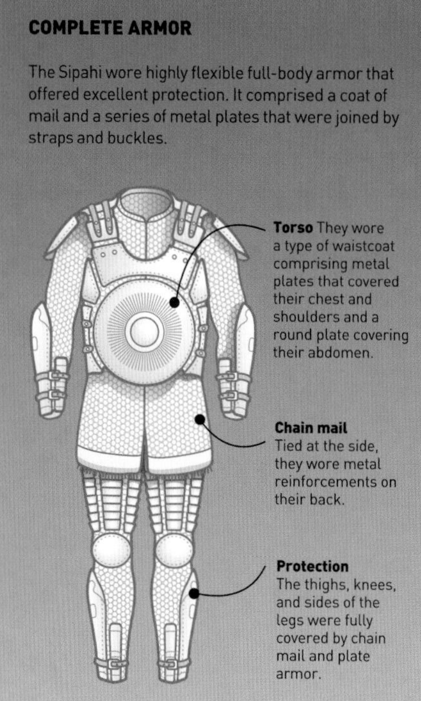
Torso They wore a type of waistcoat comprising metal plates that covered their chest and shoulders and a round plate covering their abdomen.
Chain mail Tied at the side, they wore metal reinforcements on their back.
Protection The thighs, knees, and sides of the legs were fully covered by chain mail and plate armor.

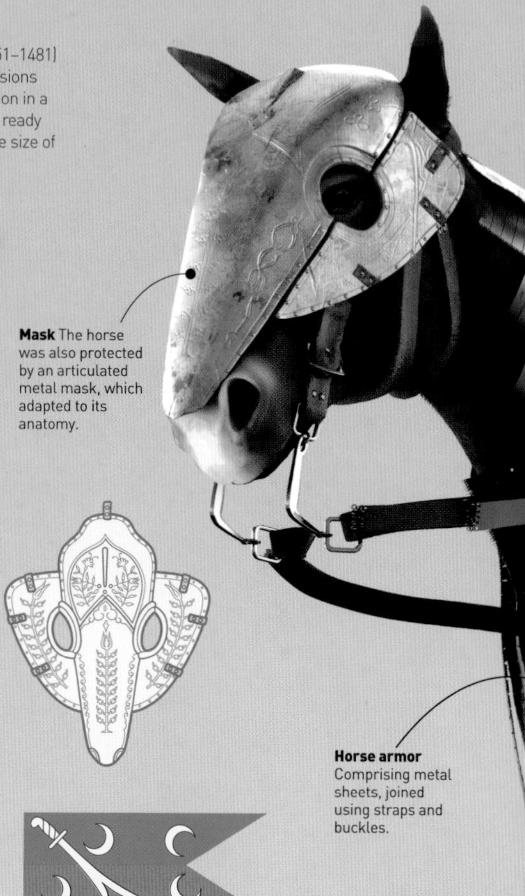
Mask The horse was also protected by an articulated metal mask, which adapted to its anatomy.
Horse armor Comprising metal sheets, joined using straps and buckles.

Standard Symbol of the elite cavalry.

OTHER WEAPONS

Among the other weapons chosen by the Sipahi were different models of ax (*aydogan*, *teber* and *sagir*) and maces (*bozdogan* and *sesper*).

Kilij The long, curved blade of this saber was designed for sweeping aside opponents with lunges and was capable of decapitating enemies with a single slash.
Shishak The helmet was equipped with hinged protectors for the nose, neck, and face.
Char aina Metal plate armor buckled together over the coat of chain mail.
Kolluk Metal plates worn on the forearms strapped over the coat of mail.
Dagger With a double-edged, curved blade. The sheath was sometimes crafted from silver.
Clothing They typically wore a skirt and belt, both made from silk.
Coat of mail Made from riveted and soldered rings.
Yatagan Another sword characteristic of the Turks.
Teber The traditional ax, with a crescent-shaped blade.
Kalkan The shield was made from wood and had a metal boss. It was covered in decorative silk.
Boots They were very heavy, made from metal sheets joined together using rows of rings.
Mount and stirrups Designed to allow the horseman to support himself while mounting the horse.

The Battle of Lepanto

When the Ottomans attacked the island of Cyprus in 1570, the Venetians called on their fellow Christians to defend their possessions in the Mediterranean. Pope Pius V responded to the call and inspired the creation of the Holy League (made up of Venice, Spain, the Papacy, Malta, and Genoa), whose fleet, under the command of John of Austria, brought an end to the Turkish threat in the Battle of Lepanto, on October 7, 1571, in what was the greatest battle between galley ships in history.

A fight on three fronts

The Battle of Lepanto was fought on three defined fronts, although in some cases, ships on one front went to the aid of others.

1 NORTH FLANK
The Turks take the initiative and try to surround the Christians by the coast. In a risky maneuver, the Christian right sector surrounds the Ottoman ships, grounding them on the coast and destroying many of them.

2 CENTRAL FLANK
The flagships of each fleet stay together and charge. All around, dozens of Christian and Ottoman galleys crowd together. After an hour and a half of combat, the Ottoman central flank is destroyed and its commander killed.

3 SOUTH FLANK
The Ottoman commander tries to open a breach between the Christian central and right flanks, but then surrounds the central flank. The Christians send for reinforcements, and, eventually, the Ottomans flee, suffering heavy losses.

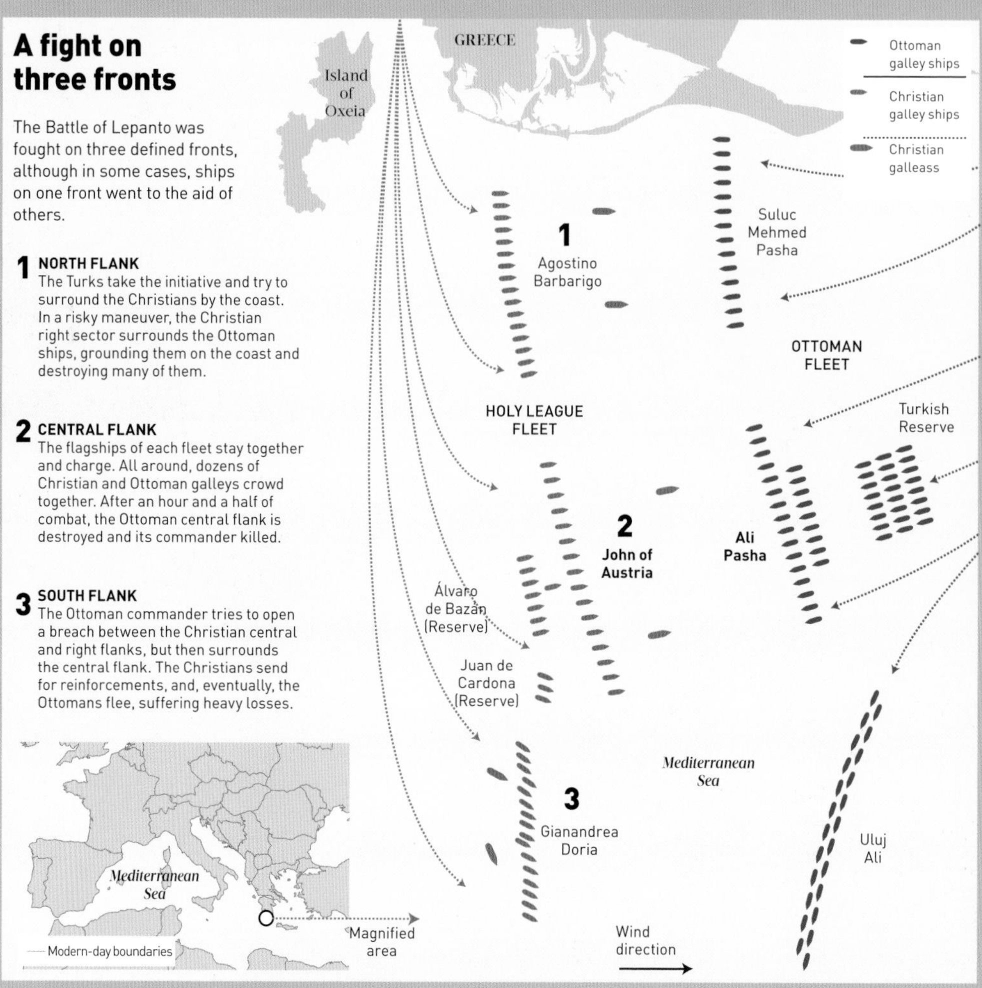
GREECE
Island of Oxeia
Ottoman galley ships
Christian galley ships
Christian galleass
1
Agostino Barbarigo
Suluc Mehmed Pasha
OTTOMAN FLEET
HOLY LEAGUE FLEET
Turkish Reserve
2
John of Austria
Ali Pasha
Álvaro de Bazán (Reserve)
Juan de Cardona (Reserve)
Mediterranean Sea
3
Gianandrea Doria
Uluj Ali
Mediterranean Sea
Modern-day boundaries
Magnified area
Wind direction

MIGUEL DE CERVANTES SAAVEDRA
The author of *Don Quixote* took part in the Battle of Lepanto when he was just 24 years old. A bullet from an harquebus left his left hand permanently paralyzed. He was therefore known as "The one-armed man from Lepanto."

The battle

A battle between galley ships began with artillery to weaken enemy ships; it was then customary for ships to attack in an attempt to board, and fight hand-to-hand.

Sailing downwind
Allowed ships to reach greater speeds, but reduced maneuverability in battle.

Sailing upwind
Used up the energy of the oarsmen and speeds were reduced, but maneuverability at short distance was improved.

Firepower
Was concentrated on the bow of the ship.

Wind direction

COMPARISON OF FORCES

Holy League

FIGHTERS ▸ Between 20,000 and 28,000

SHIPS ▸ Between 200 and 229 galley ships and 6 galleasses

Ottomans

FIGHTERS ▸ Between 16,000 and 30,000

SHIPS ▸ 280 (some 200 galley ships)

Hand-to-hand combat
The Christian soldiers had armour and firearms and so were better equipped for boarding.

Oarsmen Were usually slaves or convicts. They were shackled to the ship. If they were triumphant, they could be released as a reward.

Venetian galleasses
Were larger than the galley ships and heavily armed. They were placed at the front and caused considerable damage to enemy ships that were preparing to fight.

La Real Galley Ship

The flagship of John of Austria during the Battle of Lepanto, *La Real* was the largest galley of its time. Built in 1568 in Barcelona, it was an impressive structure and some notable works of art adorned its red and gold painted hull. In the famous battle, it had a crew of 400 sailors and soldiers and around 236 oarsmen.

The queen of the seas

Galleys dominated the seas during the sixteenth and seventeenth centuries. They were ships of impressive design, built in wood and propelled by dozens of pairs of oars and also, thanks to their large sails, by the wind.

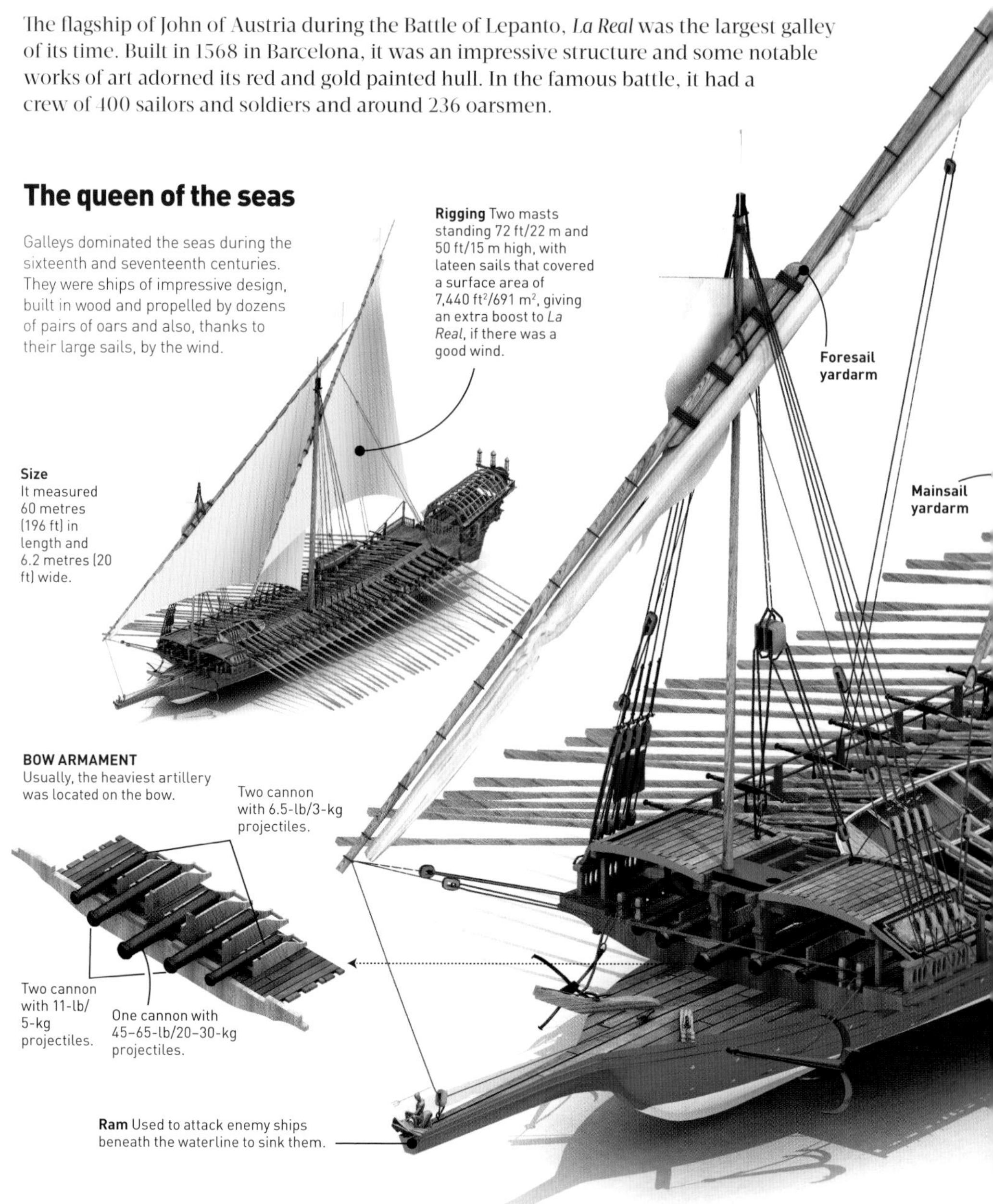

Rigging Two masts standing 72 ft/22 m and 50 ft/15 m high, with lateen sails that covered a surface area of 7,440 ft²/691 m², giving an extra boost to *La Real*, if there was a good wind.
Foresail yardarm
Mainsail yardarm
Size It measured 60 metres (196 ft) in length and 6.2 metres (20 ft) wide.
BOW ARMAMENT Usually, the heaviest artillery was located on the bow.
Two cannon with 6.5-lb/3-kg projectiles.
Two cannon with 11-lb/5-kg projectiles.
One cannon with 45–65-lb/20–30-kg projectiles.
Ram Used to attack enemy ships beneath the waterline to sink them.

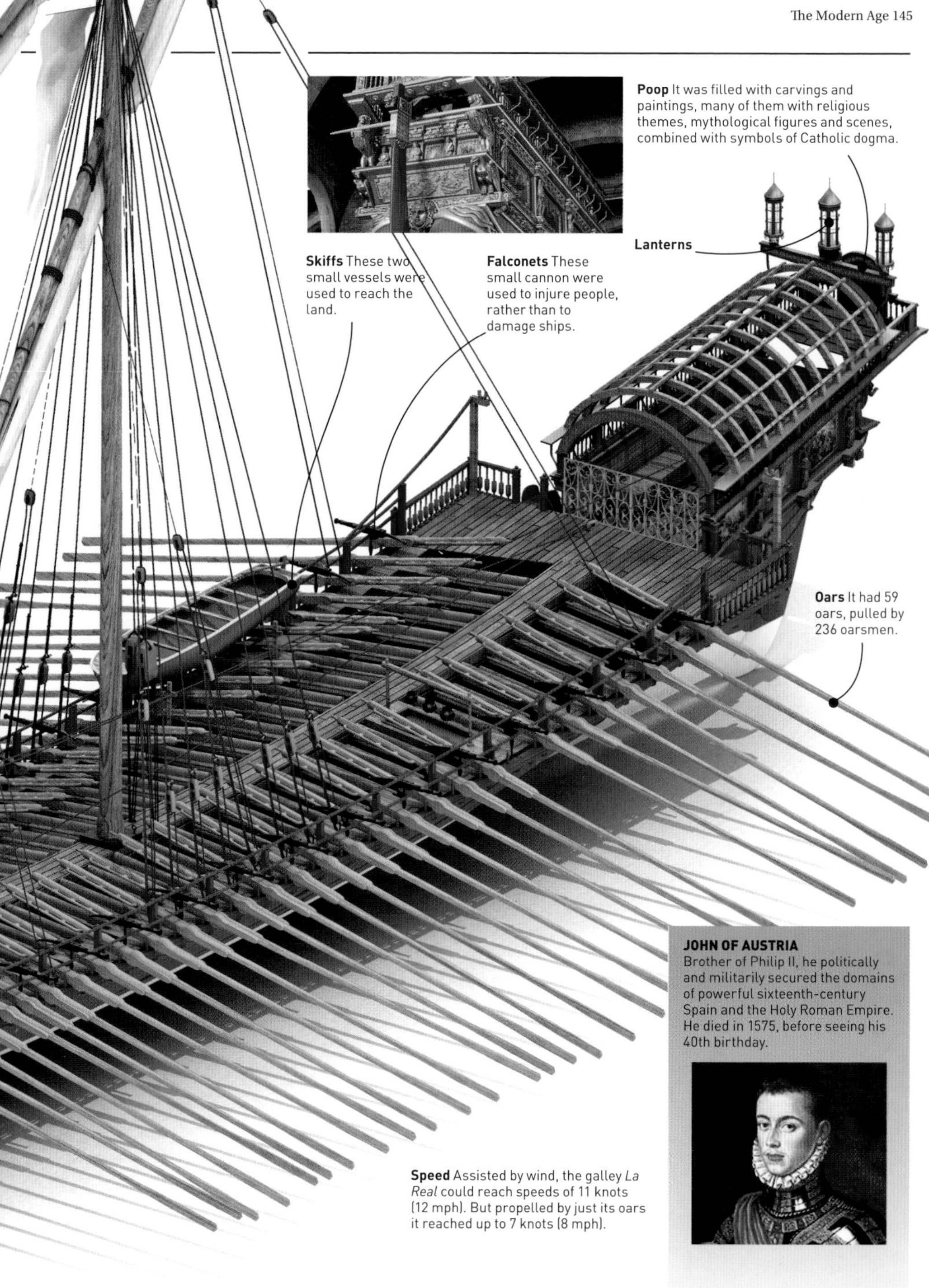
Poop It was filled with carvings and paintings, many of them with religious themes, mythological figures and scenes, combined with symbols of Catholic dogma.
Lanterns
Skiffs These two small vessels were used to reach the land.
Falconets These small cannon were used to injure people, rather than to damage ships.
Oars It had 59 oars, pulled by 236 oarsmen.
Speed Assisted by wind, the galley *La Real* could reach speeds of 11 knots (12 mph). But propelled by just its oars it reached up to 7 knots (8 mph).

JOHN OF AUSTRIA
Brother of Philip II, he politically and militarily secured the domains of powerful sixteenth-century Spain and the Holy Roman Empire. He died in 1575, before seeing his 40th birthday.

NAPOLEON'S ARMY

CITIZEN SOLDIERS

Before Napoleon, there had never been an army made up of citizen soldiers. Never before had an army assumed the dictates of a revolution like that of the French in 1789, or implemented similar ideals: sacrifice for the common good, fraternity among equals, and a military career based solely on talent. This made the army of the French emperor a corps that, over 25 years, spread through Europe in a wave of conquest of a magnitude previously unknown.

The Napoleonic army also introduced a new form of warfare in which the most important thing was not to defeat the enemy, conquer their territories, or achieve symbolic success, such as taking the capital of the opponent, but to destroy it completely. Its structure had also improved significantly. It was no longer organized according to traditional regiments of infantry, cavalry, and artillery, but divided into divisions that behaved as small autonomous armies, with all units integrated into them, so that they could act separately and cover several fronts at the same time. These autonomous combat bodies helped to improve logistics, and allowed them to maneuver around the flanks and rear guard of their enemies, which turned many of their campaigns into real masterstrokes of military strategy.

Other distinctive characteristics defined this army. They did not, for example, rely on supply lines, but lived on what they discovered on the land. Looting and pillaging provided them with as much as they needed, whether it was food, weapons, or ammunition, although such practices made the soldiers despised as well as feared. Their tactics were also flexible, and it was the first army to incorporate surveyors, engineers, and cartographers into the ranks, who were responsible for inspecting the land and making maps that helped the marshals to develop the strategy to follow during battle. They were also able to apply so-called "offensive exploitation," which was to continue to conquer after the main battle had been waged.

The artillery was another of his great strengths. Napoleon's army had concentrations of artillery, the like of which had never been seen before. At the Battle of Wagram (1809), Napoleon lined up 554 guns, the ammunition for which was provided by the so-called "supply wagons": caravans run by civilian contractors who ensured the army never ran out of projectiles. This resource gave the army greater mobility so that it could move at a speed that astonished its contemporaries. They moved at 120 paces per minute, unlike the 70 covered by their enemies. The main units of light infantry were riflemen, grenadiers, and sharpshooters, while the dragoons were in the cavalry.

Napoleon's Army

After the revolution of 1789, France had to face a series of defensive wars against coalitions of European monarchies. With the rise of Napoleon Bonaparte, the French army went on the offensive, conquering most of Europe and maintaining supremacy in the battlefield for almost a decade. Their success had much to do with Napoleon's military vision, but also with a formidable army that came to number 690,000 troops.

Tactical perfection

Napoleon based his tactics on having fast-moving forces and being highly aggressive. Unlike other armies of the time, Napoleon's army was organized into divisions each made up of infantry, cavalry, and artillery. Each constituted a small army with freedom of action and autonomy, allowing commanders to make decisions based on their own judgment—thus giving the army greater flexibility.

The creation of an empire

1789–1800 ▸ Napoleon conquers Egypt and consolidates his gains in Italy.

1801–1806 ▸ From Venice to Austria, occupying Prussia and Poland and creating the Confederation of the Rhine.

1807–1810 ▸ On annexing Spain and Portugal, the empire reaches its farthest extension.

Revolutionary army With the revolution, the royal army was replaced by another made up of citizen-soldiers recruited from among the people when, in 1793, a mass draft was declared.
Infantry In 1804, it contained around 350,000 men. They went on long marches for weeks at a time, and during battles they marched with fixed bayonets in search of close combat.

The rise of Napoleon

After successful campaigns in Italy and Egypt he returned to France as a hero. In 1799, he took control of the government and was appointed First Consul, and in 1804 was crowned Emperor of France with absolute power. He reformed the army into which he put his ideas and his personality, and instilled in his men a sense of belonging and devotion.

GENERAL WINTER
Perhaps the biggest strategic mistake was Napoleon's invasion of Russia in 1812. The Emperor achieved a pyrrhic victory at Borodino and entered Moscow, only to discover that the Russians had burned it. His famous withdrawal in the middle of the Russian winter finished off the Grande Armée. Of the 690,000 who embarked on the campaign, only 93,000 survived.

The enemy After Napoleon's coronation in 1804, Britain, Austria, Russia, and Sweden, formed the Third Coalition to confront him.

Artillery Napoleon thought the artillery fundamental and believed that the best arrangement was five cannon per 1,000 soldiers. Although he didn't achieve this figure, his artillery was the best in Europe.

The Soldiers of the Grande Armée

In 1805, Napoleon gave the name "Grande Armée" (Great Army) to the army he created to invade England. He never got to achieve his objective, although he did create a formidable military force—the largest in Europe—which had a powerful cavalry. Despite the harshness of the campaigns, the soldiers of the Grande Armée always showed great discipline and strength, driven by a deep sense of duty, patriotism, and a hunger for glory.

Infantrymen and horsemen

Napoleon dressed his cavalry in splendid uniforms and imposed rigorous training. It consisted of several bodies—cuirassiers, carbines, hussars, hunters, pikemen, and dragoons who broke enemy lines and attacked in key places of battle. The infantry were divided into regiments of light and line infantry and were able to travel hundreds of miles in a few months. They were preceded by *voltiguers* who advanced in dense columns under fire, seeking close combat.

Lines of infantry
Forming the base of the French infantry, they fought with musket and bayonet and sometimes the saber.

Voltiguers
Initiated skirmishes to break enemy lines.

Hussars
Light cavalry corps, specializing in reconnaissance and pursuit.

Mamelukes
They were a small elite body of Napoleonic cavalry made up of Egyptian soldiers.

A MULTINATIONAL FORCE
The Grande Armée was made up of French soldiers, but also those of allied or subjugated states. In its ranks there were one and a half million Gauls and over 700,000 troops from Poland, Italy, Saxony, Bavaria, and Egypt, among other countries.

Imperial guard

Made up of Napoleon's most experienced soldiers, this was the elite force of the French army. It had an infantry corps, an artillery corps, and cavalry. It was divided into two sections: the Old Guard, the most senior soldiers; and the Middle Guard and Young Guard.

Cuirassiers

They were Napoleon's heavy cavalry, an army corps that had fallen into disuse and which the emperor resurrected with 15 regiments. They were used to break up the British "square" formation.

Helmet With horsehair tail and feathers (used in parades)
Colback They wore a high cap made of bearskin.
Firepower They used a model IX, 1.75-cm caliber musket
Armor Protected them during hand-to-hand combat and from long-distance shots.
Well armed Their weapons consisted of a straight sword, two pistols, and a short carbine.
Protected feet They used hide gaiters. In their backpack they carried a spare pair.
Boots The high-leg boots were great for riding, but uncomfortable when fighting on foot.

The Battle of Austerlitz

Fought on December 2, 1805, the Battle of Austerlitz saw Napoleon's troops face an allied army of Austrians and Russians, commanded by Czar Alexander I of Russia and Austro-Hungarian Emperor Francis I. It was one of the finest demonstrations of the great ingenuity of the French Emperor, which resulted in his most memorable victory and allowed him to end the Third Coalition.

Preparation

After capturing Vienna, Napoleon continued his pursuit of the Russian army. With winter looming and the imminent arrival of allied reinforcements, the French emperor wanted to fight as soon as possible. And this he did near Austerlitz (modern-day Czech Republic), where he devised a strategy to encourage a premature attack by his opponents, anticipating their movements.

COMPARISON OF FORCES

French

MEN ▸	73,000
CANNONS ▸	130
WOUNDED ▸	8,000

Allies

MEN ▸	85,000
AUSTRIANS ▸	15,000
RUSSIANS ▸	70,000
CANNONS ▸	278
WOUNDED ▸	16,000

PRATZEN HEIGHTS
This hill was an important strategic point from where the whole battlefield could be controlled. Napoleon allowed the Allies to occupy it, letting them believe in their superiority. His strategy of deception went as planned. When the Allies launched their attack, he took Pratzen with renewed vigor.

THE CONSEQUENCES
After the defeat, Austria had to agree to peace and concede its Italian possessions. This paved the way for Napoleon to invade the south of Germany and establish the Confederation of the Rhine as a buffer state between France and Prussia.

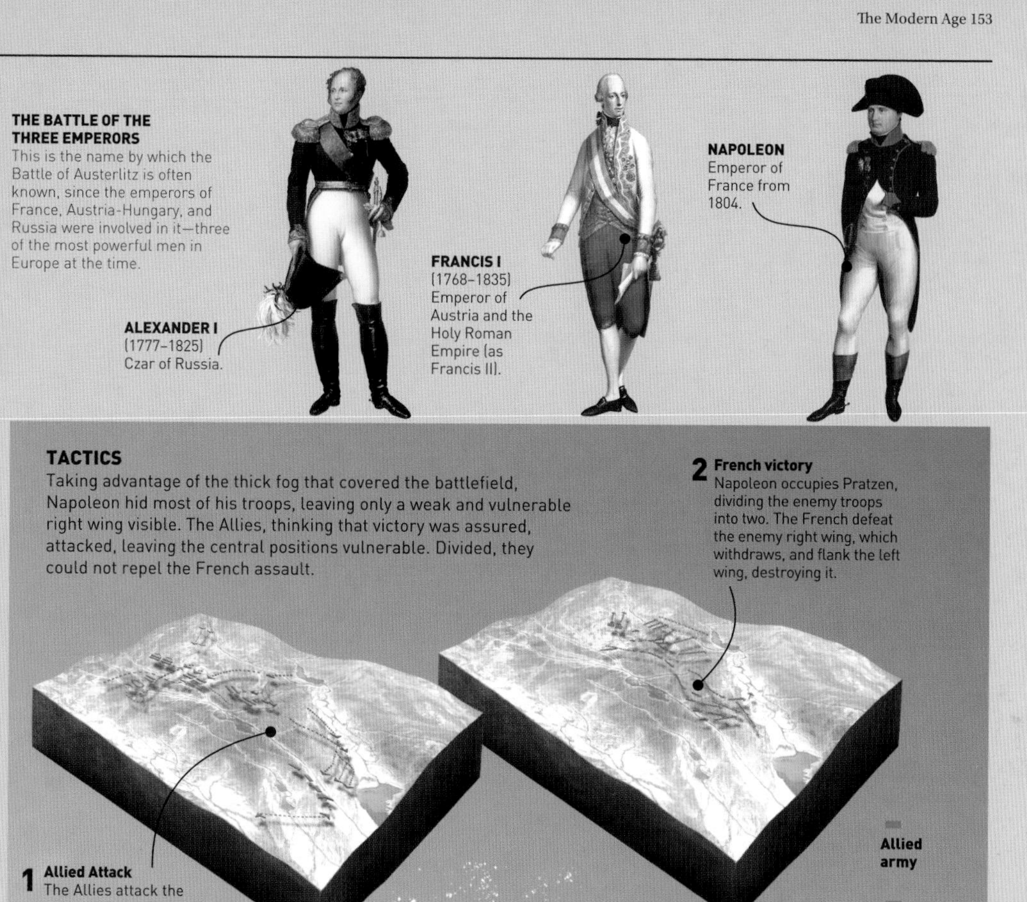

THE BATTLE OF THE THREE EMPERORS
This is the name by which the Battle of Austerlitz is often known, since the emperors of France, Austria-Hungary, and Russia were involved in it—three of the most powerful men in Europe at the time.

ALEXANDER I
(1777–1825)
Czar of Russia.

FRANCIS I
(1768–1835)
Emperor of Austria and the Holy Roman Empire (as Francis II).

NAPOLEON
Emperor of France from 1804.

TACTICS

Taking advantage of the thick fog that covered the battlefield, Napoleon hid most of his troops, leaving only a weak and vulnerable right wing visible. The Allies, thinking that victory was assured, attacked, leaving the central positions vulnerable. Divided, they could not repel the French assault.

1 Allied Attack
The Allies attack the apparently weakened French right flank. But they find that it has been reinforced and they send troops from the center in the heights of Pratzen, leaving this position exposed.

2 French victory
Napoleon occupies Pratzen, dividing the enemy troops into two. The French defeat the enemy right wing, which withdraws, and flank the left wing, destroying it.

Allied army

French army

DEATH ON THE LAKE
Attacked from all sides, Russian troops on the left flank fled across the frozen ponds of Satschan. The French opened fire on the ice with their cannon, breaking it up, and a large number of troops met their end in the freezing waters.

The Battle of Waterloo

June 18, 1815 was a landmark date in the history of Europe. That day, on the plains of Waterloo (Belgium) a battle was fought that ended the Napoleonic era. An army consisting of an allied coalition of British, Dutch, Germans, and Prussians defeated the French Emperor's imperial troops. The battle left behind a trail of thousands of dead on both sides and brought about the surrender of Napoleon, who was exiled to the remote island of St. Helena, where he died six years later.

The last great battle

Allied troops were located at a high site, where they could observe the movements of the French without being seen. In addition, three farms were fortified at the front: Hougoumont, La Haye-Sainte, and Papelotte.

COMPARISON OF FORCES

France
MEN ▸ 72,500

CANNON ▸ 246

Alliance
MEN ▸ 120,000

CANNON ▸ 290

	Alliance	France
Cavalry		
Infantry		

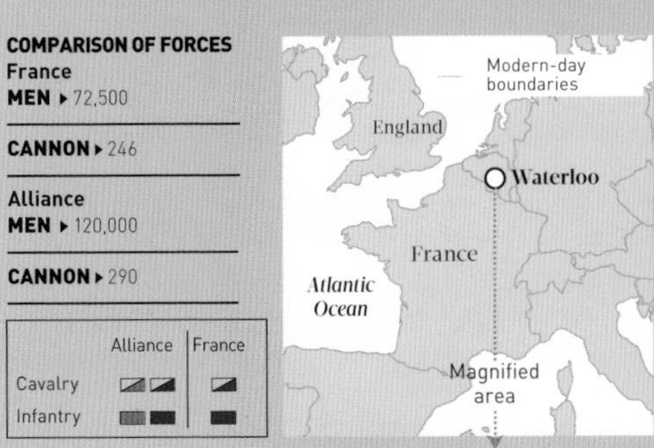
Modern-day boundaries
England
Waterloo
France
Atlantic Ocean
Magnified area

THE RETURN OF NAPOLEON
Following a previous defeat, in February 1815, after just one year Napoleon escaped from exile on the island of Elba, where he had been sent. On March 20, without having fired a single shot, he triumphantly entered Paris. The Seventh Coalition met to confront him, before it finally succumbed.

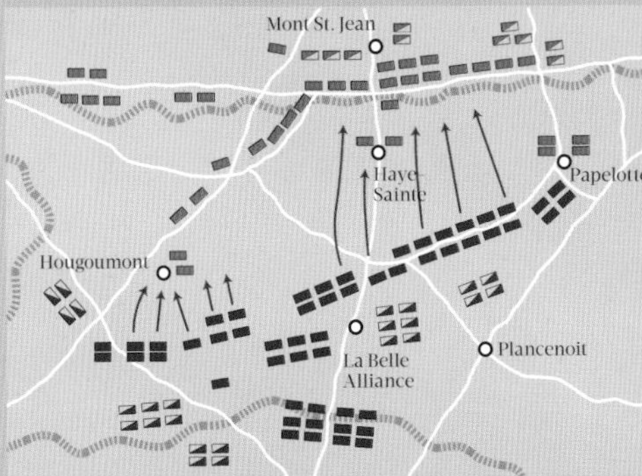
Mont St. Jean
Haye Sainte
Papelotte
Hougoumont
La Belle Alliance
Plancenoit

1 OBJECTIVE: FARMS
The battle begins with a diversionary attack on Hougoumont farm, in order to make a more full-on assault on the allied center. But the British do not fall into the trap. The struggles for the Hougoumont and Haye-Sainte farms themselves become battles that decimate the French.

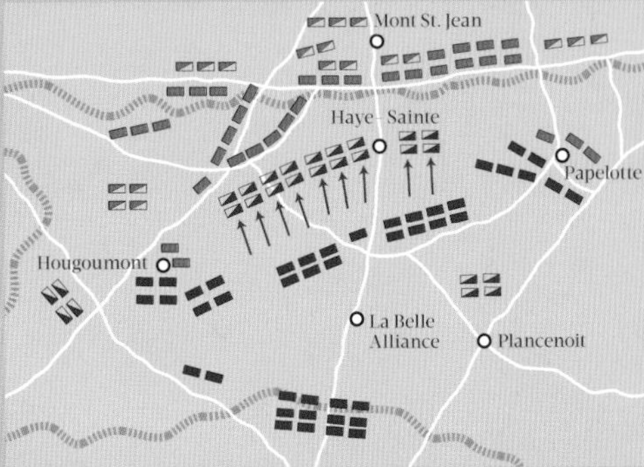
Mont St. Jean
Haye Sainte
Papelotte
Hougoumont
La Belle Alliance
Plancenoit

2 CAVALRY ATTACK
The Allies reorganize their positions. Believing they are dealing with a retreat, the French carry on with their cavalry charges. Despite these actions they are repelled by the Allies, who are arranged into squares, and able to cause serious casualties.

An impenetrable square

The cavalry could destroy a line of infantry. To avoid this, infantry were arranged into hollow squares. At Waterloo, this tactic was instrumental in repelling the terrible attacks of the imperial cavalry.

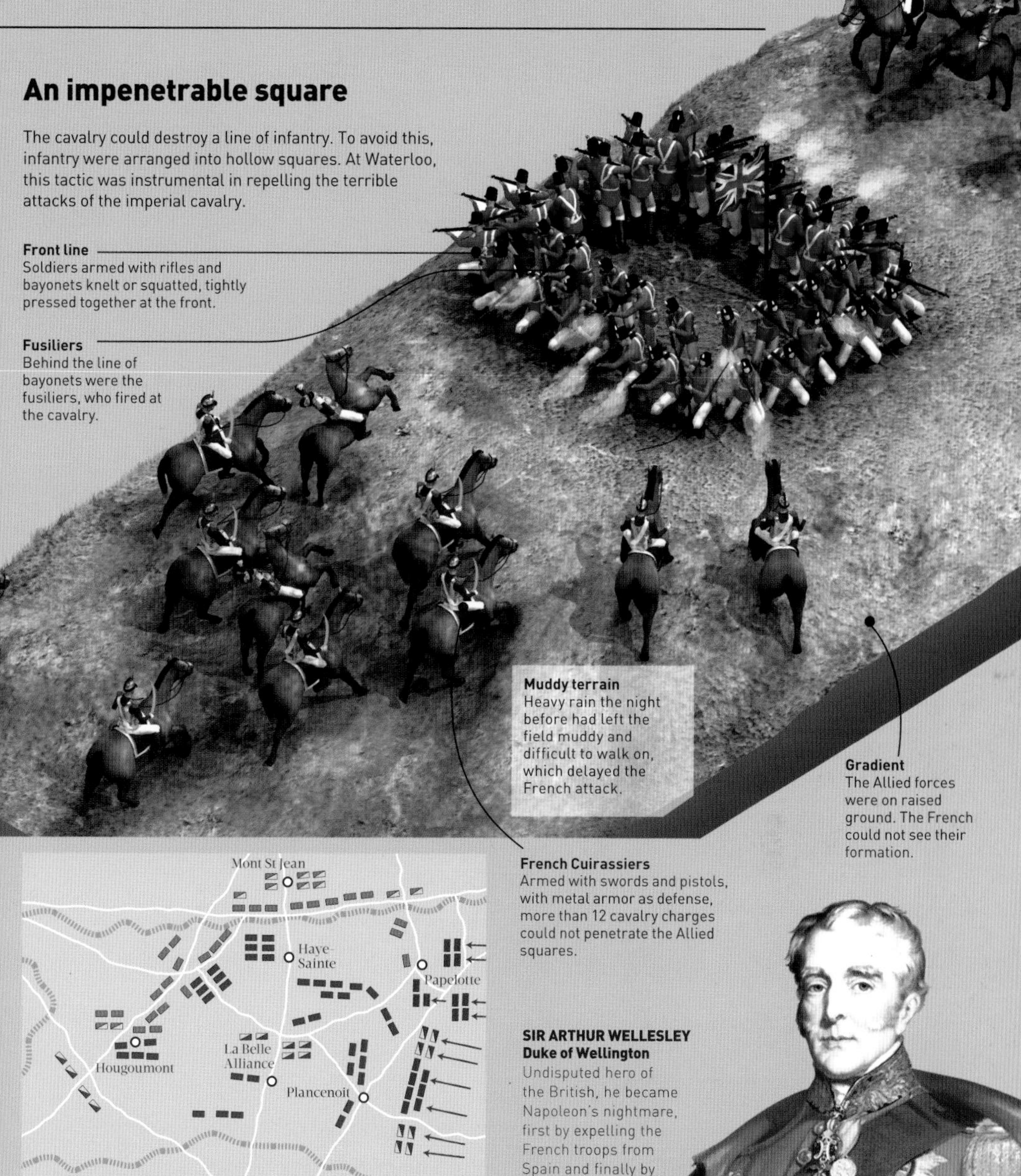
Front line
Soldiers armed with rifles and bayonets knelt or squatted, tightly pressed together at the front.
Fusiliers
Behind the line of bayonets were the fusiliers, who fired at the cavalry.
Muddy terrain
Heavy rain the night before had left the field muddy and difficult to walk on, which delayed the French attack.
Gradient
The Allied forces were on raised ground. The French could not see their formation.
French Cuirassiers
Armed with swords and pistols, with metal armor as defense, more than 12 cavalry charges could not penetrate the Allied squares.
Mont St Jean
Haye-Sainte
Papelotte
Hougoumont
La Belle Alliance
Plancenoit

3 THE FINAL BATTLE
Napoleon orders his Imperial Guard to attack the Allied center, but British forces surprise them with their devastating musket fire. Then the Prussians arrive and open a front on the right flank. Devastated, toward the end of the day the French begin fleeing in retreat.

SIR ARTHUR WELLESLEY
Duke of Wellington
Undisputed hero of the British, he became Napoleon's nightmare, first by expelling the French troops from Spain and finally by defeating him at Waterloo.

NAVAL AND MILITARY SUPREMACY

In the seventeenth century, during the English Civil War (1642–1651) there were hardly any trained troops on either side (England, Scotland, Wales, and Ireland were involved) and there was no permanent army (the Royal Horse Guards, which in 1820 became part of the British Royal Guard, wasn't formed until 1661), but by the early eighteenth century the situation had changed completely. British infantry and grenadiers were equipped with a saber, bayonet, and rifle, a weapon that was also carried by officers, and the cavalry were usually armed with short-barrelled rifles and almost always with pistols.

But one of the secrets of the British army's success during the eighteenth century lies in its mastery of the sea and control of trade routes, creating a buoyant economy. In England, the state could always raise the necessary funds to successfully wage war (the Bank of England was founded in 1694), and it kept a relatively small army in Europe while using its wealth to establish continental business alliances that also gave it a naval advantage in controlling European waters and winning battles for the colonies and maritime trade. The English Navy, for example, spent almost £19 million, an exorbitant amount at that time, between 1689 and 1697, but this resulted in the country becoming the great colonial power of the age, after ousting the Spanish, Dutch, and French.

In the late eighteenth century, the British Navy, in addition to outstripping its rivals on the European continent, had high-quality captains and crew, which transformed the character of naval confrontations with new combat tactics. It was precisely its colonial power that would allow it to maintain, for centuries, a military and naval strength born from its political and commercial wealth and the bravery of its soldiers who were called "redcoats," because of the color of their uniforms, designed to easily distinguish them from the rest of the fighters and, incidentally, to hide the blood from their wounds.

Although the British East India Company claimed in the seventeenth century that theirs was "business, not war," the fact is that they had permission from the Empire to recruit armies and even to create them, as happened in India with the Sepoys, employed native soldiers who were armed and trained like Europeans, and who proved their worth against Indian adversaries as well as against armies from Europe. The British Army, which was organized into infantry corps and light cavalry, fought wars at the ends of the known world (the Carnatic wars in India or against France in North America), and used to attack in rows of six or eight soldiers firing simultaneously. Ready to fight face to face, the English infantryman was always effective, equally when attacking with the bayonet.

Conflict in North America

The oldest British settlement in North America dates back to 1607, when the first settlers built fortified villages to defend themselves from Indian attacks. Throughout the eighteenth century, as colonization of the New World advanced, the British had to fight against the native peoples and against the French, with whom they fought for the conquest of North America.

Wolstenholme Fort

Wolstenholme, in Virginia, was one of the first British settlements. Like most towns, it had a fort where settlers could take shelter in the event of an attack, as coexisting with Native Americans brought alternating moments of peace and confrontation. The Wolstenholme Fort, for example, suffered an attack from the Powhatan in 1622, in which 400 of its 1,000 inhabitants died.

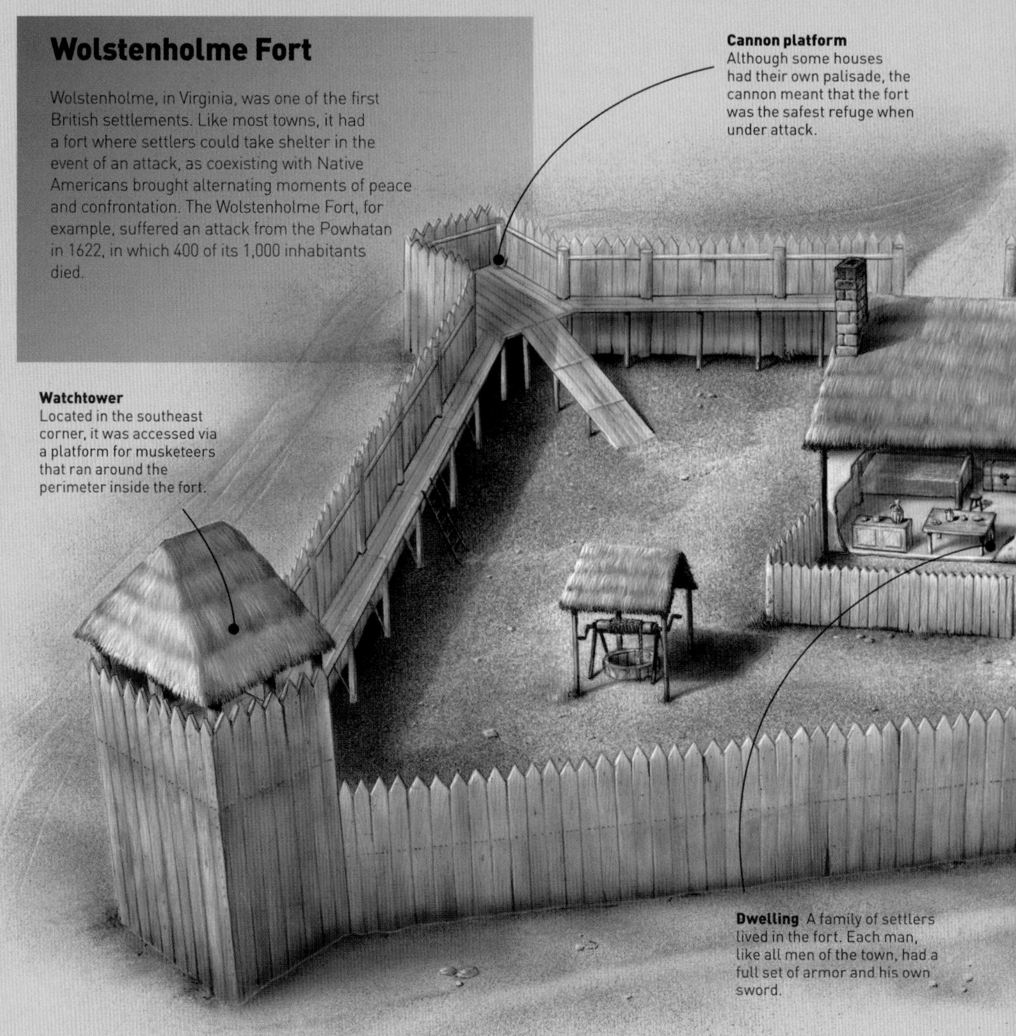
Cannon platform
Although some houses had their own palisade, the cannon meant that the fort was the safest refuge when under attack.
Watchtower
Located in the southeast corner, it was accessed via a platform for musketeers that ran around the perimeter inside the fort.
Dwelling A family of settlers lived in the fort. Each man, like all men of the town, had a full set of armor and his own sword.

French and Indian War

In the eighteenth century, the British and French disputed the colonization of North America. The confrontation, included within the conflict of the Seven Years' War raging in Europe, led to the French and Indian War (1754–1763) in America, between the British and the French, who were allied with several Native American tribes. Great Britain emerged victorious from the fight and France lost all its continental possessions.

Paddock The cattle of Wolstenholme were gathered together in this paddock every night. If the village was attacked, the livestock was put inside the fort.

Pontiac's War

After the British victory in Canada against the French, a Native American revolt broke out in the Great Lakes in 1763 with the aim of expelling the settlers. Many tribes, under the leadership of Chief Pontiac of the Ottawa tribe, attacked several British forts and settlements. The rebellion was put down, but the Native Americans forced the British government to abandon the restrictive policies they had imposed on them until then.

The siege of Fort Detroit The Native Americans captured eight British forts and cut supply lines. However, the forts of Pittsburgh and Detroit resisted.

British Redcoats

The ability of the British Empire to become a world power for almost three centuries was largely attributable to the efficiency of its army. Its troops fought on all types of terrain and in all types of climate, against all types of enemy and always fulfilling their duties; as a result, the red coats worn as part of their uniform became a symbol of the British Empire. At the same time, they represented a great paradox, given that the soldiers who wore them, the staunch defenders of the Empire, typically came from less privileged classes.

Esprit de corps

Poorly paid, housed in tiny military bases and with no basic commodities, the Redcoats represented the lowest part of an uncompromising hierarchy that imposed harsh punishments and rigid discipline. Their *esprit de corps* was intense, founded on solidarity with their colleagues and the admiration of intermediary officers, lance corporals, and sergeants from similar social backgrounds. All the above, in addition to their training and experience, the most comprehensive and modern fighting equipment, and the support of the world's best fleet, made them formidable soldiers.

SCOTS AND IRISH

Among the British troops, the presence of Scottish and Irish soldiers was notable. For example, during the American War of Independence, 60 percent of British troops were English, 24 percent were Scottish and 16 percent were Irish. Despite their historic hostility toward the English crown, these troops always fought with the utmost bravery.

French cuirassiers defeated at the Battle of Waterloo by the Highlanders and Scots Greys.

ORGANIZATION

With 104 regiments, the line infantry was the backbone of the British Army during the Napoleonic Wars. The organization of Regiment 33 can be seen here.

33

Coat of arms of Regiment 33: original (left) and modern day (right).

COMMAND OF THE REGIMENT ▸ General

COMMAND OF THE BATTALION ▸ Colonel

BATTALIONS PER REGIMENT ▸ Two

PERSONNEL PER BATTALION ▸ 1,000 soldiers

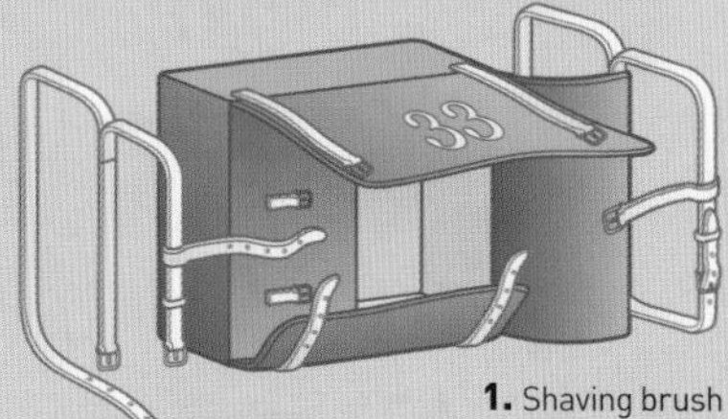
33

BACKPACK

Each infantryman carried a backpack containing all his equipment, which meant he could keep himself and his uniform in order.

1. Shaving brush
2. Soap and soap dish
3. Razor
4. Telescope
5. Cutlery
6. Journal
7. Polish brush
8. Fishing tackle
9. Tinderbox
10. Canteen

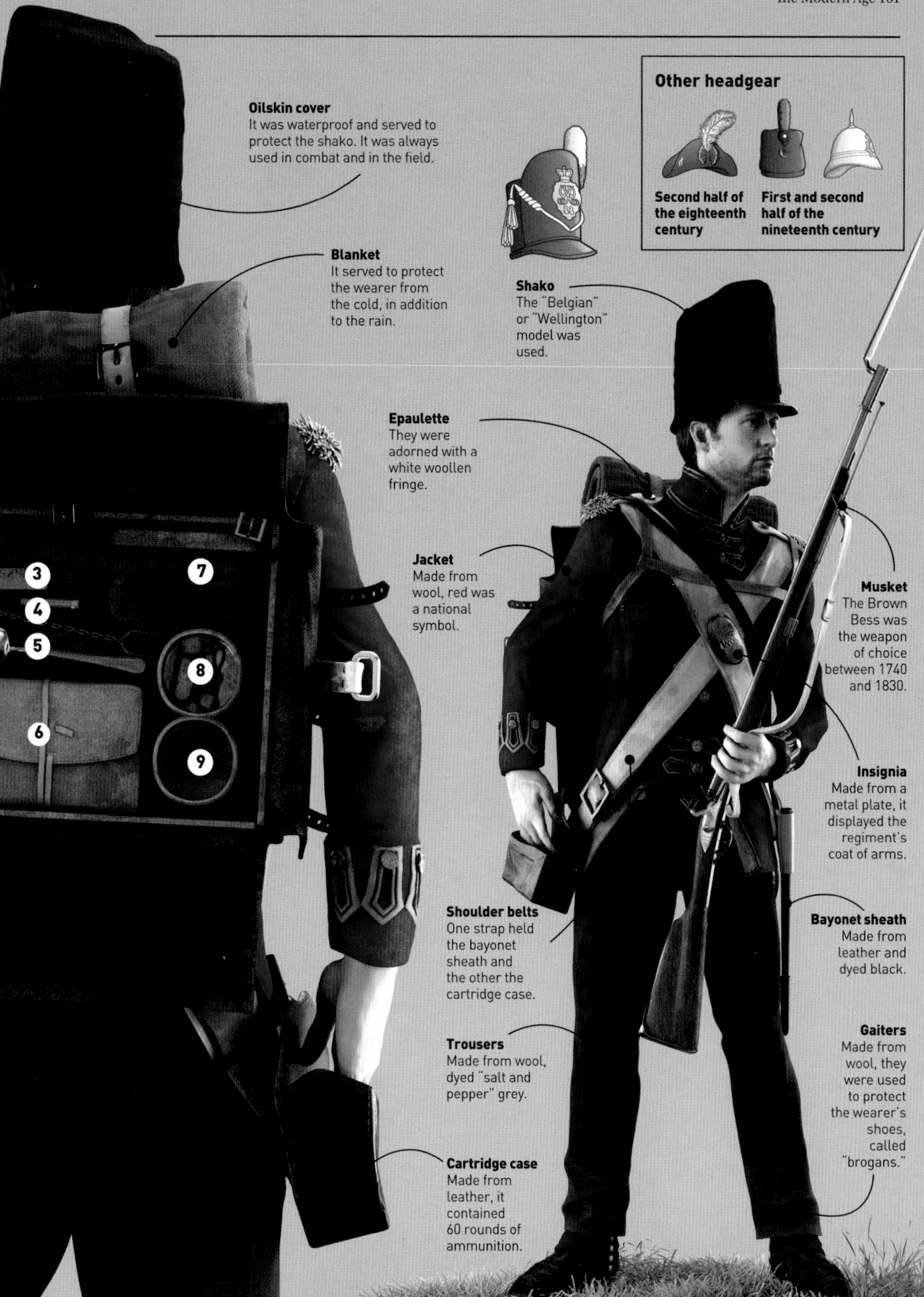
Oilskin cover
It was waterproof and served to protect the shako. It was always used in combat and in the field.
Blanket
It served to protect the wearer from the cold, in addition to the rain.
Other headgear
Second half of the eighteenth century
First and second half of the nineteenth century
Shako
The "Belgian" or "Wellington" model was used.
Epaulette
They were adorned with a white woollen fringe.
Jacket
Made from wool, red was a national symbol.
3
4
5
6
7
8
9
Musket
The Brown Bess was the weapon of choice between 1740 and 1830.
Insignia
Made from a metal plate, it displayed the regiment's coat of arms.
Shoulder belts
One strap held the bayonet sheath and the other the cartridge case.
Bayonet sheath
Made from leather and dyed black.
Trousers
Made from wool, dyed "salt and pepper" grey.
Gaiters
Made from wool, they were used to protect the wearer's shoes, called "brogans."
Cartridge case
Made from leather, it contained 60 rounds of ammunition.

The Battle of Trafalgar

On October 21, 1805, with Europe immersed in the Napoleonic Wars, the British naval fleet, under the command of Admiral Horatio Nelson, destroyed the Franco-Spanish fleet, under the command of Admiral Villeneuve, off Cape Trafalgar in southwest Spain. This overwhelming victory by Nelson, who oversaw the triumph aboard the flagship HMS *Victory*, strengthened British naval supremacy throughout the nineteenth century and ended forever Napoleon's plans to invade Britain.

Nelson's strategy

Nelson attacked the Franco-Spanish fleet when it was heading toward the Mediterranean Sea. The British Admiral's strategy was to attack in two columns, dividing the enemy formation in two and forcing them to fight at close combat. Nelson died in the battle, but won a decisive victory, destroying half the Franco-Spanish fleet.

HMS *Victory*

Built in 1765, this 227-ft/69-m vessel with three bridges had 821 crew and displaced 3,500 tons. It was Admiral Nelson's flagship.

Ships of the line

Navies of the seventeenth to nineteenth centuries adopted the line of battle tactic during combat, which is how these large vessels get their name. The most daring maneuvers consisted of firing at the waterline of enemy ships and, in the withdrawal of the ships, protecting the stern from the same fate.

How to hit the waterline

At 4,000 ft/ 1,200 m distance from the target.

Aim the cannon at the main mast

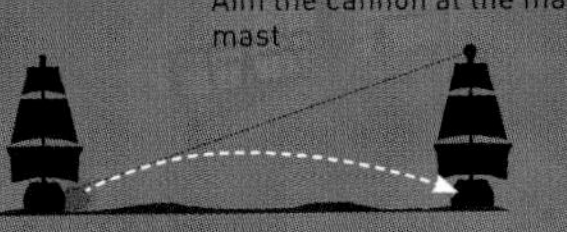

At 2,600 ft/ 800 m distance from the target.

Aim the cannon at the maintop

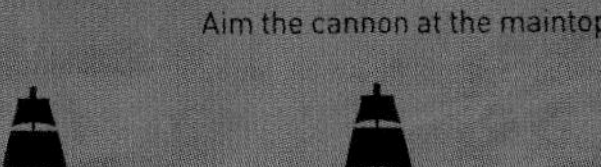

At 900–1180 ft/ 275–360 m distance from the target.

Aim the cannon directly at the waterline

Cannons Ships of the line had between 100 and 120 cannon. HMS *Victory* had 106, including guns and carronades (sliding cannon with a wheeled platform).

Masts The total weight of all three masts with yards and bowsprit, was 88 tons. They were made of pine or fir, as this timber is lighter.
Fastenings The masts were made stable by surrounding them with iron hoops and they had platforms over the yards (the horizontal poles for the sails).
Batteries The ships of the line had three batteries of cannon ready on deck to fire broadsides, except for the Spanish El Santísima Trinidad, which had four.
Hull HMS Victory spent 13 years in dry dock because her wooden hull had rotted. This was a common problem among British ships, owing to their constant vigil at sea.

COMPARISON OF FORCES

BRITISH FLEET ▸ 27 ships.

FRANCO-SPANISH FLEET ▸ 18 Spanish ships and 15 French ships.

95·1854

CHAPTER 4

THE 20th CENTURY

S·D·A·P·

THE WORLD AT WAR

Throughout the history of armies and battles fought in Europe during the twentieth century, three struggles toward the end of the nineteenth century were to play a fundamental role that would alter the correlation of the continent's powers. In all three, waged by Germany on Denmark in 1864, on Austria in 1866, and on France in 1870 and 1871, the Germans were victorious; as a result, the nation became a great power. By then, European statesmen and generals were convinced that modern wars would be brief and that nations would be unable to withstand the economic and political pressures of a long-term conflict for large periods of time. The European powers, who lived through an unprecedented period of peace between 1871 and 1914, concentrated their efforts on expanding their global reach, waging war in Africa, Asia, the Pacific, and the American continent on poorly armed indigenous peoples. The powers employed new weapons in these conflicts, such as bolt-action guns, howitzers, and machine guns; they used smokeless powder, nitrate explosives with a significant destructive power, and carriages on the cannons to prevent recoil. These weapons, together with the speeding up of the Industrial Revolution, allowed Great Britain, France, Austria, Germany, and Russia to gain greater power, sustained by colonialism. As a result, they obtained the economic resources with which they financed the two largest conflicts of the twentieth century.

In Asia, having defeated China in the First Sino-Japanese War between 1894 and 1895 and occupying Taiwan, Korea, and Manchuria, the Japanese defeated the Russians in the Russo-Japanese War. In 1904, they attacked Port Arthur, anchorage of the Russian fleet in the Pacific, with torpedoes, a tactic that would be imitated in Pearl Harbor in 1941; in 1905, the Japanese then forced Russia to abandon Korea and Manchuria, focusing their attention on the Balkans, where a group of nationalist officers had taken control of Serbia in 1903.

By then, a great arms race had taken off in Europe: Germany had constructed a significant fleet; Great Britain had a new style of battleship with large artillery and subsequently made alliances with France in 1904 and with Russia in 1907. Nonetheless, just a year later the Russians signed a treaty with Austria in which, in an exchange for rights over Bosnia and Herzegovina, their war fleet was given access to the Bosphorus. In 1911, Italy attacked Libya, while the Serbs, Bulgarians, Greeks, and Montenegrins fought a weakened Ottoman Empire. With the Czechs, Poles, and Slovaks reclaiming autonomy, and after France relocated its fleet from the Mediterranean to the North Sea in 1912, the German military notably increased its defense expenditure, recruiting more than 800,000 men, and declared an immediate "preventative war."

The trigger for World War I was the assassination of Archduke Franz Ferdinand, heir to the Austrian-

Hungarian crown, by a Serbian extremist during the former's visit to a recently annexed Bosnia on June 28, 1914. A month later, Austria declared war and bombed Belgrade. On August 1, Germany implemented the "Schlieffen Plan," named in honor of its author, Alfred von Schlieffen (1833–1913), head of the military in 1891, which consisted of advancing on two fronts: to the west, its objective was to cross Belgium, invade France, and reach Paris in a fast military operation; to the east, its aim was to attack Russia and strengthen this activity using part of the forces returning from the west. The high German command rolled out one and a half million men divided into seven armies and declared war on France on August 3. However, the breach of Belgian neutrality saw Great Britain enter the war. By November, a 450–mile/725–km front stretching from Switzerland to the English Channel had been created, which would barely change in the following three years. What had initially been considered a *blitzkrieg* (lightning strike), eventually became a war of attrition that mobilized 70 million people.

While the technological revolution transformed the nature of the war, contributing to the invention of the radio, aviation, and the construction of tanks, submarines and great battleships, officers were rooted in the tactical and operational concepts of the nineteenth century. The two great battles of 1916 barely changed things: Verdun, which became a mammoth slaughter in which more than 400,000 people were killed and 800,000 injured; and the Somme, in which the British fired 1.5 million projectiles on German positions without recording significant advances. In 1917, the Germans changed strategy, inventing what is considered modern combat: on the front line, they positioned a thin strip of machine guns before moving their strongest forces toward the center of their lines; they placed the bulk of their infantry out of range of the enemy's artillery; and they left decision-making on the battlefield to lieutenants and captains.

In February of the same year, the Russian Revolution broke out. The Germans allowed Vladimir Lenin (1870–1924) to return to Russia from Switzerland in a sealed train and provide significant amounts of money to the Bolsheviks, who signed a peace agreement with the Germans in 1918, handing over the Baltic states, Poland,

Finland, and a large part of the Ukraine in the process. In May, the German army implemented "Operation Michael" against France, mobilizing a million men and coming within 40 miles/65 km of Paris. However, the entrance of the United States into the war stopped the offensive. In reality, the German Army destroyed itself in the operation; almost all of its personnel were killed or injured in action. In September, British tanks, close to Amiens, and the offensive of the U.S. Air Force on Saint-Mihiel, had forced a breach in German lines. Meanwhile, hunger and strikes had ravaged the fabric of German society. Bulgaria and Turkey declared peace in October, with Austria signing the armistice in November. Having lost the war, Emperor Wilhelm II (1859-1941) abdicated. On November 9, Germany became a republic and on November 11, it ceased hostilities. World War I resulted in the deaths of 700,000 British; 250,000 Commonwealth subjects; 500,000 Italians; 1,100,000 Austrians; 1,300,000 French; 2,000,000 Germans, and 40 percent of the Serb population, 30 percent of the Turkish population, and 25 percent of the Romanian and Bulgarian populations. More than nine million soldiers aged between 20 and 30 died in active service. The war also had a significant impact on society, as women assumed their place in the new workforce. However, the greatest impact was the effect on people's faith in "progress" and the consequent emergence of radical left- and right-wing ideologies in Europe.

The Treaty of Versailles, signed in 1919, and the London Conference of 1922 established the war reparations to which Germany would be subjected: 140,000 million gold marks, 52 percent of which were assigned to France, 22 percent to Great Britain, 10 percent to Italy, and a similar amount to Belgium. Furthermore, Versailles also marked the collapse of the Austro-Hungarian Empire, the restoration of Poland, Denmark, and Belgium and the confiscation of Germany's overseas assets and its fleet. Such conditions were humiliating to the German military elite, who attributed their defeat to what they claimed was sabotage on the part of the Jews and Communists in the Reich, and placed responsibility for the situation at the feet of the new Weimar Republic.

In the following 20 years, while France tried to contain Germany by building the "Maginot Line" (the largest defense line in the modern world, which saw the construction of 108 forts and

the excavation of more than 250 miles/400 km of tunnels along the border with Germany and Italy), key decisions were taken that would determine the course of World War II. Starting in 1923, while the United States made a series of important loans to Europe, Germany drafted a transcendent document: "Die Truppenführung" ("Troop Command") in which a new concept of armored warfare was proposed. After the Wall Street Crash of 1929, when the United States demanded the return of its loans, the Central European economy collapsed, preparing the terrain for a new large-scale conflict.

In 1933, with Adolf Hitler being named as Chancellor, Germany embarked upon a huge rearmament program (in 1935, it had three armored divisions; by 1936 this grew to six and by 1940 to ten). Meanwhile, the British Army was barely able to finance itself up to 1939, stagnancy reigned supreme in France, and, in the U.S.S.R., the purges of Joseph Stalin (1878–1953) resulted in the disappearance of tens of thousands of military men. Around this time, the British Royal Air Force incorporated the use of radar in its planes, and the invention of sonar made British admirals believe that enemy submarines would pose no threat. Japan and the United States manufactured large armored ships and aircraft carriers, while the German *Luftwaffe* (its air force) grew.

Hitler, in addition to rearmament and the elimination of the Jews, was intent on conquering and restructuring Europe. In 1935, Benito Mussolini, the Italian Prime Minister from 1922, ordered an attack on Ethiopia using mustard gas. In 1936, General Francisco Franco rebelled against the Spanish Republic and started a civil war, with the support of Germany and Italy and with no intervention from Great Britain or France, which cost a million lives and concluded with the installation of a Fascist regime in Spain. In 1938, Hitler invaded Austria while the international community remained impassive. His next moves were to occupy Czechoslovakia in 1939 and sign a pact of non-aggression with Stalin that saw eastern Poland, the Baltic states, and Finland assigned to the latter, and the invasion of west Poland: one and a half million of the *Wehrmacht* (the German Army) were deployed and in less than 30 days, Hitler and Stalin divided up the country. In the process, 70,000 Poles died. Great Britain, who had guaranteed the independence of Poland, and France then declared war on Germany. In April 1940, the Germans attacked Denmark, and in May, took the Netherlands and Belgium, before invading France. Paris fell in June and on June 22, Philippe Pétain (1856–1951), Marshal of France, signed an armistice which saw a period of active collaboration with the Nazi regime. By this time, Mussolini had also declared war on France and Great Britain.

Just a month earlier, Winston Churchill (1874–1965) had been named British prime minister, and although Germany hoped that Great Britain would not attack, the economic support and weaponry provided by the United States were decisive. The British had an efficient air force and had been able to decipher secret transmissions between the German high command. But despite this, in August, they would come up against the *Luftwaffe*, suffering significant losses. Hitler, in turn, ventured into the Balkans in September in order to guarantee the provision of fuel from Romania. In March 1941, he destroyed Yugoslavia and bombed Belgrade, with 17,000 civilian lives lost; as a result, guerrilla warfare swept the country, which would later cause numerous German casualties. Shortly after, the 7th Flieger-Division, the first to transport paratroopers, conquered Crete.

By then, the Germans had implemented "Operation Barbarossa," with a view to invading the Soviet Union. In June 1941, they opened fire across a 2,000-mile/3,200-km front to the east. Three million soldiers, accompanied by "special action units" tasked with annihilating Jews and Communists, marched toward Leningrad. However, the German advance was stopped by problems supplying its troops and, finally, the harsh Russian winter prevented the Germans from bringing their plan to fruition. In December, the Red Army counterattacked and freed positions around Moscow. The operation cost the *Wehrmacht* more than a million lives.

On December 11, four days after the Japanese attack on Pearl Harbor, inflicting massive losses on the U.S. Pacific fleet, Hitler declared war on the United States. In August 1942, when the Americans, in addition to deciphering German naval codes, had caused significant damage to Japanese interests in the Korean Sea and in Midway, the Germans arrived at the Volga River, and in September attacked Stalingrad. The battle lasted over two months, and cost the lives of 500,000 soldiers of the Axis (Germany, Japan, Italy) and 750,000 Soviet soldiers. The Soviets' "Operation Uranus" mobilized a million soldiers, 13,000 cannons and 900 tanks against the German Sixth Army, which surrendered in January 1943.

The same year, Germany lost the arms race, and although it launched the North Africa Campaign, the initiative was a disaster. Meanwhile, the United States had brought together an enormous fleet and was producing 250 bombers every day. Its troops invaded Sicily in July, resulting in the removal of Mussolini; they took Rome and expelled the Germans through the north of Italy. Meanwhile, in the Atlantic, the Allies recorded significant successes, having deciphered the Germans' naval codes. In May, the Germans lost 41 submarines, while in Europe, the British and Americans implemented the harsh "Combined Bomber Offensive." In May 1944, the German Air Force was destroyed.

June 6, 1944 was "D-day." Five Allied infantry divisions and three paratrooper divisions landed on the beaches of Normandy. On September 2, 6,500 ships and carriers and more than 12,000 planes deployed 117,000 men, who freed Brussels. Furthermore, on the Eastern Front, the Soviet Army, following the German retreat at Kursk in 1943, had reached the Black Sea and the Carpathian Mountains. On July 20, 1944, when a group of German officers made an unsuccessful attempt against Hitler, Germany had already lost 17 divisions and more than half of another 50. That autumn, the *Wehrmacht* was on the back foot and the systematic bombing of the German transport network in winter was the final nail in the coffin of its wartime economy. In January 1945, the Soviets attacked from the east and the British and Canadians reached the Rhine from the north. In March, in the Pacific, U.S. B-29 bombers destroyed a large part of Tokyo and then Okinawa.The Japanese retaliated causing 65,000 injuries. On April 30, Hitler committed suicide. His commanders unconditionally surrendered just a week later. However, the definitive end of the war would not come until August, when on August 6 the United States dropped an atomic bomb over Hiroshima, causing 90,000 deaths, and

on August 9 over Nagasaki, causing a further 35,000 deaths. On September 2, Japan surrendered.

World War II was followed by 45 years of fragile peace—the "Cold War"—between the U.S.S.R. and the United States, who had become the two military superpowers with radically different governing styles and economies. There were years of peace in Europe, which established a military alliance with the United States in 1949 under NATO (North Atlantic Treaty Organization). However, there was not a single war-free day in the rest of the world. The collapse of colonial empires and the economic interests of the powers caused confrontations that would have terrible consequences: Korea in 1950; Malaysia in 1952; Algeria in 1954; Vietnam in 1960 and 1973; Angola in 1961; Palestine in 1948, 1956, 1967, and 1973; the Persian Gulf in 1988, 1990, and 1991, Rwanda in 1990; the Balkans in 1992; Chechnya in 1993; Zaire in 1996; and so on.

During the 1960s and 1970s, the scientific and technological revolution miniaturized nuclear weapons, improved communications and long-range ballistic missile launch systems, and completely changed military strategies and tactics. So-called "nuclear deterrence" was implemented, with weapons capable of annihilating all life forms on the planet. The computer revolution followed in the 1980s, as a result of space and military programs, which transformed the concept of war once again. Following the dissolution of the U.S.S.R. in 1991, the concept of war would go global. The progressively "richer" societies, now using satellite-controlled missile systems to protect themselves and remote-controlled robots with significant destructive capacities for "remote" warfare, are now facing new threats, such as terrorist activities against civilians, and the possible use of atomic weapons by an ever-increasing number of countries.

714

Chronology and Main Battles

During the twentieth century, science became a determining factor in the evolution of armies worldwide. The technological revolution developed conventional weapons in such a way that, in reality, they became obsolete in a short space of time. As a result, governments had to designate large sums of money to researching new attack and defense systems. Furthermore, constant rearmament was accompanied by a huge step forward in terms of communication. And war went global.

AVENGE
PEARL
HARBOR
OUR BULLETS WILL DO IT

1900

1903
A group of nationalist officers take power in Serbia

1904
The Japanese attack the Russians' Pacific fleet at Port Arthur

1905
Russo-Japanese War

1912
France transfers its Mediterranean fleet to the North Sea

1914
Archduke Franz Ferdinand is assassinated in Bosnia. World War I begins

1916
Battles of Verdun and the Somme

1917
Bolshevik Revolution in Russia

1919
Treaty of Versailles

1922
London Conference on Reparations, at which the sums of money to be paid by Germany are established

1922
The Soviet Union is created

1925
The Chinese Civil War begins

Stalin assumes power in Russia

1929
Wall Street crash. The Great Depression begins

1933
Adolf Hitler is named German Chancellor

1936
General Franco rebels against the Spanish Republic and starts the Spanish Civil War

1939
Germany and the Soviet Union sign a non-aggression pact. The invasion of Poland triggers World War II

1940
The Germans conquer Paris

1941
Japan attacks the United States at Pearl Harbor

1942
Battle of Stalingrad

1944
Normandy landings

1945
The United States drops two atomic bombs over Hiroshima and Nagasaki. End of World War II

The United Nations (U.N.) is founded by 51 countries

1946
The First Indochina War begins

1947
India and Pakistan gain independence from the British Empire

1948
Foundation of the state of Israel

1949
Creation of NATO

Proclamation of the People's Republic of China

1950
The Korean War begins

1950

THE MISSILE CRISIS
In 1962, Fidel Castro asked the U.S.S.R. for medium-range ballistic missiles, for which over 40 platforms were erected on Cuba. The Russians withdrew them in return for a promise that the United States would not invade the island.

Daily Herald
KENNEDY BLOCKADES CUBA
Daily Mirror U.S. MOVES ON CUBA—IT'S THE BIG BLOCKADE
Daily Mail
CUBA BLOCKADE
SKETCH CUBA BLOCKADED
DAILY EXPRESS
Kennedy:

In Italy and Turkey, the United States installed 30 *Jupiter* missiles in Italy and 15 in Turkey aimed toward the U.S.S.R, but withdrew them later.

1954
Algerian rebels start a battle for national liberation. The Geneva Accords implement an anticommunist autocratic regime in South Vietnam

1955
The Warsaw Pact is signed. Civil war in Sudan

The first nuclear-driven submarine is launched by the U.S.A.—the U.S.S. *Nautilus*

1956
France sends its army to Algeria. The Suez Canal crisis. The Arab-Israeli War

1960
First test of a ballistic missile, *Polaris*, with nuclear capacity in the United States

1961
Attempted invasion of Cuba at the Bay of Pigs

1962
Cuban missile crisis. Algeria gains independence from France

1964
U.S. Congress authorizes war against Vietnam

1967
The Six-Day Arab-Israeli War. Civil war in Nigeria

1970
The United States invades Cambodia to destroy North Vietnamese logistics bases

1973
The United States withdraws from Vietnam. Israeli victory in the Yom Kippur War. Cultural Revolution of Mao Zedong in China.
Oil crisis

1974
Civil war in Angola

1975
Pol Pot regime in Cambodia

1979
Islamic Revolution in Iran. The Soviet Union invades Afghanistan

1980
War breaks out between Iran and Iraq

1982
The Falklands War between Argentina and the United Kingdom

1988
The war ends between Iran and Iraq

1989
The Berlin Wall falls

1990
Iraq invades Kuwait. The Gulf War begins

1991
The Soviet Union breaks up. Chechen War. The Yugoslav Wars begin

1994
Tutsi massacre at the hands of the Hutus in Rwanda

1996
The Taliban take power in Afghanistan. Russia withdraws from Chechnya. The United States invades Iraq

1999
NATO intervenes in Kosovo

2000

2001
Islamic extremists attack the Twin Towers in New York, causing over 3,000 deaths

Famous Military Men

They mobilized millions of men and had sophisticated weapons and economic resources at their disposal that would have been unimaginable just a few years earlier. They led armies whose degree of specialization became increasingly more complex throughout the twentieth century and they faced, over the course of a decade, a progressively more developed civil society that was less willing to tolerate casualties in combat.

1890–1969

DWIGHT DAVID EISENHOWER
U.S. Commander in "Operation Torch" in North Africa (1942) and Supreme Commander of the Allied Forces during "Operation Overlord" (1944). He participated in the Normandy landings and victoriously reached Nazi Germany in 1945. In 1953, he was elected U.S. President.

1884–1943

ISOROKU YAMAMOTO
Japanese admiral, from 1939 commander-in-chief of the Combined Fleet of the Imperial Japanese Navy. He planned the attack on Pearl Harbor, but six months later suffered a serious defeat at Midway. He died after the plane he was traveling in was downed in an ambush.

1885–1945

GEORGE SMITH PATTON
U.S. military man, he commanded a tank unit during World War I and participated in World War II on the African Front. In 1944, he crossed enemy territory from Normandy to Czechoslovakia, where he stopped in 1945 owing to the Armistice.

1887–1976

BERNARD LAW MONTGOMERY
A brilliant English military officer during World War II. In 1942, he was sent to Africa, where he beat Rommel at El Alamein. He participated in the Sicily and Normandy landings in 1944. His military strategy wore down the Germans and contributed to victory in the final offensive.

"If we fail, then the whole world, including the United States, including all that we have known and cared for, will sink into the abyss of a new dark age."

Winston Churchill, *Blood, toil, sweat, and tears* (1941)

The Holocaust Memorial in Jerusalem.

MILITARY VICTIMS VS. CIVILIAN VICTIMS

Whereas during wars waged throughout the nineteenth century, military injuries accounted for 80 percent of the total, from 1945 onward, most of the approximately 50 million people killed in war were civilians. This figure reached 70 percent in Vietnam.

1888–1954

HEINZ GUDERIAN

A German military officer who developed the *blitzkrieg* (lightning strike) technique. After participating in Operation Barbarossa, he was dismissed for his rebellious character. Later he was named Chief of the General Staff of the Army, but was dismissed again in 1945.

1891–1944

ERWIN ROMMEL

A German military officer, Rommel participated in both World Wars, demonstrating great ability as a strategist. He was sent to Africa, where he kept the British at bay until 1942. Hitler forced his suicide after discovering his participation in the 1944 plot against him.

1896–1974

GEORGY KONSTANTINOVICH ZHÚKOV

Soviet military man and hero, he registered the most important victories on the Russian Front. He organized the defense in Stalingrad and the counterattack that cornered and defeated the Nazis in the city. He also led the Russian Army that took Berlin.

1912–2013

NGUYEN VO GIAP

A Vietnamese military man, he participated in an armed pro-independence group that merged with Ho Chi Minh's group in the 1940s. He was a tactical specialist at guerrilla warfare and helped his country to victory in the war against South Vietnam and the United States.

Contemporary Weapons

During the twentieth century, tanks, planes, and missiles changed military tactics and, from halfway through the century, nuclear arms converted deterrence into a strategy. Nonetheless, land-based combat retained its position as the determining factor in struggles. In this aspect, the firepower of weapons used by land troops increased exponentially and became increasingly more accurate, sophisticated, and deadly.

Rifles

Repeating rifles in World War I gave way to more accurate and quicker self-loading rifles in World War II. In the 1990s, the incorporation of more powerful ammunition helped increase the target distance, while decreasing the rifle's size and weight.

Lee Enfield Manually loading repeating rifle, used by the British infantry in World War I.

Sturmgewehr 44 Self-reloading assault rifle, produced by Germany in 1944–5, combining the features of a submachine gun and an automatic firearm.

MP5KA Submachine gun produced by the German company Heckler & Koch since the 1960s, it measures just 13 in/ 33 cm.

AK-47 Automatic assault rifle designed by Mikhail Kalashnikov and adopted by the Soviet Army in 1949. Cheap, simple, and long lasting, it is frequently used by guerrillas and national liberation movements.

Pistols

Used by officers in the main armies in the two World Wars, they were later almost entirely relegated to use solely in the security and police sectors.

Luger P08 Employed by the German Army, it incorporated the Parabellum cartridge that would become a standard worldwide.

CZ 805 Assault rifle fitted with a telescopic sight for snipers, produced since 2009 by the Czech company Czub, which exports it to 100 countries.

Homemade weapons

In contrast to the increasingly sophisticated weapons used by national armies, irregular forces have sought ways of manufacturing their own weapons. Examples can be seen in the weapons manufactured by resistance groups during World War II.

Grenades made at home by the Norwegian resistance.

29ct.
VIM

Land mine camouflaged in the bottle of a cleaning product, made by the Danish resistance.

Machine guns

The first fixed-mounting machine guns were supplemented at the beginning of the century by light machine guns. During World War I, they were decisive in trench warfare and, from World War II onward, they were made lighter. Recently, materials such as plastic and fiberglass have been incorporated into their production.

Vickers MK.1 Machine gun Employed by the British Army in 1922, it was manufactured until 1968.

Tank machine gun used by the Soviet Army during World War II.

Antitank weaponry

Grenade launchers and mobile rocket launchers (such as the U.S. bazooka) became commonplace during World War II. Since then, they have become standard weaponry in all modern conflicts.

Panzerfaust 60 Used by the Wehrmacht, this model was disposed of after a single use.

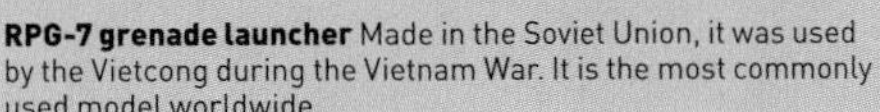

RPG-7 grenade launcher Made in the Soviet Union, it was used by the Vietcong during the Vietnam War. It is the most commonly used model worldwide.

Trench Warfare

The conduct of World War I made it clear that classic military tactics had been rendered obsolete. Evolution and the firepower of weapons resulted in mobile warfare being replaced by position warfare, with a new predominant setting–the trenches. The romantic times in which an image of glory in combat reigned were now over. Now, war was about mud, resistance, suffering, and death in passageways measuring between 3–6 ft/1–2 m deep.

Daily life on the battlefield

The Western Front became an out-of-this-world scene: land scorched by heavy artillery, craters, barbed wire, and endless lines of trenches. Here, soldiers withstood the cold, humidity, and bombings, waiting for the moment at which the alarm would sound, informing them that they must leave the protection of the trench and launch an attack on enemy lines, under relentless machine-gun fire.

Rear guard
The heavy artillery was located 6 miles/10 km from the front line and moved forward as the infantry progressed.

Support trench
This served as a reserve to the front line. It was usually occupied by shelters located over 33 ft/10 m underground to withstand the direct impact of heavy artillery.

La Voie Sacrée
The route that supplied the defenses on the French front. Between 3,000 and 3,500 trucks crossed this route on a daily basis, transporting soldiers, war supplies, and evacuating casualties.

No Man's Land
Otherwise known as the battlefield; that is to say, the piece of land between the two enemy trench lines. Mines were usually planted in this wretched muddy zone, littered with bomb craters.
Fences
The trenches were protected by large, intertwined rows of barbed-wire fences. It was extremely difficult for the enemy infantry to pass them.
Aviation
Planes often flew over the trenches, whether to fire machine guns at the enemy, or to warn of an imminent attack.
Tunnels
Some German shelters were connected by tunnels, facilitating the transport of soldiers without being exposed to enemy fire.
Front line
The front trenches were the most dangerous. Soldiers had to take cover both from enemy fire and the artillery coming from the support trench, located behind them.
Fire step
The side that faced the enemy was called the "parapet" and was equipped with a support area for shooting.
Trench, board, and sump

IN DETAIL

The trenches were fortifications carved into the soil and designed in a winding way to minimize the effect of cluster bombs and limit the sight line in the event of an enemy breach.

Battles for position

During winter 1914, the Western Front remained stable. Armies took shelter in endless lines of trenches, running for around 450 miles/725 km from the English Channel to the Alps, perfectly protected by fences, machine guns, and repeating rifles. The defenses offered a significant advantage, where both sides were able to prepare new attacking tactics to take enemy positions, including the indiscriminate use of a whole host of gases.

Assault on strongholds

The armies had to vary their strategies in order to overcome their enemies' complex defensive strongholds. Great battles gave way to small assault forces taking advantage of artillery in order to breach enemy lines. They often took action at night, to surprise their enemy and avoid machine-gun fire.

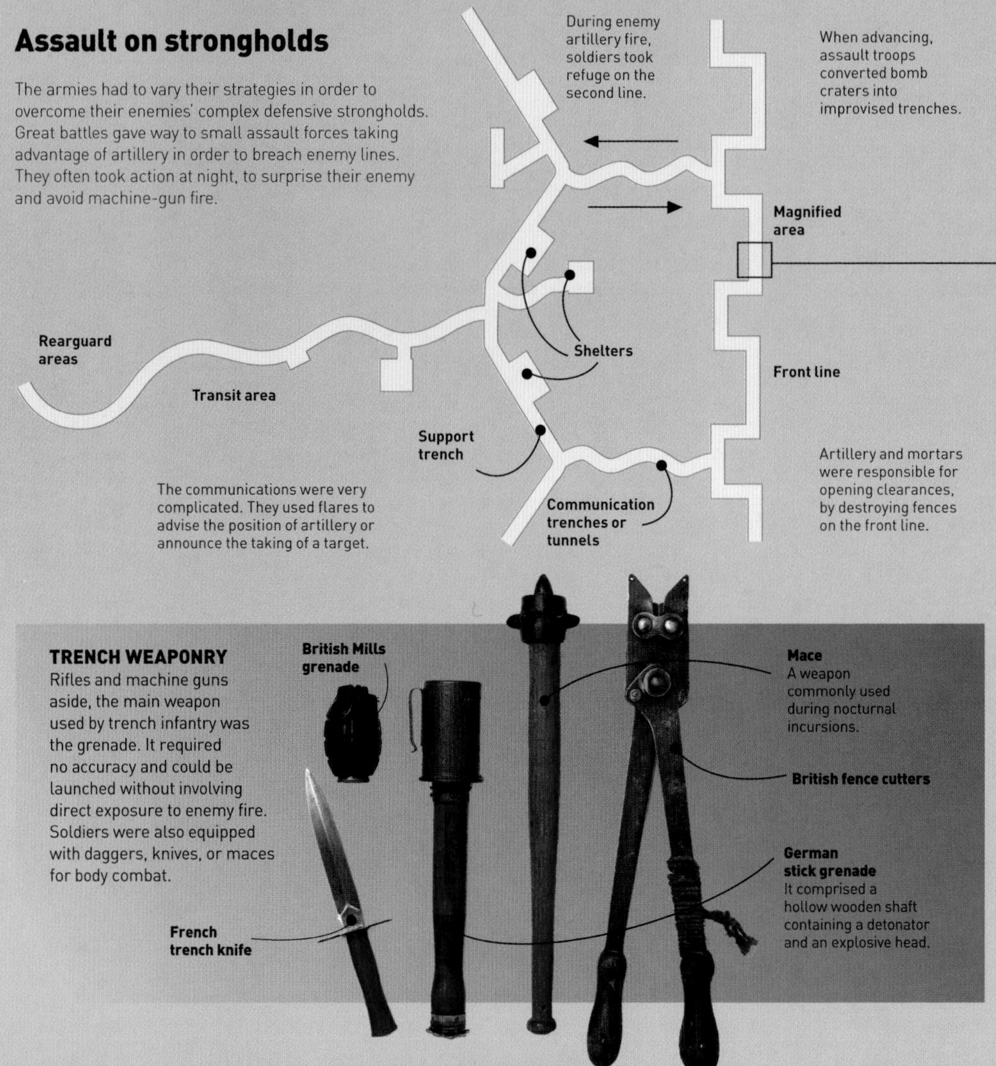
During enemy artillery fire, soldiers took refuge on the second line.
When advancing, assault troops converted bomb craters into improvised trenches.
Magnified area
Rearguard areas
Shelters
Front line
Transit area
Support trench
Artillery and mortars were responsible for opening clearances, by destroying fences on the front line.
The communications were very complicated. They used flares to advise the position of artillery or announce the taking of a target.
Communication trenches or tunnels
British Mills grenade
Mace
A weapon commonly used during nocturnal incursions.
British fence cutters
German stick grenade
It comprised a hollow wooden shaft containing a detonator and an explosive head.
French trench knife

TRENCH WEAPONRY

Rifles and machine guns aside, the main weapon used by trench infantry was the grenade. It required no accuracy and could be launched without involving direct exposure to enemy fire. Soldiers were also equipped with daggers, knives, or maces for body combat.

Barbed wire
It was stealthily erected overnight and required daily maintenance. Fences could be 30 in/ 75 cm in height and several feet wide.

Sandbags
Used as a support when firing. Gaps were normally opened up between bags to help vision without being seen. Alternatively, very primitive periscopes were used.

Fire step

Rear side, or "parados"
Offered protection against cluster bombs and served as a parapet for the enemy when they took a trench.

Positioning advantage

At the beginning of World War I, rifle and machine-gun fire, in addition to large fences, made trenches practically impregnable.

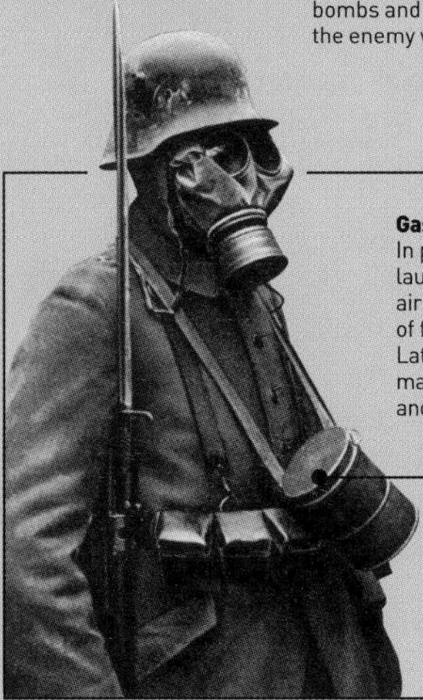

Gas projectiles
In principle, gas was launched into the air, taking advantage of favorable winds. Later, projectiles were manufactured for artillery and mortars.

Masks
The use of gas resulted in the appearance of gas masks, seen here on a German soldier (1917).

CHEMICAL WARFARE

In August 1914, gas was used for the first time as a weapon against enemy trenches. First, tear gas and chlorine gases were deployed; later, these would be replaced by more deadly agents, such as phosgene and mustard gas.

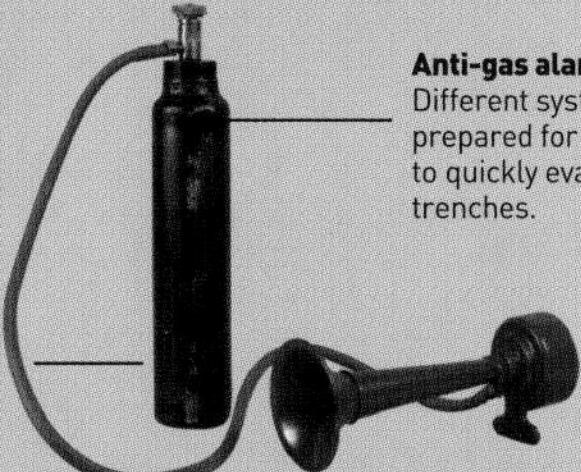

Anti-gas alarm
Different systems were prepared for soldiers to quickly evacuate the trenches.

The Battle of the Somme

On July 1, 1916, the offensive of British and French troops on German positions in the Somme region, on the Western Front, clearly demonstrated the enormous cruelty of trench warfare during World War I. Although the Allies would finally drive back the Second German Army under the command of Fritz von Below, there were tens of thousands of casualties on both sides while just 6 miles/10 km of headway was made into enemy territory.

Objective: relieve Verdun

In the face of significant German pressure on the important enclave of Verdun, the French commander-in-chief, Joseph Joffre, proposed a significant offensive around the River Somme to his British counterpart, Douglas Haig. The objective was to force the Germans to mobilize their personnel in Verdun. The first attack on the German trenches, which were well-prepared and in a clearly advantageous position, resulted in a massacre of the inexperienced British infantry. The Allied block learned from its mistakes and after a siege that lasted for months, it pushed back the enemy line after taking Beaumont-Hamel on November 13, 1916.

ROAD TOWARD CAMBRAI
SWABIA STRONGHOLD
LEIPZIG STRONGHOLD
High Wood
Delville Wood
Leuze Wood
Mametz Wood
Trônes Wood
WATERLOT FARM
River Ancre
BRITISH ZONE
River Somme
FRENCH ZONE

Front line on July 1 1916
Front line on August 1 1916
Final front line on November 20, 1916
Main German bunkers

July 1
The land offensive clashes with the powerful defensive positions of the Germans.

July 14
Having learned their lesson, the Allied Forces launch a skilled nighttime attack that breaks the second German line.

November 13
The Allies take Beaumont-Hamel and the German Army withdraws to the Hindenburg Line.

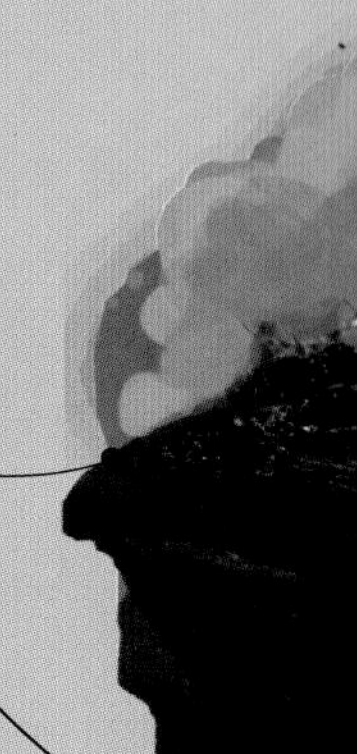

Incline
The slope of the land offered the Germans an additional advantage, as they benefited from a good view along the lines.

Highly prepared
The Germans had constructed an efficient network of trenches in the 20 miles/32 km to their line, with underground shelters and fortified strongholds.

GERMAN SOLDIER
In 1916, metal helmets, *stahlhelm*, were already in use, rather than the leather *pickelhaube*.

BRITISH SOLDIER
Well-armed with a Lee Enfield rifle, one of the best of the Great War.

Most units that participated in the Battle of the Somme comprised British volunteers and troops from Commonwealth countries such as South Africa, Canada, New Zealand, and Australia. In total 420,000 casualties were recorded.

Miserable conditions
In the trenches, soldiers lived in cold, humid, rat-infested conditions. Around the Somme, autumn rains worsened these conditions further still.

Frustrated attack

The British artillery had bombed German positions for a week to prepare the land for its infantry. However, one third of the 1.5 million projectiles launched were defective and the German line was barely weakened. As a result, on July 1, British soldiers were easy prey for German fire. Around 60,000 casualties were recorded in a single day.

Sterile attack
British soldiers were highly exposed to enemy fire. Many fell on the battlefield and did not even reach the German line.

Firepower
The standard issue German rifle, the Mauser Gewehr 98, in addition to the Maxim machine guns, razed the Allied troops on their offensive of July 1 1916.

Airships

The Great War also converted our skies. Before the introduction of fighter planes, which intensified combat, cities were attacked from the sky by enormous, significantly vulnerable, aluminum-structure dirigibles full of gas: airships. They were first used on reconnaissance missions. However, the Germans quickly identified their potential as a weapon to combat the powerful British navy and to bomb British soil.

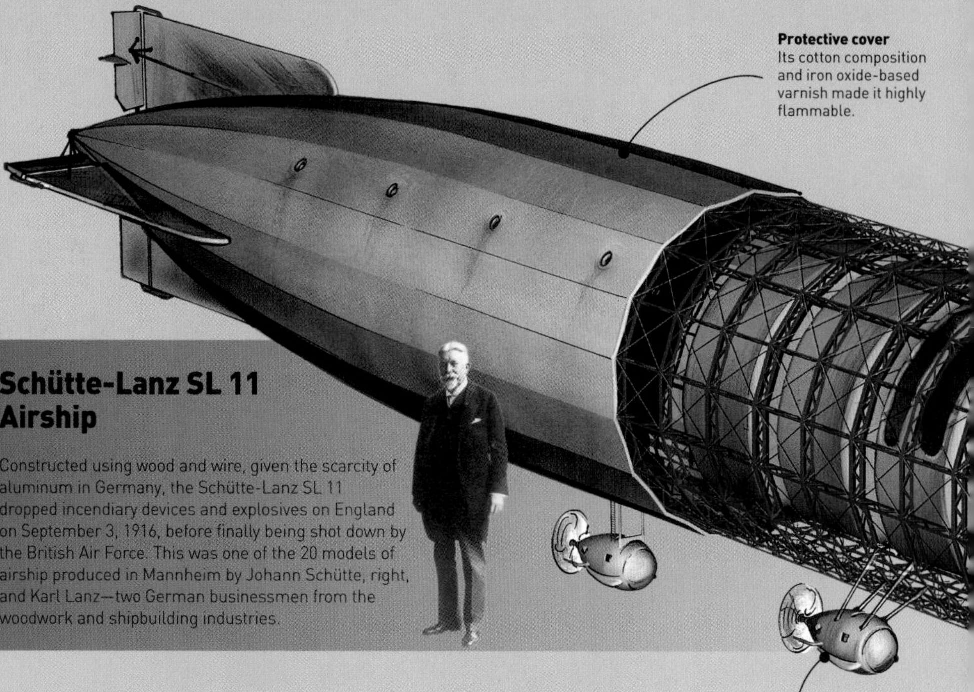

Protective cover
Its cotton composition and iron oxide-based varnish made it highly flammable.

Schütte-Lanz SL 11 Airship

Constructed using wood and wire, given the scarcity of aluminum in Germany, the Schütte-Lanz SL 11 dropped incendiary devices and explosives on England on September 3, 1916, before finally being shot down by the British Air Force. This was one of the 20 models of airship produced in Mannheim by Johann Schütte, right, and Karl Lanz—two German businessmen from the woodwork and shipbuilding industries.

Engine nacelle
The main nacelle. It was equipped with four Maybach HSLu piston engines with a unit capacity of 240 hp.

INSIDE THE GONDOLA
The control platform or gondola on the Schütte-Lanz SL 11 was equipped with two rudders, one for direction and another for height, to control the airship and to keep it level. It was also fitted with a compass, an altimeter, and a barograph as basic navigation tools.

IN BREACH OF THE HAGUE AGREEMENT
On August 24, 1914, a German airship dropped several bombs over the Belgian city of Antwerp, resulting in numerous victims. In doing so, Germany breached the 1899 Hague Conventions for the first time, which prohibited discharging bombs from balloons and similar devices.

Technical information

Length ▸ 570 ft/174 m

Height ▸ 66 ft/20 m

Volume ▸ 1,126,500 cu ft/31,900 m³

Speed ▸ 59 mph/95 km/h

Number of engines ▸ 4

Unit capacity ▸ 240 hp

Payload ▸ 21 tons

Cells
Filled with hydrogen, a gas so flammable that it would be replaced by helium. Consumption of fuel made the airship lighter, and this lift was compensated by allowing gas to escape.

Structure
The rings, or circular girders, were joined to the horizontal girders, with struts used in a cross shape. They were then covered by thin sheets.

Weaponry
In addition to bombs, the Schütte-Lanz 11 SL was equipped with a firing post at the bow with 7.92-mm Parabellum machine guns installed on steerable mounts.

Control platform
Also known as a gondola, the engines and radio were operated from here and the airship's course was set, via height and direction rudders, and upper and lower flaps, all of which were located at the stern.

Pneumatic landing wheel

S.L.

Enigma, the Secret Machine

During World War II, the Germans used a revolutionary electromagnetic machine that encoded and decoded messages by means of a rotor cipher system. Thus, they were able to communicate messages without the Allied Forces understanding their content. When the Enigma machine's encryption system was finally discovered, the Nazis lost a strategic advantage that contributed to accelerating the end of the conflict.

THE ALLIES—AGAINST THE ROPES
Encoded communications offered the German Navy a significant advantage in the North Atlantic region. Nazi submarines received a constant flow of information, thanks to which they could forecast Allied operations and attack the supply convoys arriving from the United States. It is calculated that around 100,000 Enigma machines were produced.

An Enigma cipher machine on the armored vehicle (Sd.KFz.251) of German General Heinz Guderian, May 1940.

Reflector
Rotor signals were "reflected" using a fixed cable, thus enabling messages to be decoded. Therefore, when the receiver typed the encoded letter, the original appeared.

Rotors
In its commercial form, the Enigma used three rotors. For military purposes, a further two rollers were introduced, multiplying the number of possible combinations.

Lampboard
Beneath the letters, small bulbs were illuminated using a 4.5-volt battery.

Plugboard
This panel of pins enabled letters to be connected using cables, making the level of encryption more complex. For example, by connecting A to R, the letter R was sent to the rotors when the letter A was pressed.

Millions of codes

In 1918, German engineer Arthur Scherbius patented an ingenious cipher machine, which was introduced and manufactured five years later under the name "Enigma". In 1933, the Nazis nationalized the company and distributed the device throughout their forces. The Enigma consisted of a mechanical keyboard, like the one on a typewriter, connected to a plugboard fitted with the 26 letters of the alphabet. When a key was pressed, an order was sent by means of a circuit through three rotors each equipped with 26 positions. In turn, these spun each time and an electrical pathway lit the resulting output letter.

Additional pins
In addition to the pins on the front panel, some machines were also equipped with these pins beneath the cover to make encryption even more complicated.

Initial sequence
Here, the starting position of the three rotors can be seen; for example, DHR, which had to be set by the receiver in order to decode the message with the receiving Enigma machine.

MARIAN REJEWSKI
This Polish mathematician worked out how to decode the Enigma codes. Thanks to his discoveries, British cryptographers at Bletchley Park, headed by Professor Alan Turing, were able to decode Nazi messages.

Enigma operators used secret books that pre-established which codes, or rotor combinations, should be used on a given date.

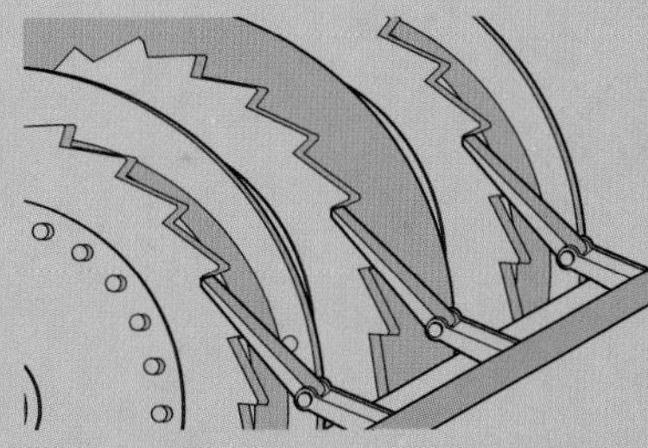

By modifying the position of each rotor, a different code was established for encoding messages.

The Aircraft of World War II

Aviation played a significant role during World War II. In addition to being essential in decisive aerial combats, planes were an essential part of military strategy, supporting the progress of land troops or bombing enemy positions. During the conflict, their instrumentation was progressively perfected, with some becoming authentic legends of the skies.

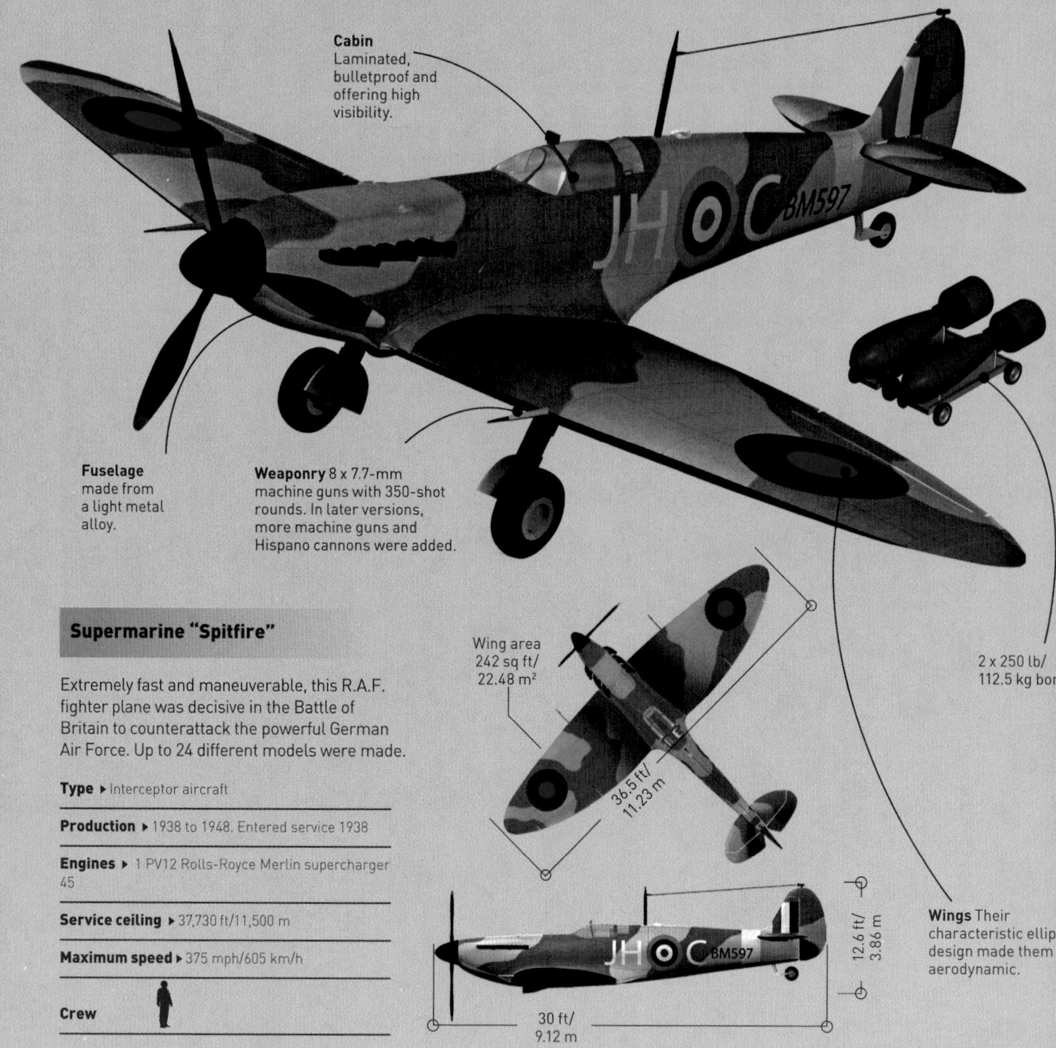
Cabin Laminated, bulletproof and offering high visibility.
JH
C
BM597
Fuselage made from a light metal alloy.
Weaponry 8 x 7.7-mm machine guns with 350-shot rounds. In later versions, more machine guns and Hispano cannons were added.
Wing area 242 sq ft/ 22.48 m²
36.5 ft/ 11.23 m
2 x 250 lb/ 112.5 kg bor
12.6 ft/ 3.86 m
30 ft/ 9.12 m
Wings Their characteristic ellip design made them aerodynamic.

Supermarine "Spitfire"

Extremely fast and maneuverable, this R.A.F. fighter plane was decisive in the Battle of Britain to counterattack the powerful German Air Force. Up to 24 different models were made.

Type ▸ Interceptor aircraft

Production ▸ 1938 to 1948. Entered service 1938

Engines ▸ 1 PV12 Rolls-Royce Merlin supercharger 45

Service ceiling ▸ 37,730 ft/11,500 m

Maximum speed ▸ 375 mph/605 km/h

Crew

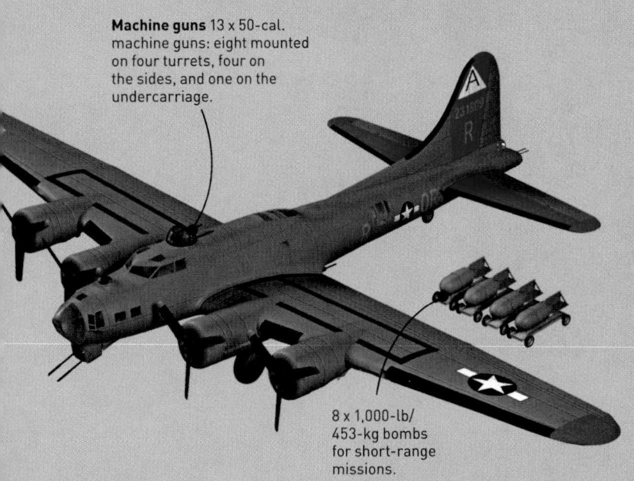
Machine guns 13 x 50-cal. machine guns: eight mounted on four turrets, four on the sides, and one on the undercarriage.
8 x 1,000-lb/ 453-kg bombs for short-range missions.

Boeing B-17 "Flying Fortress"

The main aircraft used by the U.S. Army Air Forces in Europe. Measuring almost 75 ft/ 23 m in length and with a wingspan of 102 ft/31 m, it was one of the most reliable bombers of the war.

Type ▸ Four-engine heavy bomber

Production ▸ 1938 to 1945

Engines ▸ 4 radial Wright R-1820-97 "Cyclones"

Service ceiling ▸ 35,000 ft/10,668 m

Maximum speed ▸ 287 mph/462 km/h

Crew 

tsubishi A6M-2 "Zero"

fighter aircraft, belonging to the anese Imperial Army, surprised the es given its speed, maneuverability, and ponry.

e ▸ Fighter bomber

duction ▸ 1939 to 1945 (entered service in 1941)

ne ▸ 1 x 14-cylinder radial Nakajima Sakae 21

ice ceiling ▸ 32,800 ft/10,000 m

imum speed ▸ 339 mph/545 km/h

w 

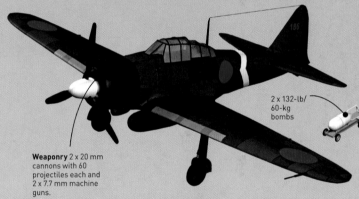

Weaponry 2 x 20 mm cannons with 60 projectiles each and 2 x 7.7 mm machine guns.

2 x 132-lb/ 60-kg bombs

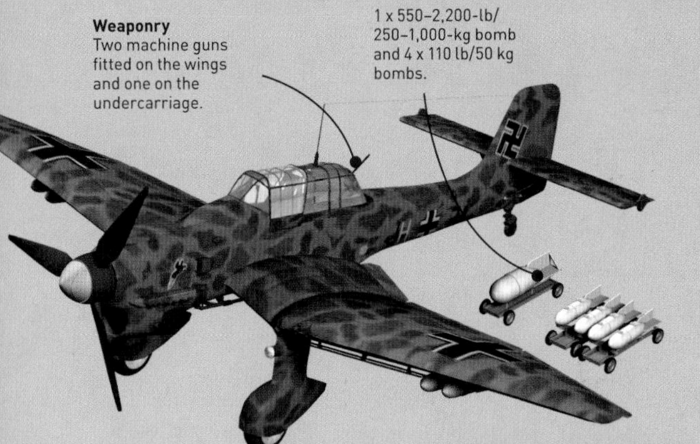
Weaponry Two machine guns fitted on the wings and one on the undercarriage.
1 x 550–2,200-lb/ 250–1,000-kg bomb and 4 x 110 lb/50 kg bombs.

Junkers JU-87 "Stuka"

Used by the *Luftwaffe* as aerial artillery support units, and despite being vulnerable to fighter aircraft attacks, they were potent, highly accurate attack aircraft.

Type ▸ Dive bombers

Production ▸ 1937 to 1944

Engine ▸ 1 x 1,200-hp Junkers Jumo 211 Da

Service ceiling ▸ 26,245 ft/8,000 m

Maximum speed ▸ 211 mph/340 km/h

Crew 

R.A.F. pilots

When Hitler, after his victory in France, decided to invade Great Britain, he knew that any attempt would fail unless he was able to control the country's air space first. Therefore, between July 10 and October 31, 1940, the *Luftwaffe* launched the greatest aerial campaign known until then. However, the British Royal Air Force, despite having fewer servicemen and pilots with barely any combat experience, employed titanic efforts to repress Hitler's plans.

Thin on the ground, but brave nonetheless

When the Battle of Britain began, the Germans had 2,550 planes compared with Britain's 1,963. Most R.A.F. pilots were volunteers with a good knowledge of flying, but only a limited number had been involved in combat before. Winston Churchill said of them: "Never in the field of human conflict was so much owed by so many to so few." Thereafter, they were known as "The Few."

ACES OF THE SKY

The greatest R.A.F. pilots (British, from the Commonwealth, or exiled from nations conquered by the Nazis) in the Battle of Britain were: Eric Lock (English, shot down 21), Archie McKellar (Scottish, 19), James Lacey (English, 18), Josef František (Czech, 17), Witold Urbanowicz (Polish, 15) and Brian Carbury (New Zealander, 15).

Douglas Bader, a British pilot who had lost his legs, shot down 12 planes during the Battle of Britain.

AERIAL COMBAT TACTICS

Bomber attack

1. Formation of a line behind the enemy.
2. Division into two sections, forming a downward step.
3. Positioning on the enemy's tail and attacking in columns of three.

R.A.F. Spitfires
German bombers

Evasion faced with numerical superiority

1. Two BF 109 dive into attack.
2. The Spitfire descends sharply while shooting.
3. The second German plane remains out of the line of fire.
4. The Spitfire fires a burst and escapes.

GENERAL CHARACTERISTICS

The information corresponds to the Royal Air Force during the Battle of Britain.

R.A.F. General Staff Flag.

ARDUA · AD
PER
ASTRA

Insignia of the Royal Air Force.

High command ▸ Chief of the Air Staff Sir Hugh Dowding

Squadrons ▸ 51

Number of planes ▸ 900 (700 were Spitfires or Hurricanes)

Pilots ▸ 1,200

Goggles Mk III
The model introduced in 1935 was fitted with celluloid lenses.

Oxygen mask and microphone
The mask was type B, and the plane features a type E microphone.

Helmet and headphones
The type-B helmet was made of leather and was equipped with radio communication headphones.

Leather jacket
The jacket was essential to survive the cold temperatures experienced at high altitudes.

Mask

RAF jacket
Like the rest of the uniform, it was made of twill and had a row of buttons with two breast pockets and two side pockets.

Microphone

LS-type life jacket
Pilots often painted them yellow to make them easier to spot at sea.

Irvin parachute
The harness had a quick-release mechanism, and the ring to deploy the parachute was located beneath the left forearm.

Container rucksack

Release cord

Boots
The upper part of the 1939 model was made from vulcanized canvas, which made them more comfortable.

Release mechanism
A buckle made it easy to quickly open the parachute.

Everhot bag
These chemical heat pouches were placed inside the pilot's boots.

Trousers
Also made from twill, they were the gray-blue color typically associated with the R.A.F.

The Atomic Bomb

In 1941, the United States, dragged into World War II by the bombing at Pearl Harbor, started to develop the atomic bomb. The operation was called the Manhattan Project and was led by Dr. J. Robert Oppenheimer. On August 6 and 9, 1945, the world experienced the consequences of this weapon for the first time: around 100,000 people died instantly and two cities were completely destroyed.

The objectives

The bombed cities were both over 3 miles/5 km in diameter. In addition to causing significant actual harm, the United States sought to deal Japan a definitive psychological blow.

Hiroshim
Kokura
Nagasaki

August 9
11.01 a.m.
Bomb detonates over Nagasaki.

Yakushi
Magnified area →
RYŪKYŪ ISLANDS
Okinawa

The B-29 *Enola Gay*
The plane was baptized by Paul Tibbets, commander of the B-29, in honor of his mother.

Cannons

To transport the 9,127-lb /4,140-k atomic bomb, all cannons with th exception of the 20-mm cannon f to the tail were removed.

THE NUCLEAR EXPLOSION
The uranium bomb "Little Boy" was launched from a height of 31,000 ft/9,450 m and, after a fall of almost one minute, it exploded 1,970 ft/600 m above ground level, close to the center of Hiroshima.

The air heats to 18 million degrees and a fireball is produced.

Everything is vaporized.	All structures are destroyed.	Large structures collapse.	All flammables ignite.	Second-degree burns.
Mortality rate: 98%	Mortality rate: 90%	Mortality rate: 65%	Mortality rate: 50%	Mortality rate: 15%

Hypocenter

Distance	0 ft/0 km	0.6 miles/0.9 km	1.1 miles/1.8 km	2 miles/3.2 km	2.9 miles/4.6 km	3.4 miles/5.5 km
Time	0 seconds	0.20 seconds	0.30 seconds	0.52 seconds	1.20 seconds	1.30 seconds

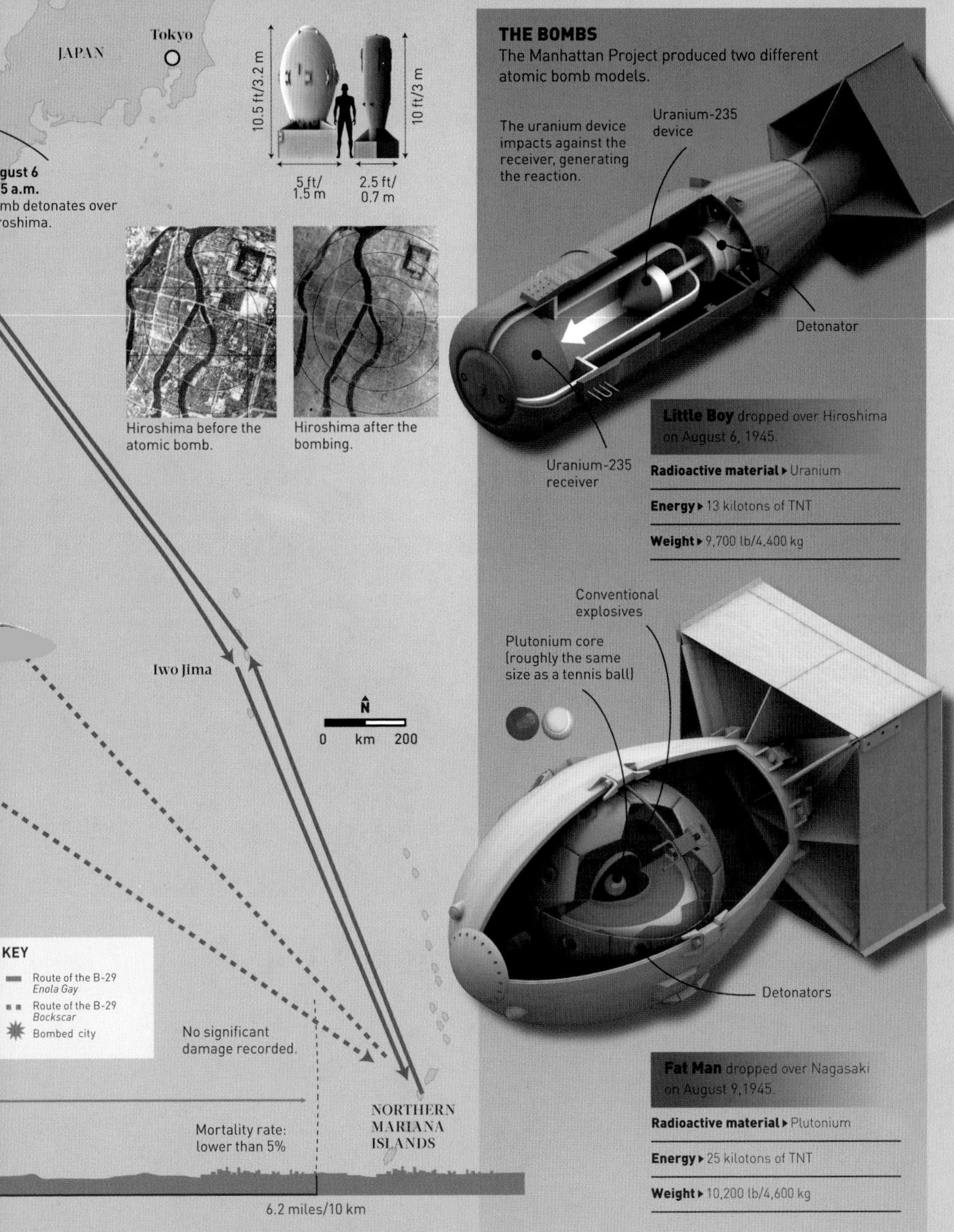

Tokyo
JAPAN
10.5 ft/3.2 m
10 ft/3 m
5 ft/ 1.5 m
2.5 ft/ 0.7 m
ugust 6
15 a.m.
omb detonates over
roshima.
Iwo Jima
N
0 km 200
KEY
Route of the B-29 *Enola Gay*
Route of the B-29 *Bockscar*
Bombed city
No significant damage recorded.
Mortality rate: lower than 5%
6.2 miles/10 km
NORTHERN MARIANA ISLANDS

Hiroshima before the atomic bomb.

Hiroshima after the bombing.

THE BOMBS

The Manhattan Project produced two different atomic bomb models.

The uranium device impacts against the receiver, generating the reaction.
Uranium-235 device
Detonator
Uranium-235 receiver

Little Boy dropped over Hiroshima on August 6, 1945.

Radioactive material ▸ Uranium

Energy ▸ 13 kilotons of TNT

Weight ▸ 9,700 lb/4,400 kg

Conventional explosives
Plutonium core (roughly the same size as a tennis ball)
Detonators

Fat Man dropped over Nagasaki on August 9,1945.

Radioactive material ▸ Plutonium

Energy ▸ 25 kilotons of TNT

Weight ▸ 10,200 lb/4,600 kg

Attack Helicopters

The first helicopters served as support to land units, offering greater mobility. It was during the 1970s, and the Vietnam War, that development began on designing attack models that were faster and equipped with greater firepower. Today's models are sophisticated devices fitted with night-vision systems and antiradar devices, in addition to being capable of launching powerful guided missiles.

KA-52 Alligator

Designed for the Russian Armed Forces by Kamov, it is equipped with antitank and antiaircraft features, to execute reconnaissance missions and support ground troops.

Type ▸ All-purpose attack helicopter

Entered service ▸ 2010

Engines ▸ 2 x VK-2500 d

Primary users ▸ Russia

Crew

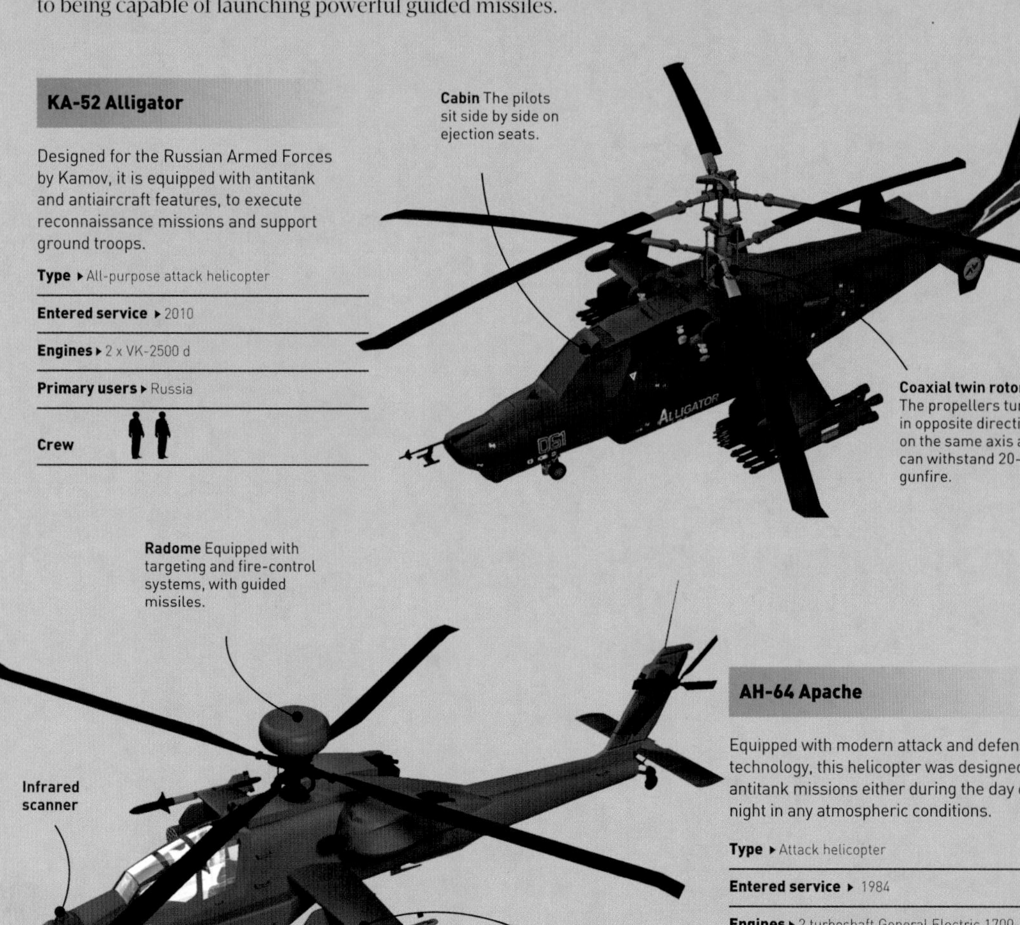
Cabin The pilots sit side by side on ejection seats.
Coaxial twin rotors The propellers turn in opposite directio on the same axis ar can withstand 20-n gunfire.
ALLIGATOR
Radome Equipped with targeting and fire-control systems, with guided missiles.
Infrared scanner
Machine guns Fire 625 projectiles per minute.
Wings Capable of holding up to 16 antitank missiles, rockets, and antiaircraft missiles, in addition to external fuel tanks.

AH-64 Apache

Equipped with modern attack and defense technology, this helicopter was designed antitank missions either during the day or night in any atmospheric conditions.

Type ▸ Attack helicopter

Entered service ▸ 1984

Engines ▸ 2 turboshaft General Electric 1700-G

Primary users ▸ U.S.A., Great Britain, Israel, J among others

Crew

UH-1 Huey

Widely used in Vietnam to transport troops and for evacuation, attack, and armed escort purposes. Today, it is the most widely used in the world and has been implemented in 40 countries.

Type ▸ Multipurpose utility helicopter

Entered service ▸ 1959

Engine ▸ 1 turboshaft Lycoming T53-L-13

Primary users ▸ U.S.A., Japan, Australia, the Philippines, among others.

Crew 

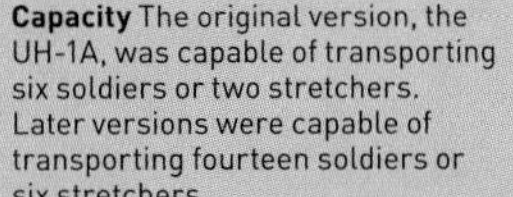

Capacity The original version, the UH-1A, was capable of transporting six soldiers or two stretchers. Later versions were capable of transporting fourteen soldiers or six stretchers.

Weaponry Armed versions are equipped with three machine guns and two pods for seven rockets each.

UH-60 Black Hawk

Tactically speaking, this helicopter is extremely important given its capacity to deploy troops on difficult terrain in aerial assault operations.

Type ▸ Tactical transport utility helicopter

Entered service ▸ 1979

Engines ▸ 2 turboshaft General Electric T700-GE

Primary users ▸ U.S.A., Korea, Turkey, Colombia, among others.

Crew 

Electronics Fitted with avionics, GPS.

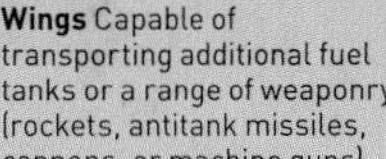

Wings Capable of transporting additional fuel tanks or a range of weaponry (rockets, antitank missiles, cannons, or machine guns).

Technology Detection-avoidance, nocturnal-vision, and obstacle-detection systems.

Capacity 38 troops

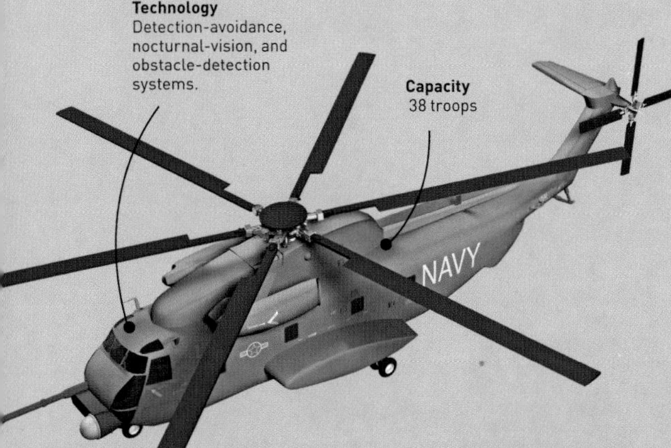
NAVY

MH-53 J Pave Low III

Technologically advanced, its main mission was to deploy, supply, and collect special forces from enemy territory. Used in Iraq and the Middle East.

Type ▸ Combat search and rescue helicopter

Entered service ▸ 1981, retired in 2008

Engines ▸ 2 turboshaft General Electric T64-GE-415

Primary users ▸ U.S.A.

Crew 

British Paratroopers

The British Parachute Regiment was created on June 22, 1940 at the behest of Winston Churchill, who had been impressed by the skill of German parachutists during operations in Scandinavia and the Netherlands. In the short space of time available to create a new combat force, it was largely based on the German model. On February 10, 1941, during "Operation Colossus," the Red Devils had their baptism of fire.

Intensive training

The first British paratroopers comprised of volunteers from different regiments of the air force and army who were trained for airborne operations. The success of "Operation Colossus" underscored the usefulness of the new force, which would be expanded. In addition to harsh physical training, a platoon had to be able to march 50 miles/80 km in 24 hours; their induction included an intensive parachute course that lasted 12 days. They also learned attack and defense techniques for fortifications, bridges, and railroads.

THE PARACHUTE

The Type X model, used by the British Army during World War II, was developed in 1940 by Raymond Quilter of GQ, along with Leslie Irvin, another manufacturer in the same sector. It was replaced in the 1960s by Type XP, which differed mainly in being bigger. In turn, this was replaced by GQ LLP Mk1 in 1993.

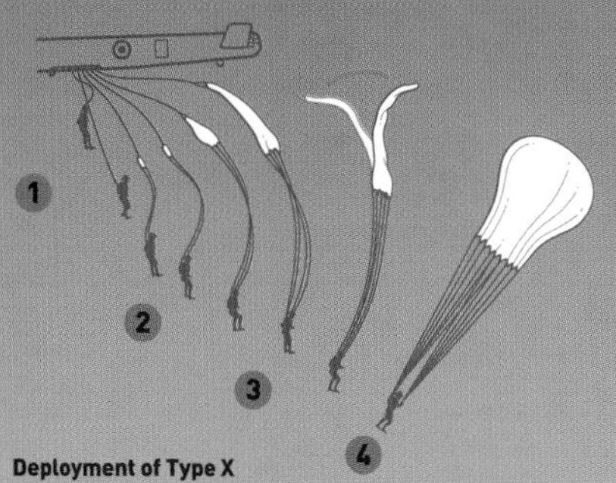
1
2
3
4

Deployment of Type X

1. When jumping, the push automatically releases the parachute.
2. The cords fully extend.
3. The chute then opens.
4. A hole at the top serves to steer the fall.

GENERAL CHARACTERISTICS

British paratroopers received the nickname "The Red Devils" from their German counterparts following their fierce combat during the Tunisia Campaign (1942).

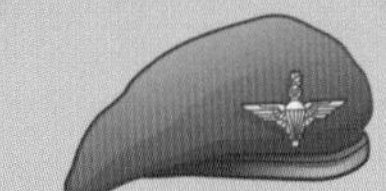

Insignia and Beret
The insignia is the image of the hero Bellerophon on the winged Pegasus.

High command ▸ Prince of Wales

Current structure ▸ Four battallions

Major operations ▸ Slapstick (1943), Tonga (1944), Market Garden (1944), Varsity (1945).

Commanding officers ▸ Sir Roland Gibbs, Anthony Farrar-Hockley

Motto ▸ *Ready for anything*

WEAPONRY

They used the Lee Enfield No. 4 rifle, the Sten Mk II submachine gun, light Bren machine guns, and Browning pistols.

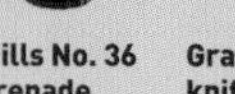

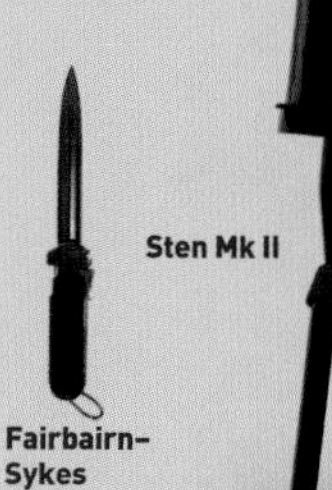

Mills No. 36 grenade

Gravity knife

Fairbairn–Sykes fighting knife

Sten Mk II

FULL EQUIPMENT

Similar in origin to the uniform of German paratroopers, it gradually evolved until it retained its own features. The 1943 version continued in service for over a decade after the end of World War II.

Helmet
The most commonly used models were Mk I and Mk II, both made from steel.

Jacket
The "Smoke" or Denison jacket was introduced in 1942; an improved version would be released in 1944.

Straps
A harness firmly held the soldier to his parachute.

Oversmock
Worn over the uniform to prevent equipment getting tangled in the parachute.

Type X Parachute
A silk chute measuring 23.5 ft/7.14 m in diameter and with 28 cords measuring 25 ft/7.6 m in length.

Trousers
Equipped with a secret pocket designed to hide the Fairbairn-Sykes fighting knife.

Jump bag
Allowed the soldier to carry all his weapons and equipment with him.

Hiking boots
The standard British infantry footwear was used.

HIMARS Rocket Launchers

The arms industry evolves to respond to current warfare, as has been the case in regions of conflict such as Iraq or Afghanistan. An example of this is the U.S. Army HIMARS rocket launcher: a light, easily transportable vehicle capable of hitting its target from a great distance with maximum precision and efficiency. Since their deployment in 2005, these sophisticated trucks equipped with rocket launchers have fired 2,500 projectiles.

Deadly weapon

HIMARS, or the High Mobility Artillery Rocket System, was developed in the United States by Lockheed Martin (missile launcher) and BAE Systems (vehicle). It is a device designed to attack artillery positions, antiaircraft defenses, military or logistics vehicles, or concentrations of troops from a given distance (up to 186 miles/300 km), with the advantage of being able to abandon its firing position quickly, before being located and counterattacked.

Armored cabin
Only three people—the driver, the gunner, and the section chief—travel in this cabin, protected against small weapons and gases.
Launcher
Employs a hydraulic lift system. It takes around 15 minutes to prepare the shot, but less than 20 seconds to take aim.
Light
The truck weighs just 24,000 lb/12 tons, meaning it can be transported on a Hercules C-130, one of the most common U.S. Air Force aircraft.

PAD

HIMARS can launch six guided missiles (GMLRS) to a distance of up to 43 miles/70 km, or a tactical ATACMS missile, with a range of up to 186 miles/300 km. Its level of accuracy is excellent, thanks to the GPS system incorporated on the projectiles.

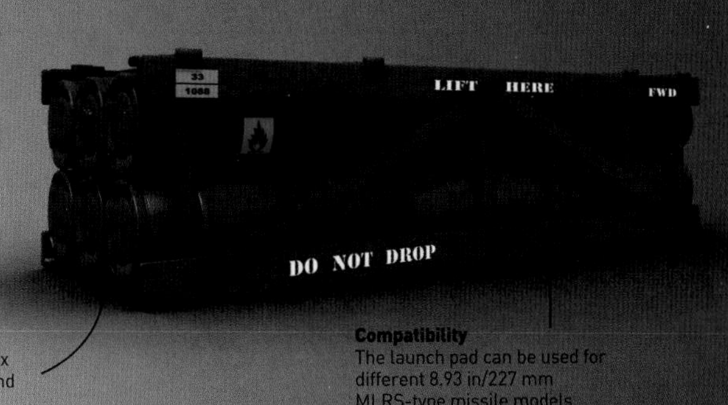
33
1088
LIFT HERE
FWD
DO NOT DROP

Six in less than a minute
The launch sequence for a six GMLRS-missile load is around 45 seconds.

Compatibility
The launch pad can be used for different 8.93 in/227 mm MLRS-type missile models.

HIMARS technical data

Rocket launcher manufacturer ▸ Lockheed Martin

Truck manufacturer ▸ BAE Systems

Country ▸ U.S.A.

Range ▸ GMLRS: 43 miles/70 km
ATACMS: 186 m/300 km

Cost ▸ $3 million

Maximum speed ▸ 58 mph/94 km/h

Operational range ▸ 298 miles/480 km

6x6 drive
Unlike tracked vehicles, on which rocket launchers were previously installed, these trucks are extremely fast and can access complex terrain.

M31 MISSILES

The first M26 projectiles used by HIMARS, with a range of just 20 miles/32 km, would eventually give way to the new GMLRS M31 guided missiles. One of the main advantages of this extremely accurate weapon, with just a 33-ft/10-m margin of error, is that it reduces collateral damage.

GPS
Guide and control device, with GPS antenna.

Explosive core
Each M31 contains around 200 lb/90 kg of controlled fragmentation explosives.

Multifuse
Equipped with three different adjustments, depending on the target: bunkers, open-air target, etc.

GMLRS motor

Child Soldiers

Perhaps the most abhorrent feature of armed conflicts, the use of children to fight as soldiers is a practice that dates back centuries, and to this day it is still a characteristic of war worldwide. They are recruited forcibly, separated from their families and used as cannon fodder or subjected to a whole host of abuses. The childhood of a young soldier is the practice's first victim. Various organizations worldwide fight to eradicate this practice and rehabilitate its victims.

Children of war

The U.N. estimates that there are more than 250,000 child soldiers, whereas Amnesty International sets the figure at over 300,000. Various NGOs, such as Amnesty International, Entreculturas, Fundación El Compromiso, and Save the Children, have claimed that children under the age of 18 are recruited in more than 17 countries: Afghanistan, Chad, Colombia, the Philippines, India, Iraq, Libya, Mali, Myanmar, Pakistan, Central African Republic, the Democratic Republic of Congo, Somalia, Sudan, South Sudan, Thailand, and Yemen. They are considered cheap, obedient, and manipulable labor, and are less conscious of danger than adults.

HISTORY

Records of children participating in military campaigns have existed since ancient times, although mainly as auxiliary support. During the two World Wars, thousands of adolescents fought.

Child soldier of the Red Army in 1945.

Frau im
Luftschutz!

Propaganda of the Hitler Youth movement.

GENERAL CHARACTERISTICS

In 2002, the Optional Protocol to the Convention on the Rights of the Child raised the recruitment age from 15 to 18 years, with many countries ignoring this international rule.

250,000–300,000

is the estimated number of child soldiers currently participating in different conflicts worldwide.

STOP USING CHILD SOLDIERS
www.child-soldiers.org

Insignia
Child Soldiers is one of the many organizations that seeks to eradicate the use of children as soldiers.

HORRIFYING STATISTICS

Some NGOs claim that the number of countries that recruit minors for the purpose of combat is significantly higher than the 17 countries named, raising the number to 86 nations.

Ages ▸ Between 8 and 18 years

Released and reintegrated ▸ More than 100,000 since 1998

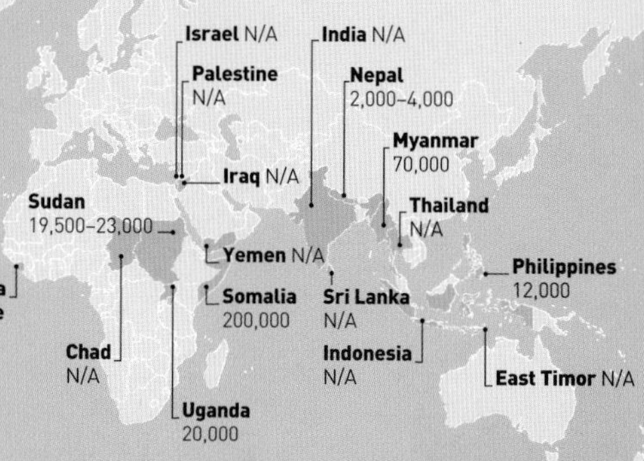
Colombia 14,000
Sierra Leone N/A
Sudan 19,500–23,000
Chad N/A
Uganda 20,000
Israel N/A
Palestine N/A
Iraq N/A
Yemen N/A
Somalia 200,000
India N/A
Nepal 2,000–4,000
Myanmar 70,000
Thailand N/A
Sri Lanka N/A
Indonesia N/A
Philippines 12,000
East Timor N/A

YOUNG MILITIA

Children sent into combat use an extremely heterogeneous set of equipment, depending on the armed forces to which they belong—in most cases, irregular militia groups.

Berets
It is only very occasionally that boys are equipped with protective helmets.
The African drama
Currently, Africa is the continent where the highest percentage of child soldiers can be found. This image shows an African child soldier.
Uniform
They are provided with only the most basic uniform: a shirt and trousers at best.
Cartridges
Vietnamese-style holders, designed to hold curved AK-47 clips.
AK-47 rifle
The weapon most commonly used by unconventional troops worldwide.
Footwear
Generally, civilian and everyday footwear is used: flip-flops, sandals, or trainers.
Recruited in Southeast Asia
Thousands of children participate in the frequent conflicts that ignite in the region. In the image, a child soldier from Southeast Asia can be seen.
Missions
They are forced to serve as decoys, as bodyguards to their superiors, or to detect enemy positions.
Volunteers
Some minors join armies after their families are broken up as a result of the conflict.
Western weaponry
They also use Western weaponry, such as the M-16 rifle.

GIRL SOLDIERS

Forty percent of child soldiers are girls; in addition to fighting in battles, they are used to cross minefields and as sex slaves.

Vietnam
Young girl soldiers.

"Star Wars"

On March 23, 1983, Ronald Reagan announced a new national defense program that would render atomic weapons "impotent and obsolete." He was referring to the Strategic Defense Initiative (SDI), a project that would employ cutting-edge weapon, computing and communications technologies to create a defense system capable of stopping a massive Soviet nuclear missile attack. The program, popularly known as "Star Wars," ended up in decline.

A very expensive project

Under the Reagan Administration, the SDI program received more than $23 billion worth of funding. For six years, the sum dedicated to the Defense Initiative grew exponentially, growing by increments of more than 100 percent year on year. In 1989, it accounted for 17 percent of the Defense Department budget earmarked for research. With the end of the Cold War, the project gradually fell into decline. In 1993, President Bill Clinton changed its name to the Ballistic Missile Defense Organization, significantly reducing its budget.

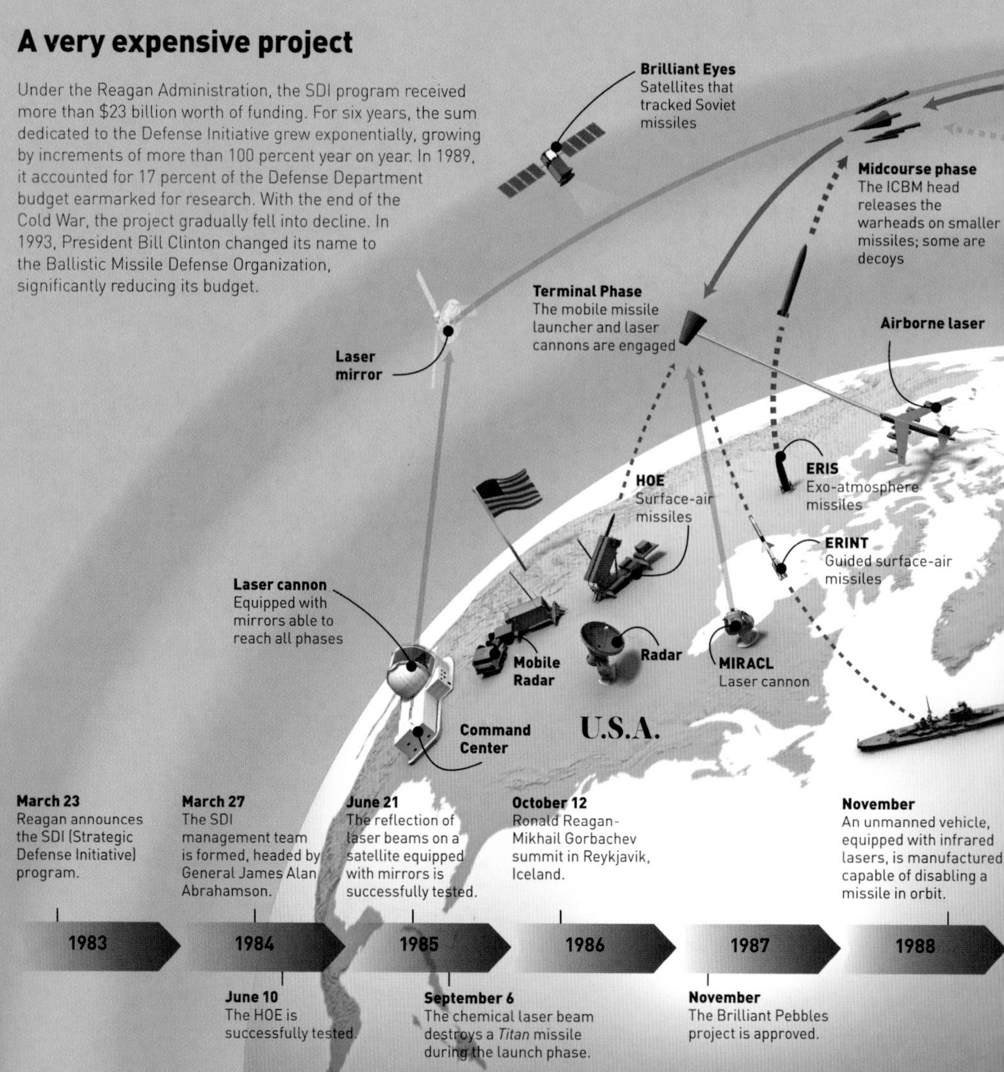
Brilliant Eyes
Satellites that tracked Soviet missiles
Midcourse phase
The ICBM head releases the warheads on smaller missiles; some are decoys
Terminal Phase
The mobile missile launcher and laser cannons are engaged
Airborne laser
Laser mirror
HOE
Surface-air missiles
ERIS
Exo-atmosphere missiles
ERINT
Guided surface-air missiles
Laser cannon
Equipped with mirrors able to reach all phases
Mobile Radar
Radar
MIRACL
Laser cannon
Command Center
U.S.A.

March 23
Reagan announces the SDI (Strategic Defense Initiative) program.

March 27
The SDI management team is formed, headed by General James Alan Abrahamson.

June 21
The reflection of laser beams on a satellite equipped with mirrors is successfully tested.

October 12
Ronald Reagan-Mikhail Gorbachev summit in Reykjavik, Iceland.

November
An unmanned vehicle, equipped with infrared lasers, is manufactured capable of disabling a missile in orbit.

1983 | 1984 | 1985 | 1986 | 1987 | 1988

June 10
The HOE is successfully tested.

September 6
The chemical laser beam destroys a *Titan* missile during the launch phase.

November
The Brilliant Pebbles project is approved.

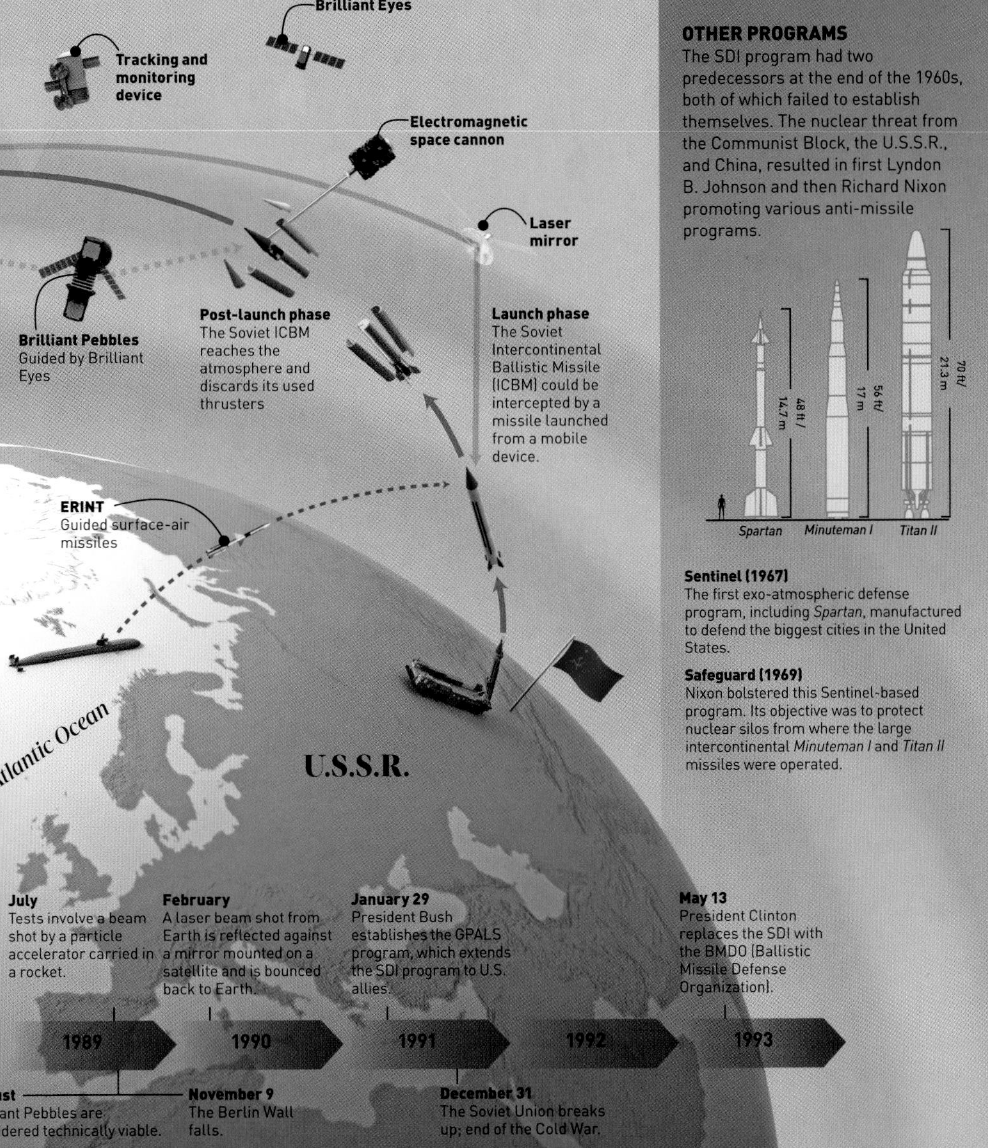
KEY
Soviet nuclear missile
U.S. missiles
Beam shot from Earth
Projectiles launched from Brilliant Pebbles
Brilliant Eyes
Tracking and monitoring device
Electromagnetic space cannon
Laser mirror
Post-launch phase
The Soviet ICBM reaches the atmosphere and discards its used thrusters
Launch phase
The Soviet Intercontinental Ballistic Missile (ICBM) could be intercepted by a missile launched from a mobile device.
Brilliant Pebbles
Guided by Brilliant Eyes
ERINT
Guided surface-air missiles
Atlantic Ocean
U.S.S.R.
48 ft / 14.7 m
56 ft/ 17 m
70 ft/ 21.3 m
Spartan
Minuteman I
Titan II
July
Tests involve a beam shot by a particle accelerator carried in a rocket.
February
A laser beam shot from Earth is reflected against a mirror mounted on a satellite and is bounced back to Earth.
January 29
President Bush establishes the GPALS program, which extends the SDI program to U.S. allies.
May 13
President Clinton replaces the SDI with the BMDO (Ballistic Missile Defense Organization).
1989
1990
1991
1992
1993
gust
liant Pebbles are
sidered technically viable.
November 9
The Berlin Wall falls.
December 31
The Soviet Union breaks up; end of the Cold War.

OTHER PROGRAMS

The SDI program had two predecessors at the end of the 1960s, both of which failed to establish themselves. The nuclear threat from the Communist Block, the U.S.S.R., and China, resulted in first Lyndon B. Johnson and then Richard Nixon promoting various anti-missile programs.

Sentinel (1967)
The first exo-atmospheric defense program, including *Spartan*, manufactured to defend the biggest cities in the United States.

Safeguard (1969)
Nixon bolstered this Sentinel-based program. Its objective was to protect nuclear silos from where the large intercontinental *Minuteman I* and *Titan II* missiles were operated.

The Army of the Future

Weapons, helmets, camouflage, bulletproof vests ... The technological development of all these elements, and many others, point toward a soldier operating as an independent combat unit, intercommunicating with his or her peers, but self-sufficient and equipped for combat in all situations, terrain, and conditions. Using nanotechnology, the arms industry is currently working on alternatives that help create intelligent uniforms to protect soldiers.

Land Warrior

As part of the transformation experienced by the U.S. Armed Forces since 9/11, the Land Warrior program was implemented in Iraq in 2007. Its objectives were to increase the deadliness of individual soldiers, increase their survival capacity, and equip them with comprehensive command, communication, and control devices. However, the program was cancelled due to the excessive weight of the equipment (20 lb/9 kg) and the logistical problems involved in recharging the batteries that supplied the cutting-edge technology systems.

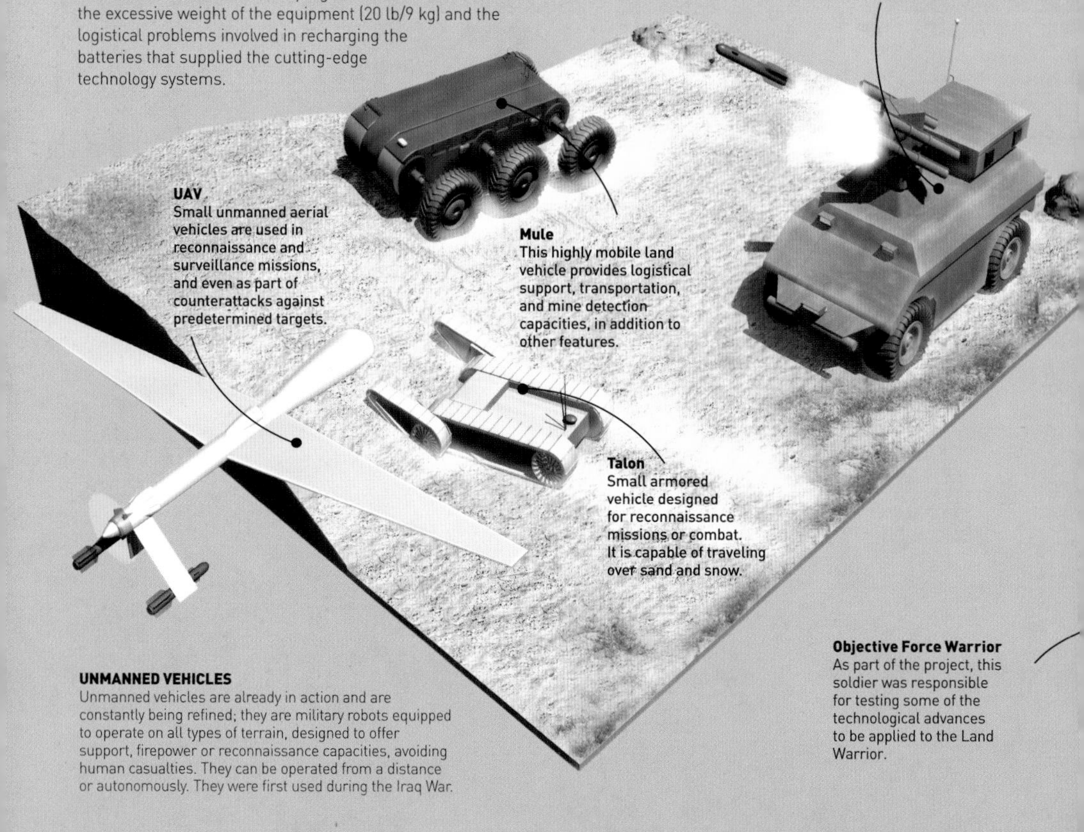

Cougar
Unmanned land-attack vehicle with significant firepower, designed to be resistant to mines and homemade bombs.

UAV
Small unmanned aerial vehicles are used in reconnaissance and surveillance missions, and even as part of counterattacks against predetermined targets.

Mule
This highly mobile land vehicle provides logistical support, transportation, and mine detection capacities, in addition to other features.

Talon
Small armored vehicle designed for reconnaissance missions or combat. It is capable of traveling over sand and snow.

UNMANNED VEHICLES
Unmanned vehicles are already in action and are constantly being refined; they are military robots equipped to operate on all types of terrain, designed to offer support, firepower or reconnaissance capacities, avoiding human casualties. They can be operated from a distance or autonomously. They were first used during the Iraq War.

Objective Force Warrior
As part of the project, this soldier was responsible for testing some of the technological advances to be applied to the Land Warrior.

Robo Troop

For 2030, the U.S. Army's objective is to apply developing technologies to a combatant provisionally named Robo Troop. Some of these technologies were tested in Iraq with the Land Warrior. However others, such as the exoskeleton, are still in the initial development stages.

Helmet
Equipped with an internal gas mask, stereoscopic night vision, biometric target identifier, satellite communication, and automatic voice translator.

Visor
Rather than using direct sight, the soldier would be able to observe his/her surroundings by means of an HUD system.

DRAGON RUNNER
A military robot used for urban combat in places difficult for a soldier to access. Weighing just 9 lb/4 kg, it can be transported in a backpack. In 2010, the British Army purchased 100 units to be used in Afghanistan.

Weaponry
Kevlar shields would be replaced by intelligent fabric equipped with nanotechnology, which would become harder upon detecting an approaching bullet. A screen with useful combat information and a GPS system would be incorporated onto the combatant's wrist.

Weapon
It can reach 3,280 ft/1,000 m and can fire two types of ammunition: conventional 4.5 mm bullets, or 15 mm guided explosive bullets.

Exoeskeleton
Designed to quadruple the natural strength of the soldiers' legs and back, it can run faster, jump higher, and lift more weight.

Camouflage
The outer fabric of the suit automatically changes color, adapting to the environment, just like a chameleon. Thanks to nanotechnology, fabrics that offer invisibility or transparency are currently being developed.

THE IMPERIAL JAPANESE ARMY

FOLLOWING THE WESTERN MODEL

In Japan, after 300 years of Tokugawa shogunate governance and 200 years of peace, the Boshin War (1868–1869) had made way for the Meiji period and the Westernization of the country; as a result, a completely new army was born, following the European model. The new armed forces, baptized as the Imperial Army, replaced the Samurai armies. Troops no longer belonged to noblemen, and began to respond directly to the emperor, who bestowed wide-reaching powers on his highest officers for the purposes of military planning and strategy.

By the mid-nineteenth century, the United States had pressured Japan into opening itself to trade. It was not to be, however. Japanese society was the only non-Western society to adopt Western military weapons and uses, to later use them against their inventors. By 1873, the government had enforced obligatory military service on all men aged over 21, who had to serve for three years, and entrust their training to French officers by means of the so-called military missions to Japan (1872–1880 and 1884–1889). In principle, the Japanese Army was to follow the Napoleonic model. However, following the Prussian victory in the 1870 war against France, the emperor, fascinated by the Prussian model, contracted German officers (Major Jacob Meckel and Captain von Blankenbourg, among others) to train military officers between 1886 and 1890.

The Imperial Army therefore adopted the Prussian military model and ensured its separation from civilian powers and its undivided loyalty to the emperor, who was named the sole commander-in-chief of the army and the navy. Each of the six regional heads of divisions were replaced, and at the top of the chain of command, an extremely powerful headquarters was set up, capable of forcing the removal of a cabinet and preventing the creation of a new one. This headquarters was responsible for the General Staff Office, Army Ministry and two General Inspection Offices: one for military training and another for aviation.

Furthermore, several Italian and Dutch officers worked on training the Japanese Army during these years to employ Western weapons and military tactics. Its navy was tutored and trained by the British Navy, and the development of its armed forces was the responsibility of French Commander Jacques-Paul Faure between 1918 and 1919.

Japan tested its new army during the 1894–5 Sino-Japanese War and the 1904–5 Russo-Japanese War, in which they attacked and besieged Port Arthur and used flares, grenades, and poisonous gases for the first time. It also featured prominently in the Manchurian invasion and World War II. It was dissolved by the North American authorities in 1945, following the Japanese surrender.

Soldiers of the Japanese Imperial Army

The sweeping progress of the Japanese Imperial Army during the war against China during the 1930s and the offensive against the Allied Forces in Asia and the Pacific from 1941 to 1942, gave an impression of invincibility. However, the Allied counterattack that began in Guadalcanal and New Guinea midway through 1942 exposed internal fractures in the army that were the result of modern, well-trained armed forces restrained by almost primitive traditions.

Value and fanaticism

The strictly hierarchical structure of Japanese society was reflected in its army. Mistreatment of rank-and-file soldiers was commonplace and all soldiers not of Japanese origin (Koreans and Taiwanese, for example) suffered significant racial abuse. However, Japanese soldiers had a series of characteristics that made them a difficult adversary for the Allied troops: their ability to adapt to the most adverse conditions, blind obedience to superiors, culture of suicide, and a code of honor that never allowed them to surrender.

THE ZANRY

Zanry is the Japanese term for "straggler" and refers to a number of Japanese Army combatants who, loyal to the concept of never surrendering, hid in the most remote parts of the islands on which they were fighting, and remained there for years without ever realizing the war had ended. One of them was Lieutenant Hiroo Onoda (below).

Onoda spent 30 years hiding on the Philippine island of Lubang. He refused to surrender until he received orders from Major Taniguchi, his superior during World War II. This happened in 1974.

GENERAL CHARACTERISTICS

The Japanese Imperial Army was the Empire's official ground force from 1867 to 1945.

War flag
The Rising Sun of the Empire.

Cap and star
Worn beneath the helmet.

High command ▸ Imperial Headquarters

Number of divisions ▸ 51 (in 1941)

Total personnel ▸ 6,100,000 (between 1941 and 1945)

War cry ▸ *Tenno Heika Banzai* (Long Live the Emperor)

OTHER WEAPONS

In addition to the standard rifle, each soldier was equipped with grenades. Each platoon had a heavy support machine gun, a grenade launcher, and a subrifle.

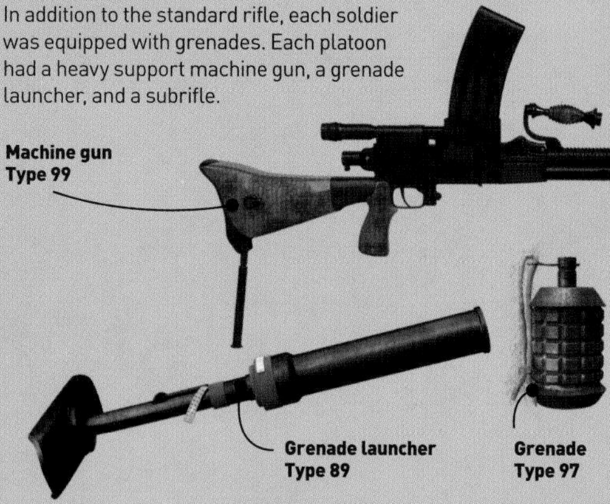
Machine gun
Type 99
Grenade launcher
Type 89
Grenade
Type 97

Tetsukabuto
The Type 92 helmet was introduced in 1932. It was made from poor quality steel; as a result, it was not always bulletproof and splinterproof.
Rifle
The Type 99 Arisaka, the standard Japanese Imperial Army supply. It had a bolt-action mechanism and was 0.303 in/7.7 mm caliber.
Kessen fuku
The elbows and collar on this battle jacket were reinforced.
Backpack
In the field, soldiers wore a backpack containing their equipment.
Straps
Comprising a belt and two criss-cross straps—one for the canteen and another for the pouch.
Gaiters
Bandages were used as gaiters. They were fastened using elastic reinforcement.
Canteen
Similar to the Afrika Korps supply, although it had no cover and was fastened to the straps.
Ammunition cartridge holders
Four in total, two of which were reserves located to the rear of the belt.
Trousers
They were usually wrapped with bandages, which served as protection against insects in tropical Asian jungles.

IWO JIMA DEFENSES

In 1945, to defend this strategic island, the Japanese excavated a series of underground tunnels with cunning traps to surprise U.S. marines.

Snipers
They sheltered in hideouts excavated into the volcanic rock.

Galleries
They crossed the entire island and had secret exits.

Attack at Pearl Harbor

The unexpected Japanese attack on the U.S. naval base in the Pacific Ocean, with no formal declaration of war having been made, sought to weaken the military strength of its enemy in order to control Southeast Asia unopposed. However, its only goal was to unleash the rage of the U.S. industrial machine, which immediately entered World War II, tipping the balance of the conflict in favor of the Allied powers.

Surprise offensive

On the morning of December 7, 1941, having made no previous declaration of war, Japan attacked the U.S. naval base of Pearl Harbor, on the islands of Hawaii. The Japanese Air Force sank the majority of the U.S. Pacific fleet, significantly damaging its aerial power and resulting in thousands of casualties. However, it did not discover its aircraft carriers among the vessels docked in the Hawaiian port, the main target of the Japanese attack.

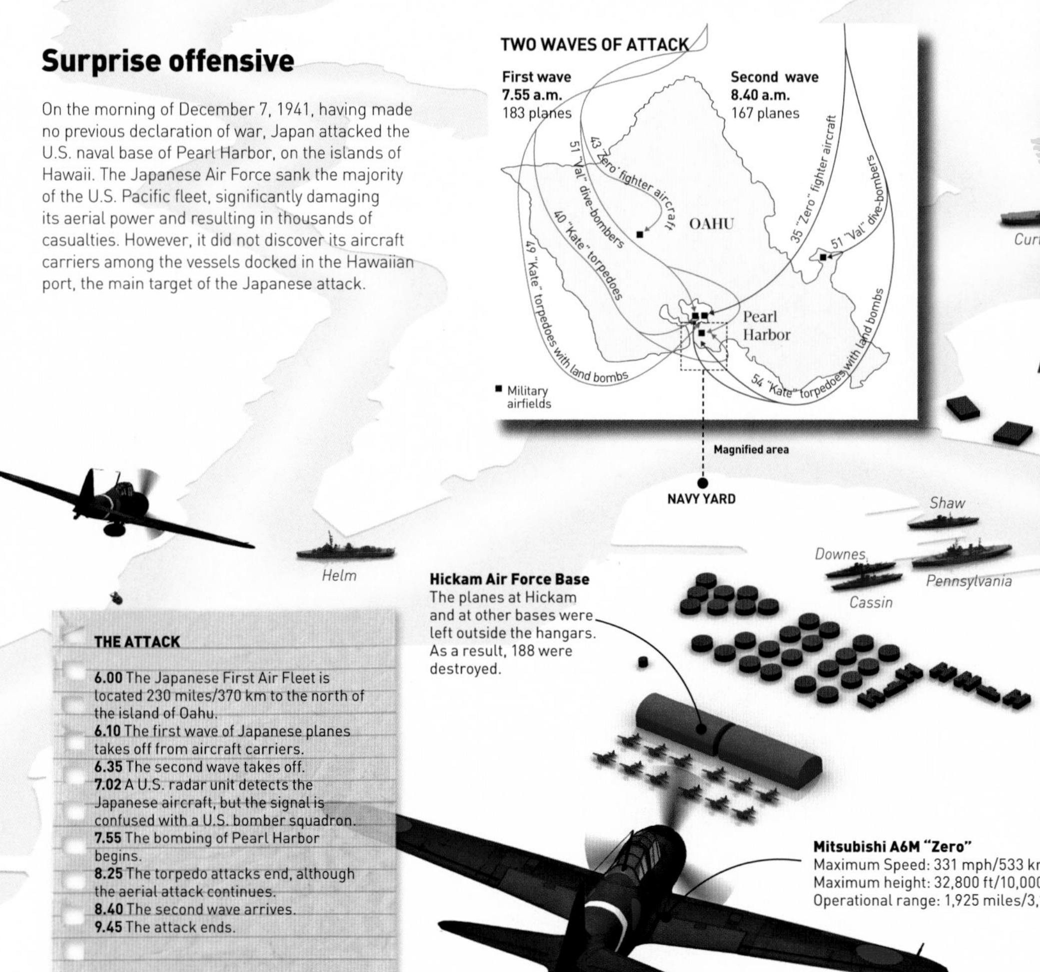

TWO WAVES OF ATTACK
First wave
7.55 a.m.
183 planes
Second wave
8.40 a.m.
167 planes
43 "Zero" fighter aircraft
51 "Val" dive-bombers
40 "Kate" torpedoes
49 "Kate" torpedoes with land bombs
OAHU
35 "Zero" fighter aircraft
51 "Val" dive-bombers
Pearl Harbor
54 "Kate" torpedoes with land bombs
Military airfields
Magnified area
NAVY YARD
Shaw
Curtis
Helm
Downes
Pennsylvania
Cassin

Hickam Air Force Base
The planes at Hickam and at other bases were left outside the hangars. As a result, 188 were destroyed.

THE ATTACK

6.00 The Japanese First Air Fleet is located 230 miles/370 km to the north of the island of Oahu.
6.10 The first wave of Japanese planes takes off from aircraft carriers.
6.35 The second wave takes off.
7.02 A U.S. radar unit detects the Japanese aircraft, but the signal is confused with a U.S. bomber squadron.
7.55 The bombing of Pearl Harbor begins.
8.25 The torpedo attacks end, although the aerial attack continues.
8.40 The second wave arrives.
9.45 The attack ends.

Mitsubishi A6M "Zero"
Maximum Speed: 331 mph/533 km
Maximum height: 32,800 ft/10,000
Operational range: 1,925 miles/3,1

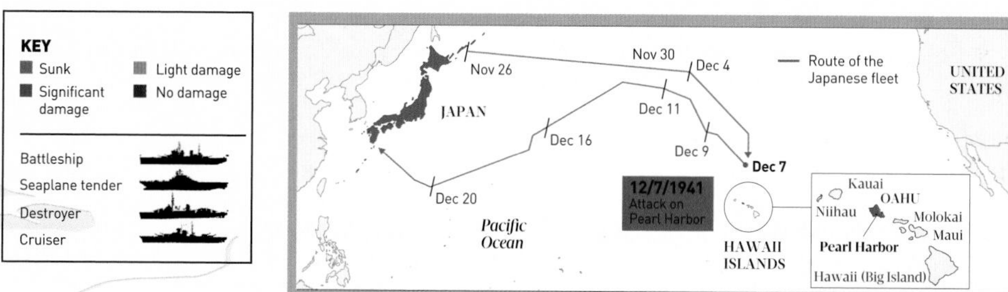
KEY
Sunk
Light damage
Significant damage
No damage
Battleship
Seaplane tender
Destroyer
Cruiser
Nov 26
Nov 30
Dec 4
Route of the Japanese fleet
UNITED STATES
JAPAN
Dec 11
Dec 16
Dec 9
Dec 7
Dec 20
12/7/1941
Attack on Pearl Harbor
Pacific Ocean
HAWAII ISLANDS
Kauai
OAHU
Niihau
Molokai
Maui
Pearl Harbor
Hawaii (Big Island)

HUMAN CASUALTIES

U.S.A. **2,402**

Military: 2,345
Civilians: 57

Japan **65**

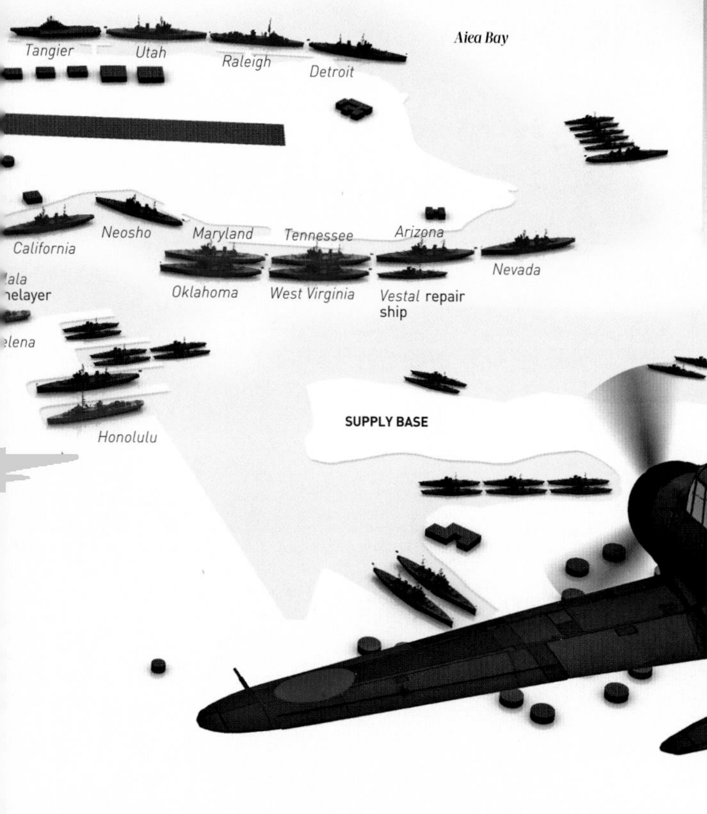

OTHER AIRCRAFT

Nakajima B5N2 "Kate"
Maximum speed: 217 mph/350 km/h
Maximum height: 25,065 ft/7,640 m
Operational range: 685 miles/1,100 km

Aichi D3A "Val"
Maximum speed: 242 mph/389 km/h
Maximum height: 30,500 ft/9,300 m
Operational range: 915 miles/1,473 km
Load: one 550-lb/250-kg bomb

PEARL CITY

usa

Aiea Bay

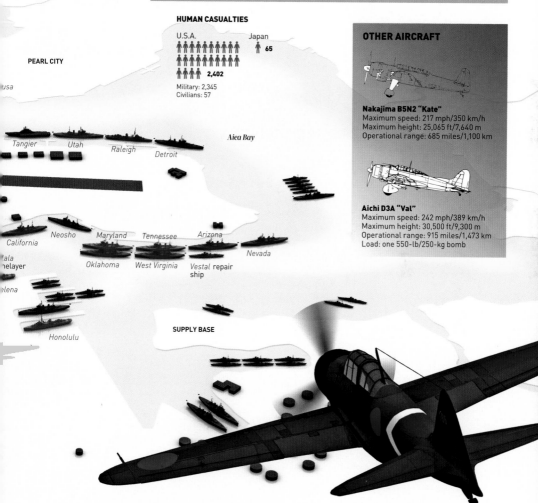

Tangier *Utah* *Raleigh* *Detroit*

California *Neosho* *Maryland* *Tennessee* *Arizona* *Nevada*

Oklahoma *West Virginia* *Vestal* repair ship

ala
nelayer

elena

SUPPLY BASE

Honolulu

Battleship Mikasa

At the end of the nineteenth century, Japan arose from its slumber and embarked upon a rapid industrialization and economic development process that would soon see the country convert into a world power. Such power was demonstrated during the 1904–5 Russo–Japanese War, sparked by the Russian expansion into East Asia and its desire to conquer Korea. The stunning Japanese victory underscored the superiority of its navy, the backbone of which were battleships and heavy armored warships.

The Japanese fleet

Japan entrusted the construction of its fleet to Great Britain, France, and Italy, all interested in curbing Russian power in Asia. The first Japanese battleship, the *Hiei*, was launched in 1877 from the British shipyards, just like the *Mikasa* (1900). The fleet was completed by the capture of Chinese battleships and the construction of replica European battleships.

FEATURES OF THE MIKASA

433 ft/
132 m
7.5 ft/
2.3 m

Displacement 15,440 tons **Speed** 18 knots

Control bridge
Reinforced with steel armor plating, it was the nerve center of the battleship. Officers would meet here to take decisions and lead a crew of 850 people.

Artillery
Its main cannons aside, the *Mikasa* was equipped with a further 46 cannons to increase its firepower: 14 x 6.06 in/154 mm caliber, 20 x 2.99 in/76 mm, 8 x 1.85 in/47 mm and 4 x 1.38 in/35 mm .

Flagship

The *Mikasa*, Admiral Togo's flagship, was decisive in the Japanese victories in the attack on Port Arthur (1904) and the naval Battle of Tsushima (1905). After exploding due to a short circuit, it was rebuilt in 1922 as a national monument at the Military Port of Yokosuka in Japan.

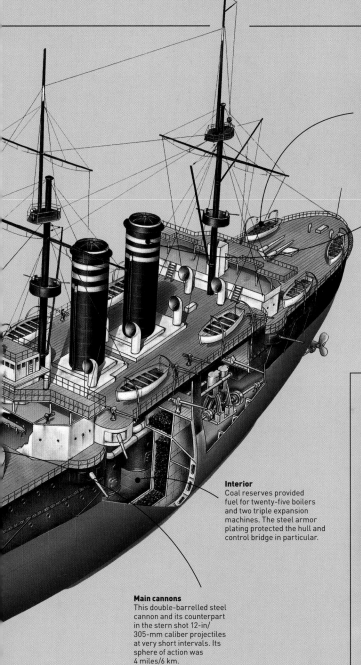

Lifeboat
Strategically located in case a torpedo should cause a leak and lead to a slow-sinking process. The devices were rendered useless if an explosion occurred in the magazine or in the boilers.

Steam
The steam propulsion system gave the battleships an advantage over sail boats during the Crimean War (1854-1855). The fumes and steam generated during combustion were released through large chimneys.

Interior
Coal reserves provided fuel for twenty-five boilers and two triple expansion machines. The steel armor plating protected the hull and control bridge in particular.

Main cannons
This double-barrelled steel cannon and its counterpart in the stern shot 12-in/305-mm caliber projectiles at very short intervals. Its sphere of action was 4 miles/6 km.

THE ADMIRAL WHO RESTORED JAPANESE PRIDE
The star among Japanese officers during the battles against China and Russia was Admiral Heihachiro Togo (1848–1934), the architect of the Imperial Navy. His strategy was decisive at the Battle of Tsushima (May 27, 1905). Russia lost practically its entire fleet and 4,380 soldiers; Japan, on the other hand, lost 3 torpedo boats and recorded just 117 casualties.

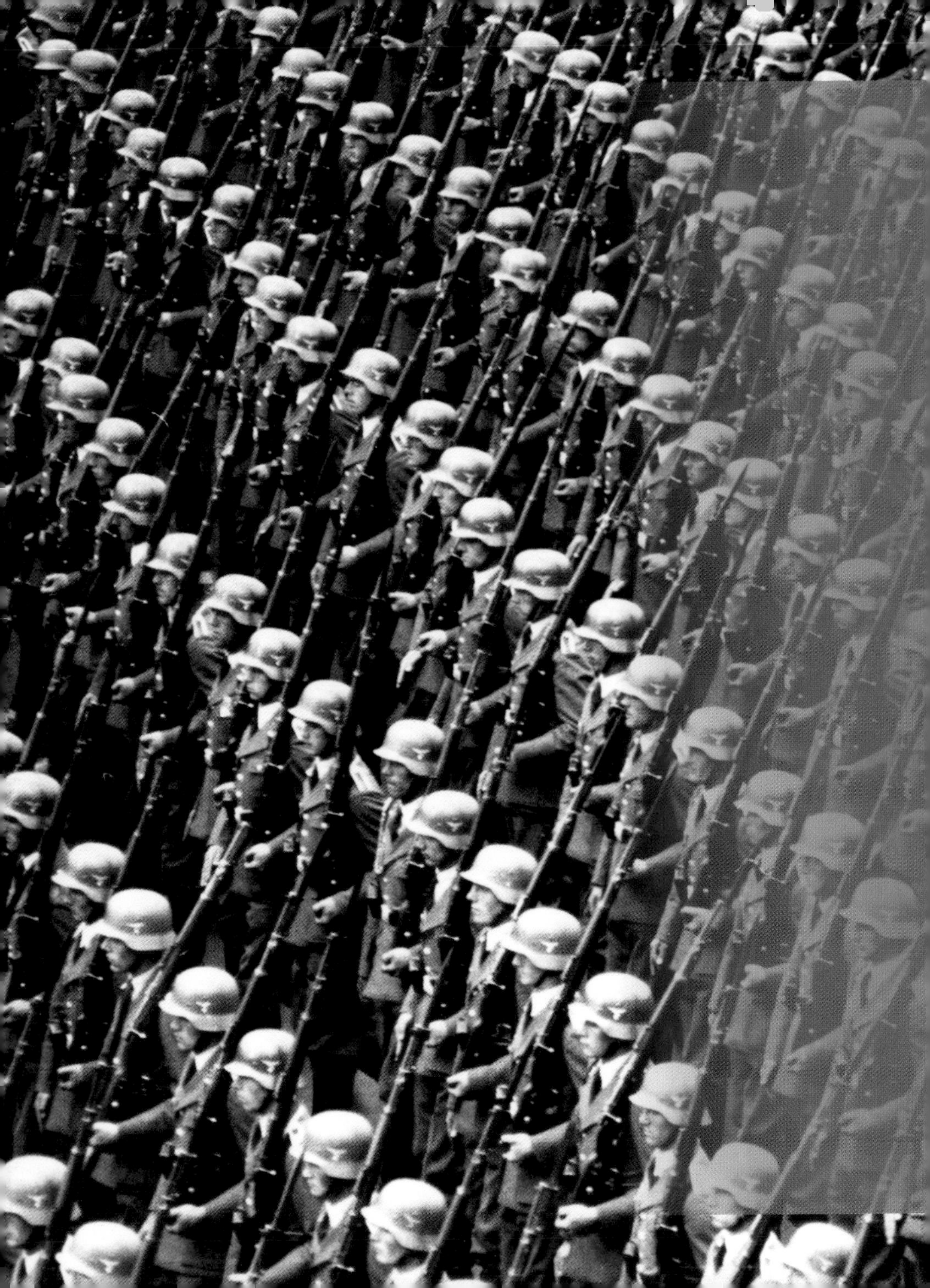

THE PERFECT WAR MACHINE

It existed for just ten years, between 1935 and 1945, but it was one of the most effective and powerful armies of its time. The *Wehrmacht*, literally the "defense force," replaced the Reichswehr, the German armed forces of the Weimar Republic, two years after Adolf Hitler was named German Chancellor. Organized, among others, by Generals Heinz Guderian, von Reichenau and Jodl, it replaced old military tactics with the so-called *blitzkrieg*, or "lightning strike," which involved quickly deploying troops that included armored divisions, infantry, mobile artillery, and aviation to support ground troops. The use of light weaponry, mobile assault, and logistics squadrons and a chain of command that facilitated autonomy in squadron activities if their officers fell in combat, in addition to an indisputable technical superiority and high level of discipline, contributed to its glowing successes during the first years of World War II. In fact, many armies would later copy its organization.

Among the motives for its success, it must also be noted that the high level of training received by its officers, and the creation and application of swift and mass tactics, allowed it to achieve its goals not only quickly, but also extremely effectively. Impeccable logistics and the use of cutting-edge weapons such as powerful and rapid tanks and a mighty air force were all key to the success. Between 1939 and 1940, it comprised more than twelve million soldiers, organized into companies (of 180 men); battalions (four companies); regiments (two companies, artillery, and antitank units, and three battalions—one reconnaissance, one general staff, and one support); divisions (comprising three regiments, or 17,000 men), army corps, and army groups. However, following the Battle of Kursk, in 1943, and especially from 1944 onward, the *Wehrmacht* no longer had enough soldiers to maintain its territorial war gains and had already incorporated practically all German men aged between 16 and 65 into its ranks. They were known as the *Volkssturm* ("people's army") and in reality, due to a lack of military training, served the army as cannon fodder in the final battles of World War II.

Also used by the Nazi regime for looting purposes and to annihilate those who it believed belonged to an "inferior race," the *Wehrmacht* was accomplice to the Holocaust. As a result, many of its commanders and chiefs of staff were found guilty of war crimes at the Nuremberg Trials following the war. It was decisively defeated in 1945, although until 1946 not all its units were officially declared as having been dissolved. That same year, Germany was banned from having an army; this ban was lifted in 1955, when the *Bundeswehr* was created.

Soldiers of the Third Reich

The personification of discipline and unrivaled professionalism; extremely well-equipped, motivated, and trained; aggressive in attack and pervasive in defense, German soldiers are considered the best infantry combatants of World War II. While it is often maintained that their superiority was attributable to the high level of technology they employed, access to such technology was restricted to small units, especially toward the end of the war. Their key was the training they received.

Perfect tactics and discipline

The Germans adjusted their training based on the combat experience they gradually acquired. The strategy involved mission-type tactics (*auftragstaktik*), in which directives were given, granting subordinate leaders the decision-making freedom to give orders depending on changes in combat. This bestowed an enormous level of tactical flexibility on the *Wehrmacht* and required a high level of individual capacity among the troops.

Special color
The gray-green color of the *Wehrmacht*'s uniform was called *feldgrau*. The tunic (*feldbluse*) and trousers (*hessen*) were made from wool cloth.
Leather cartridge cases
Capable of holding two clips of five cartridges.
Stielgranate
The stick grenade was ignited by unscrewing the base and pulling the cord underneath.
Rifle
The Karabiner 98 Kurz was the standard rifle of the *Wehrmacht* infantry troops. It had a chamber capable of holding 5 x 7.92-mm cartridges.
Bread pouch and canteen with mug
Boots
Made from leather and dyed black. The soles were reinforced using hobnails and heel irons.
Eagle
Represented the *Wehrmacht*.
Shield
With the colors of the national flag.

SYMBOLS

German helmets featured decals with symbols that identified the army corps to which the soldier belonged: army, navy, air force, SS, etc.

Clip with
32 x 9-mm
caliber
cartridges.
Its discharge rate
was 500 shots
per minute.
Cover of the open
tragbusche
Mask and filter
Lenses
Spare
lenses

Helmet The *stalhelm* was made of steel and weighed almost 2.2 lb/1 kg.

Kochgeschirr
Made from aluminum, it was used to transport cooking utensils.

Camouflage poncho
It served as a blanket and, by joining several together, a tent.

Trench spade
Stored alongside the bayonet, which measured 10 in/25 cm and had a Bakelite handle.

EVOLUTION OF THE UNIFORM

From 1943 onward, several changes were made to the uniform to make it more modern and functional. Hiking boots replaced calf-high boots, and camouflage was incorporated for most units, not just elite ranks, in addition to helmet covers.

MASCHINENPISTOLE 40

The squadron leader used an MP-40, the German machine gun par excellence.

CASE AND GAS MASK

Gas attacks during World War I resulted in the need for antigas equipment. The metal case held a mask and container with lenses.

Full equipment
The *tragbusche* was also equipped with a cloth to clean the lens. At the front, it also held antigas intoxication pills and a bottle containing liquid and gauzes for decontamination.

The Invasion of France

Between May and June 1940, one of the most stunning events of World War II and the entire history of armed conflicts occurred: the invasion of France by German troops. For the operation to succeed, the power and strategic capacity of the German forces was essential. This contrasted with the errors committed by the French-British Allies in their defensive attempts and left them on the brink of disaster. The Germans took Paris and would remain in France for four years.

Perfect coordination

The Allies expected a massive invasion from the Low Countries. However, the Germans divided into three groups; each had a specific objective and, unexpectedly, they concentrated the bulk of the attack in the Ardennes forest. The factor of surprise and the perfect coordination between groups were key.

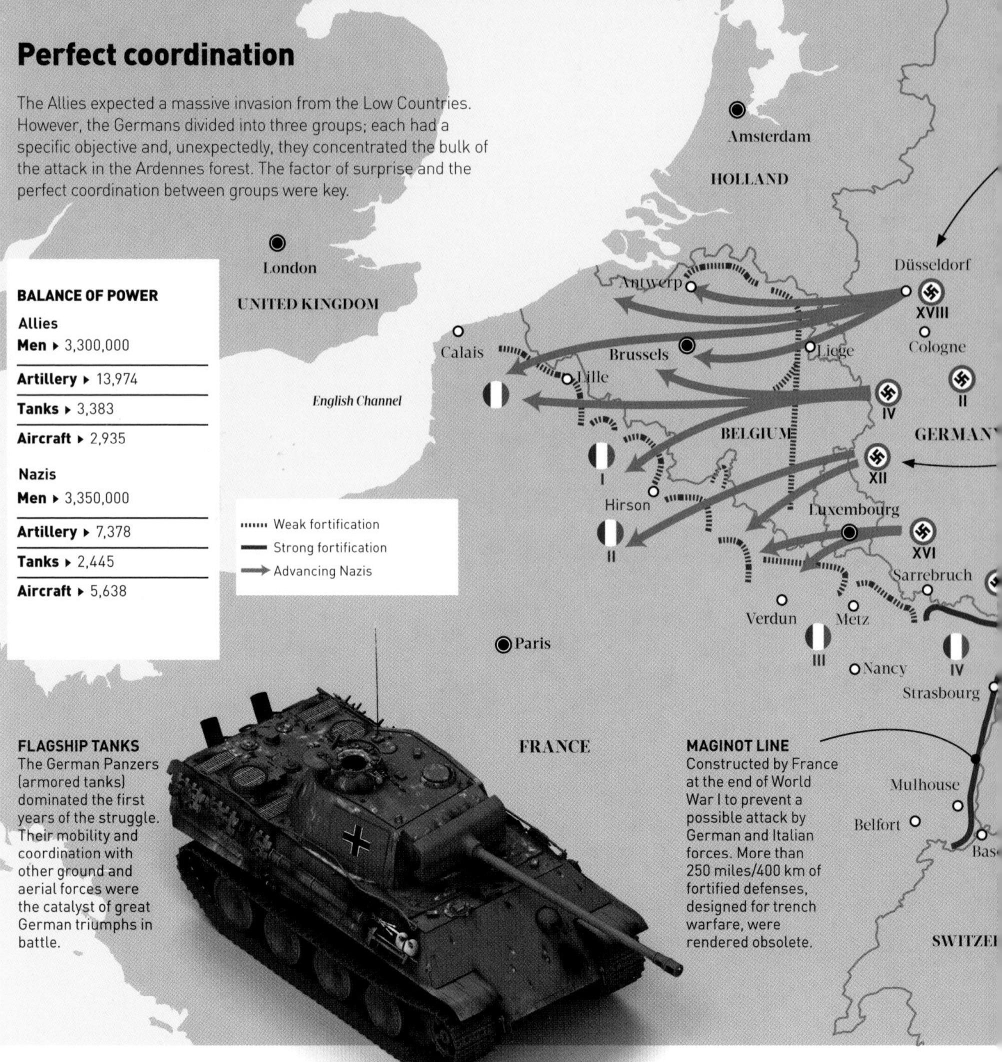
Amsterdam
HOLLAND
London
UNITED KINGDOM
Düsseldorf
Antwerp
XVIII
Cologne
Calais
Brussels
Liège
Lille
English Channel
IV
II
BELGIUM
GERMANY
I
XII
Hirson
Luxembourg
II
XVI
Sarrebruch
Verdun
Metz
Paris
III
Nancy
IV
Strasbourg
FRANCE
Mulhouse
Belfort
Basel
SWITZERLAND
Weak fortification
Strong fortification
Advancing Nazis

BALANCE OF POWER

Allies

Men ▸	3,300,000
Artillery ▸	13,974
Tanks ▸	3,383
Aircraft ▸	2,935

Nazis

Men ▸	3,350,000
Artillery ▸	7,378
Tanks ▸	2,445
Aircraft ▸	5,638

FLAGSHIP TANKS
The German Panzers (armored tanks) dominated the first years of the struggle. Their mobility and coordination with other ground and aerial forces were the catalyst of great German triumphs in battle.

MAGINOT LINE
Constructed by France at the end of World War I to prevent a possible attack by German and Italian forces. More than 250 miles/400 km of fortified defenses, designed for trench warfare, were rendered obsolete.

FINAL INVASION
In light of the casualties suffered by the French defense troops, the Germans launched a massive attack at the beginning of June. By the end of the month, they arrived in Paris. Here, Hitler can be seen in front of the Eiffel Tower on June 23.

Aerial attack

The German *Stuka* were the weapons of the sky during the first years of the conflict. Lethal and terrifying (pilots turned on sirens to generate an intimidating sound), they served to break armed enemy lines.

GROUP B
Launched into battle on May 10, 1940, efficiently invading Luxembourg, Holland, and Belgium. Thus, they distracted and rounded up the British and French forces.

Berlin

GROUP A
Responsible for the bulk of the invasion. They surprisingly sent the armored vehicles into the Ardennes forest. When they emerged, they had broken the French defensive lines and surrounded the British and French troops to the north, who suffered a genuine disaster.

GROUP C
They contained the French forces protecting the Maginot Line, to prevent them assisting the defenses attacked by Group A.

1 The pilot locked on to his target and programmed the automatic recovery system at the desired height.

2 The plane nosedived at an angle of between 65° and 80°, at more than 300 mph/500 km/h. Its sirens terrorized its targets.

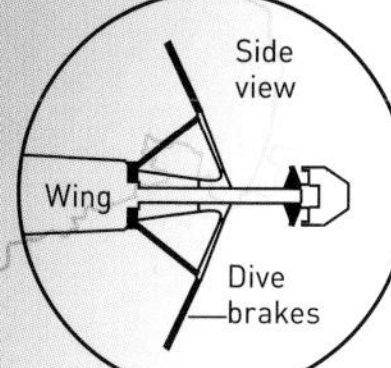

Side view
Wing
Dive brakes

When leveling out, the dive brakes allowed the *Stuka* to maintain a constant speed and a stable position to help the pilot to take aim.

3 From a height of 1,650 ft/500 m, the pilot dropped the bomb or engaged the machine gun. Meanwhile, the automatic system started the height-recovery process.

4,900 ft/ 1,500 m

1,650 ft/ 500 m

The Blitzkrieg

During the first years of the war, the German Army surprised the Allies with an innovative and highly efficient tactic: the *blitzkreig*, or "lightning strike." It was founded on the speed of combined troops, in which the actions of aviation and tanks were vital. Using this tactic, between September 1939, with the invasion of Poland, and June 1940, with the fall of France, the Germans took control of half of Europe.

HEINZ WILHELM GUDERIAN
(1888–1954)
Creator of the Panzer (tank) divisions and the man responsible for developing and applying the *blitzkrieg* doctrine in the Polish and French campaigns, he was responsible for the tank divisions.

ERICH VON MANSTEIN
(1887–1973)
He participated in the Polish campaign, adopting and perfecting the *blitzkrieg* tactic during the invasion of France, during which he was the main ideologist of the Nazi plan of attack.

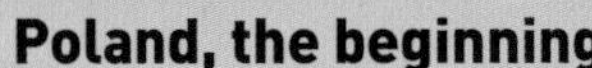

Poland, the beginning

The German Army first employed its rapid offensive tactic in the invasion of Poland. The attack began on September 1, 1939, and in just three weeks the operation was over. However, the *blitzkrieg* was most potent during the invasion of France.

The invasion
German troops entering Poland in September 1939.

Other tanks
In May 1940, the Germans h
a few Panzer III. The bulk o
armed forces comprised th
Panzer I and II.

GERMAN PARATROOPERS
As part of the *blitzkrieg*, Germans were the first to use paratroopers as a combat force. This represents just another example of the way the German Army utilized all the forces at its disposal in addition to demonstrating its modern take on warfare. One of the paratroopers' most notable actions was to take the supposedly impregnable Fort Eben-Emael in Belgium, the first time gliders had been used in history.

erial support
ıe *Stuka* bombers ɔsedived above the fixed .lied positions (such as e artillery, for example) suppress them.

Panzers in action
The pinnacle of German tanks was the Panzer III, used in the Battle of France. It was superior to the French R-35 and H-35.

Speed as the key

The *blitzkrieg* tactic consisted of a combined attack employing armed forces and highly mobile infantrymen, concentrated in a single location and supported by the artillery and aircraft. It sought to occupy strategic points that would ensure victory as quickly as possible. In order to do so, speed and surprise were key in neutralizing the enemy's reaction.

Great mobility
The Germans had light armed vehicles, such as the SdKfz-222, which were faster and more mobile than the tanks.

avorable terrain
ɔr the *blitzkrieg* to be ıccessful, the terrain ıd to be flat and ıstacle free.

The German U-Boats

Between 1939 and 1943, German submarines decimated the British war and merchant fleets in the Atlantic. Around twelve million tons of boats were sunk over the course of the conflict by the *Kriegsmarine* (the German Navy). The U-Boats (from the German *Untersee boot*, or submarine) played a pivotal role in these attacks: they attacked in groups, at night and on the surface. Given their tactics, their crews were called *Grauen Wölfe* (Gray Wolves).

Attack strategies

The pinnacle of German submarine victories came in the summer of 1942, when eight million tons of Allied boats were sunk. This was to change from mid-1943. Then, the use of sonar and escort aircraft carriers, full aerial coverage, and the decoding of German messages allowed the Allies to neutralize them.

Torpedo tubes
These two torpedo tubes were close to the living quarters of the crew; the other two were at the stern, close to the propeller. The U-47 was capable of carrying 14 torpedoes.

Technical information

Length ▸ 220 ft/67 m

Breadth ▸ 20 ft/6.2 m

Depth ▸ 15 ft/4.7 m

Displacement ▸ 753 tons

Submersion displacement ▸ 857 tons

Surface speed ▸ 20 mph/32 km/h

Submerged speed ▸ 9 mph/15 km/h

The U-47 submarine

On October 14, 1939, at the command of Günther Prien, the submarine entered the Scottish anchorage at Scapa Flow, an extremely important base for the British Navy, sank HMS *Royal Oak* (a 29,150-ton battleship with 786 men) and returned triumphant. In March 1941, it was sunk with all its crew.

GÜNTHER PRIEN
(1908–1941)
While in command of the U-47, 30 Allied boats were sunk. After his achievements at Scapa Flow, his fame grew and he received the Iron Cross. He died aged 32 on board the U-47.

KARL DÖNITZ
(1891–1980)
Great Admiral, responsible for the submarine divisions and the commander-in-chief of the Kriegsmarine from 1943. He proposed using U-boats to attack in groups.

TORPEDOES

Invented in 1866 by an Austrian Officer, Giovanni Luppis, they traveled in a straight line and left a wake, but their impact was lethal. They were capable of traveling 6 miles/10 km.

Torpedoes being loaded on a U-boat.

ontrol room
.ocated between the fficers' room and the etty officers' room, it vas from here that the eriscopes on the turret vere employed; one was ong distance.

Machine room
Fitted with compressed air tanks, electric motors, and diesel engines.

Batteries
The submarines were powered with electrical systems. The low level of power resulted in U-boats only being able to travel under water for short periods, with strategic stops planned to recharge.

Cannons
This one, measuring 3.5 in/88 mm in diameter, was located between the hatch and the turret. The antiaircraft cannon, measuring 0.8 in/20 mm in diameter, was positioned behind the turret.

LIFE ABOARD A SUBMARINE

The U-boats carried little water, smelled of oil and fuel, and were overcrowded. On board there were two toilets and 25 bunk beds for 50 crew members. Missions were endless and bravery was required to overcome claustrophobia and the high risk of perishing in combat or due to technical problems.

Hitler's bunker

The New Chancellery bunker in Berlin, a refuge from aerial attacks and the underground headquarters of the Third Reich, was Adolf Hitler's final place of residence, from January 16, 1945 until his suicide on April 30 of the same year, by which time the Soviets had entered the German capital. Its walls were around 13 ft/4 m thick and its concrete roof was bombproof. However, by the end of the war, most of it had been destroyed.

An underground refuge

Hitler's bunker was divided into two sections. The first level (located 21 ft/6.4 m beneath the surface) housed the *vorbunker*, built in 1936, where sanitary, administrative, and personal support services were located. At a lower level (30 ft/9 m deep) was the *führerbunker*, completed in 1943, which housed the residence of Adolf Hitler and Eva Braun, accompanied by their guards and personal assistants, in addition to Joseph Goebbels.

Incineration
Just a few yards from the exit to the Chancellery gardens, the bodies of Hitler and Eva Braun were incinerated.

38
37
30 ft/
9 m
1
2
3
4
10
10
36

THE FÜHRERBUNKER (LOWER FLOOR)

1-2 Hitler's doctors' rooms
3 Goebbels' cabinet and bedroom
4 Secretary's office
5-6 Switchboard
7 Heating and ventilation machines and electricity generators
8-9 Corridors and conference rooms
10 Members of security and Hitler's pets
11 Map room
12 Hitler's cabinet
13 Eva Braun's lounge and bedroom
14 Hitler's bedroom
15 Hitler's lounge
16 Hitler's bathroom and wardrobe
17 Bathrooms and toilets
18 Connection between bunkers
36 Concrete tower, ventilation, and emergency exit

THE VORBUNKER (UPPER FLOOR)

19 Pantries
20 Storage and kitchen space
21-22 Corridors
23 Canteen
24-27 Goebbels family bedrooms
28-29 Staff bedrooms
30 Machine and ventilation rooms
31 Health centers
32 Entrance to the bunker
33 Security and technical team office
34 Passage to the Old Chancellery and the bunker of the New Chancellery
35 Passage to the Ministry of Foreign Affairs and the garden of the Ministry of Foreign Affairs
37 Exit to the New Chancellery garden
38 Unfinished concrete tower

Generators
The noise of the engines, diesel electricity generators, and ventilation and water extraction pumps, were constant and filled the atmosphere.

BUNKER SUICIDES

Adolf Hitler and Eva Braun: suicide, April 30, 1945
Helga, Hilde, Helmut, Holde, Hedda, and Heide Goebbels: killed by their parents, May 1, 1945
Joseph and Magda Goebbels: suicide, May 1, 1945
General Franz Schädle: suicide, May 1, 1945
General Hans Krebs: suicide, May 2, 1945
General Wilhelm Burgdorf: suicide, May 2, 1945

Left to right: Adolf Hitler, Magda and Joseph Goebbels, Eva Braun.

North wall of the Old Chancellery
Garden wall
Ground level
Floor
Reinforced concrete ceiling
21 ft/ 6.4 m
35
30
33
28
27
29
32
26
24
23
25
33
22
34
21
20
20
31
18
20
7
20
19
20
19
VORBUNKER
9
17
13
17
16
15
FÜHRERBUNKER
14 ft/ 4.2 m
Reinforced concrete wall

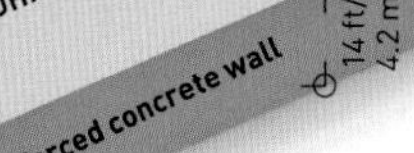

Security
All the bunker doors were airtight, in case of a gas attack.

Underground corridors
The Führer's refuge was connected to the Old Chancellery and the bunker of the New Chancellery, in addition to the Ministry of Foreign Affairs.

Cabinet
It was on the sofa in this room that the lifeless bodies of Hitler and Eva Braun were found.

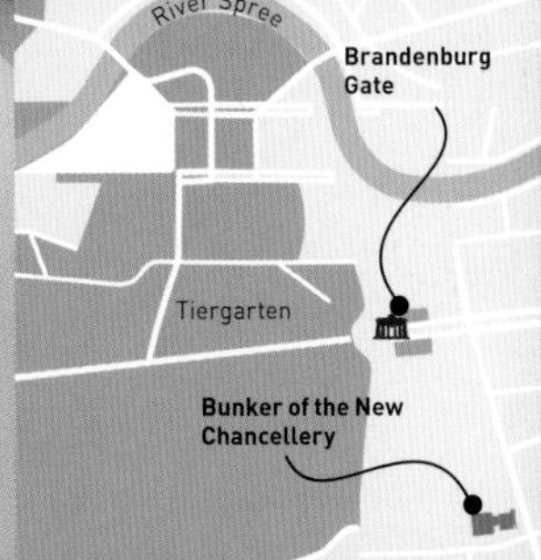
River Spree
Brandenburg Gate
Tiergarten
Bunker of the New Chancellery

FROM REVOLUTION TO MAJOR POWER

Created in the wake of the Russian Revolution of 1917 and organized by Leon Trotsky (1870–1940), then named by the Bolsheviks as War Commissioner, the Soviet Army, officially called the "Workers' and Peasants' Red Army," due to the color of the working-class flag, was initially created to support the fight of the people against capitalism during the Russian Civil War.

Trotsky, using volunteers with no military training, managed to create an army corps that, over time, would become one of the most powerful in the world. To this end, he called upon officers from the dissolved Russian Imperial Army, many of whom responded: more than 58,000 former civil servants, among whom 10,000 were employees of the former Czarist administration, worked beneath him, in addition to 214,000 former junior officers, responsible for training the new troops. Several generals from the old empire even formed part of the Red Army, such as Mikhail Tukhachevsky, who became a distinguished commander in the new military power, responding to the Revolutionary Military Council (*Revvoyensoviet*) which was presided over by Trotsky himself. The initial anarchy among troops was later transformed into strict discipline, which was put to the test in battles against the antirevolutionary "White Army" in 1919 and in the Polish–Soviet War of 1920, during which the Red Army reached Warsaw.

Having previously comprised almost five million men, in 1922, the year in which the Soviet Union was founded, due to the poor economic situation, the army had been reduced to just 500,000 personnel. It would only be after the death of Lenin in 1924, Stalin's rise to power, and Trotsky's subsequent exile, that the Red Army would regain strength. During the 1930s, with the significant development of the Soviet arms industry, which was capable of manufacturing powerful aircraft and highly resistant armor, it grew to one and a half million men. By 1933, when the country was manufacturing 3,000 tanks each year and had its own elite paratrooper regiment, the Soviet Army boasted the world's first armored unit. Despite the size of the army being reduced toward the end of the 1930s due to Stalin's purges, which cost the lives or resulted in the deportation of millions of military men, from 1941 onward it successfully faced the Nazi army—its troops would eventually be the first to take Berlin, raising the red flag above the German Reichstag building. Following World War II, the Red Army became one of the most important in the world, participating in the repression of uprisings in Hungary (1956) and Czechoslovakia (1968). Its final battle was in Afghanistan between 1980 and 1988. In the 1990s, it was dissolved and became the Armed Forces of the Russian Federation.

Soviet Soldiers

It is indisputable that the Red Army played a key role during World War II. In addition to recording the majority of human casualties, with 13,600,000 fatalities (four times more than the German army), its activities were decisive. After victory in Stalingrad, its unstoppable advance forced the Germans to withdraw the majority of their forces from the west, helping the advance of the U.S.A. and its allies on that front.

Its motivation: bravery

Prior to 1941, the Red Army encountered numerous problems and deficiencies due to the purges of Joseph Stalin. Afterward, it was reborn and became one of the most powerful forces worldwide, with a high level of training and equipment. Soviet soldiers during the war were highly disciplined and motivated (further still after the victories at Stalingrad and Kursk) to feel part of the patriotic crusade against Fascism. Most soldiers were from rural areas.

Perchatkye
These fabric gloves were made from brown or beige wool.

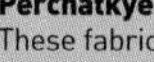

Pouch
To house the soldier's gas mask.

Cartridge case
Soldiers used the Mosin-Nagant rifle, and carried ammunition in their cartridge holders.

Spade
All combatants carried a spade to dig trenches and shelters.

Valenki
Boots designed to resist glacial temperatures, made from compressed felt.

Vatnie sharovari
These padded trousers had knee reinforcements and adjustments on the ankles.

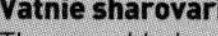

GENERAL CHARACTERISTICS

During peacetime, there were 1,800,000 men in the Red Army, which could increase to 11,000,000 in the event of mobilization. They were called to the ranks for over 20 years, from the age of 20 to 41.

Shield
The emblem of the Soviet Armed Forces.

Memorial
To fallen soldiers during World War II.

High command ▸ Marshal, followed by generals

Total army corps in 1941 ▸ 100

Historic victories ▸ Stalingrad, Kursk, Berlin

Great generals ▸ Georgy Zhukov, Semyon Timoshenko, Ivan Konev

Motto ▸ *Not One Step Backward!*

apka-ushanka
nthetic fur hat,
ich replaced
e helmet during
nter.
PPSh-41
This weapon was sturdy and required little maintenance. Its discharge rate was 900 rounds per minute.
Clip
A copy of the clip on the Finnish Suomi M31 subrifle. It had capacity to hold 71 cartridges.
1
2
3
4
Waterproofs
Tent and trench cover
Telogreika
A padded jacket worn over the combat jacket, or *gymnastiorka*.
Subrifle cartridge holder
It had a round shape for PPSh clips.
RGD-33 grenade
It could be launched up to 100 ft/30 m and had an effective explosion radius of 50 ft/15 m.

PRACTICAL AND COMFORTABLE

The Red Army uniform was designed to be comfortable, simple and practical. With temperatures ranging from -76°F to 104°F, they had to provide warmth in winter and be cool in summer.

PLASCH-PALATKA

A versatile and practical item of clothing that served as waterproofs, sleeping bag, and even a tent, when several were joined together. It was wrapped up in just four steps.

ADAPTATION OF THE UNIFORM

During World War II, the uniform varied depending on the geographical destination of the troops. Above, the warm location uniform is shown.

The Battle of Stalingrad

Considered one of the most deadly in history, costing hundreds of thousands of lives, the Battle of Stalingrad, fought between August 1942 and February 1943, represented a turning point in World War II. The Soviet victory thwarted Hitler's plans of controlling the hydrocarbon reserves of the Caucasus and destroyed the once glorious German 6th Army, which had invaded Paris and other large areas of Eastern Europe. Stalingrad was the beginning of the end for the Third Reich.

A game of pincers

Although the bulk of the battle took place on the streets, there were two decisive moments in Stalingrad: the German attack and the Soviet counterattack using the pincer movement.

BALANCE OF POWER

Axis

MEN ▸ 700,000

ARTILLERY ▸ 10,250

TANKS ▸ 500

AIRCRAFT ▸ 732

Soviets

MEN ▸ +1,000,000

ARTILLERY ▸ 13,000

TANKS ▸ 900

AIRCRAFT ▸ 1,115

USSR

Moscow

Stalingrad

EUROPE

FRIEDRICH PAULUS

Commander of the German Sixth Army, he attained the rank of field marshal just days before surrender. Unlike his predecessors, who committed suicide before capture, Paulus gave himself up. Captured by the Soviets, he was freed ten years later.

VASILY CHUIKOV

Named Commander of the Soviet 62nd Army a month after combat began, with the city he was tasked with defending in ruins and against a chaotic military and social backdrop. However, he turned it around. His motto before battle was "We will defend the city or die in the attempt."

Boguchar

Kantemirovskaya

Elanskaya

Chertkovo

V. Buzinovka

Ilovinskaya

River Volga

Dubovka

Voloshinov

Kashari

Medvezhi

Milerovo

Stalingrad

Leninsk

Morosovsk

Sovetski

Plodovitoye

Tormosin

Kotelnikovski

Sadovoye

Shebalin

Soviet front

Movement of Soviet troops

Movement of German troops

Boguchar
Kashari
Kantemirovskaya
Elanskaya
V. Buzinovka
Chertkovo
Ilovinskaya
River Volga
Dubovka
Medvezhi
Stalingrad
Voloshinov
Leninsk
Milerovo
Sovetski
Plodovitoye
Tormosin
Morosovsk
Sadovoye
Kotelnikovski
Shebalin

1 GERMANY BEGINS THE ATTACK

In July, Hitler mobilizes a significant military force which occupies cities on route to the city of Stalingrad. Confident of a quick triumph, at the end of August, aerial bombardments begin, which leave the city in ruins, and in September the Germans enter the city. However, the Soviets plan precise house-by-house guerrilla warfare tactics.

2 SOVIET COUNTERATTACK

On November 19, with the city practically in the hands of the invader, the Soviets begin a counterattack on the flanks defended by weak Romanian forces, and using a pincer movement, besiege the German forces in Stalingrad who, decimated by artillery, hunger, cold, and illness, surrender on January 31. On February 2, a ceasefire is declared.

House by house

Conscious of their inferior ability to wage large-scale combat, the Soviets took the decision to defend the city on the streets; this forced the Germans to fight house by house, thwarting their plans for a quick occupation of Stalingrad.

Aviation Hitler trusted in aviation to supply provisions to the troops trapped in Stalingrad, but this failed.
Ruins The initial devastating German aerial bombardment left 90 percent of the city in ruins.
Snipers They were key to the battle. The struggle would involve outstanding individuals and duels.
Tanks and armored vehicles A cornerstone of the German forces, their use in street combat was extremely limited.
301
German soldiers Around 290,000 fought inside the city. There were 200,000 casualties and 90,000 prisoners taken, most of whom died in Soviet prisoner-of-war camps.
Civilians The Soviet leader, Josef Stalin, prohibited civilians from leaving the city. This way, his soldiers would fight more bravely to defend them.
Soviet soldiers They hid in the ruins of buildings and forced the Germans to participate in house-by-house combat.

Soviet Tanks

The dissolved Soviet Union constructed some of the most emblematic lightweight and heavyweight armored vehicles of all time. Many models were, if not determining factors, at least fundamental to the development and the results of entire wars. Among the most famous was the T-34, produced between 1940 and 1958; it was one of the great emblems of the Red Army during World War II, during which almost 40,000 units were built.

T-34, an impeccable weapon

Quick and agile, this tank's efficiency was attributable to its excellent balance on the battlefield and its capacity to travel over ice and swampland. On the other hand, while the T-34 was comparable with other enemy models, especially German models, given their firepower and armor, it really stood out due to the low cost and quick production time in replacing those lost in battle.

Armor ▸ 2.5 in/63 mm

Cannon ▸ 3 in/76 mm

Speed ▸ 33 mph/53 km/h

Weight ▸ 26 tons

8 ft /2.5 m
10 ft/3 m
22 ft/6.7 m
Radio antenna
Cannon The T-34 was equipped with a 3 in/76 mm cannon. From 1943, it was replaced by a 3.4 in/86 mm cannon, to combat the new, better-armored German tanks.
Machine gun It used drum magazines.
Steering levers Used to turn the tank.
Armor From 1941, the different parts were armored using steel of between 1.8 and 2.5 in/45 and 63 mm; however, it was vulnerable to certain German tanks.
Pedals To accelerate and brake.

Other Red Army tanks

T-18
Although considered a failure, the T-18 represented the Soviet arms industry's first steps in producing tanks between 1928 and 1931.

Armor ▸ 0.5 in/16 mm

Cannon ▸ 1.5 in/37 mm

Speed ▸ 10 mph/17 km/h

Weight ▸ 5.9 tons

KV-1
Heavily armored heavyweight tank, almost indestructible by German tanks. It received the nickname "Nazi-killer."

Armor ▸ 3.5 in/90 mm

Cannon ▸ 3 in/76.2 mm

Speed ▸ 22 mph/35 km/h

Weight ▸ 45 tons

Periscope Used by the gunner to take aim.
Turret crew Comprising two men: the commanding gunner and the loader.
Engine It generated 500 horsepower using its 12-cylinder engine, which ran on diesel.
Exhaust pipes
Caterpillar tread Distributed the weight of the tank to prevent it sinking in the mud.
Ammunition Boxes were stored under the tank's floor. However, to facilitate access to rounds during combat, some were placed in easy-to-access holds.
Front crew Comprising two men: the tank driver and the machine gunner.

-2

KV-2 was designed as the fect heavyweight tank to destroy ifications toward the end of World II.

nor ▸ 4.5 in/110 mm

non ▸ 6 in/152 mm

ed ▸ 21 mph/34 km/h

ight ▸ 54 tons

T-72

One of the most popular Soviet tanks in modern-day Russia and worldwide. It entered service in 1971 and is currently manufactured in half a dozen countries.

Armour ▸ 100 mm (4 inches)

Cannon ▸ 125 mm (5 inches)

Speed ▸ 34 km/h (21 mph)

Weight ▸ 54 tonnes

PREPARED FOR VICTORY

The People's Liberation Army of China (PLA), which today has the largest ground force in the world, was founded in 1927. This was just 16 years after the Xinhai Revolution, which saw the end of the Qing Dynasty, after the first alliance between the Chinese Communist Party and the Kuomintang (Chinese Nationalist Party) led by Chiang Kai-chek was sealed. Initially known as the Chinese Red Army, after the second Sino-Japanese War (1937-1945), the retreat of the Kuomintang to Taiwan in 1949, and its triumph in the Chinese Civil War, the Chinese Communist Party gave it its current name.

From 1950, and following its intervention in the Korean War, the army (also known as the People's Volunteer Army) moved from being a peasant force to become a modern and well-equipped organization, with a significant number of personnel and an increasingly relevant role in national politics and the economy. Nonetheless, starting in the 1960s, an important demobilization process began. This coincided with the entity being made professional and its weapons, and military strategy and planning being overhauled. These changes would be put to the test in 1979 during a series of important military actions along the country's border with Vietnam. During the 1980s, it reduced the size of its ground troops once again, becoming a small, more mobile structure equipped with cutting-edge technology. Between 1985 and 1987 it demobilized a million men; and between 1996 and 2000, during the so-called "Ninth Five-Year Plan," a further 500,000 were demobilized. By 1993, Chinese President Jiang Zemin had implemented a "revolution of the military" which would convert the PLA into a force capable of "local wars under high-tech conditions."

Despite such notable scaling back, the army's current ground forces include 18 army groups, each of which has between 50,000 and 60,000 men divided into combined arms units. It is estimated that there may be approximately 1,600,000 personnel, divided into more than 60 divisions and 80 brigades, of which at least 40 percent are mobile or armed according to a report by the International Institute for Strategic Studies published in 2006. In addition to its reserves of at least 1,500,000 personnel, the People's Liberation Army of China boasts special operations forces, a distinguished air force, potent surface-to-air missiles, specialists in long-range precision attacks, and units of electronic warfare trained in information technology. Furthermore, it has a significant navy fleet at its disposal, in addition to marines specializing in CQC (Close Quarters Combat).

Indeed the PLA is clearly a force to be reckoned with, and underpins China's position as a world leader.

Soldiers of the People's Army

The People's Liberation Army (PLA) of China is not only the largest in the world, but most probably, the largest of all time. However, when it was founded, on August 1, 1927, it was a small army of peasants and rebel soldiers. Originally named the Red Army, it led the Chinese Communist Party to victory in the Chinese Civil War against the Kuomintang. It adopted its current name in June 1946.

Fatherland and revolution

The PLA was created in Nanchang, when a number of military garrisons rebelled against their Kuomintang superiors. In 1934, Nanchang was attacked by the Nationalists, forcing the Communists to embark upon a retreat known as the Long March, during which thousands more supporters subscribed to the PLA cause. During the 1937 Japanese invasion, the PLA and the Nationalists united efforts to expel the invaders. However, between 1945 and 1949, the PLA demonstrated the extent of its bravery during the civil war, entirely defeating the Kuomintang troops.

AN ARRAY OF WEAPONRY

Initially, German weaponry was employed, which was produced in China. However, American, English, French, and Russian weaponry was soon incorporated, in addition to that taken from the Japanese.

Traditional knives
A group of Chinese combatants, fighting the Japanese, display their traditional *dadao* knives.

GENERAL CHARACTERISTICS

The Chinese usually refer to their army as *Bayi*, which means "eight one," referring to the date on which this force was created.

八一

LPA insignia
In the center, it reads: "Bayi."

"Mao"-type hat
The symbol of the LPA for decades.

High command ▸ Central Military Commission of the Chinese Communist Party

Structure ▸ Seven military districts and three fleets

Total personnel (without reserves) ▸ 2,285,000

Historic victories ▸ Siege of Changchun (1948), Battle of Jinzhou (1948), Sino-Indian War (1962)

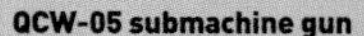

MODERN WEAPONRY
Internal production of weapons was established by the modernization program undertaken by the PLA from the 1970s. Since 2001, troops have been equipped with advanced handheld weapons designed by Jianshe Industries.

QCW-05 submachine gun

QBU-88 sniper rifle

POPULAR UNIFORM

Toward the end of the Civil War in 1949, the uniform had already been standardized significantly. However, certain details highlighted its peasant past.

Uniform
The basic uniform was similar to that of the Nationalists. However, the colour khaki was predominant, and it featured distinctive characteristics such as stars and red stripes.
Hanyang 88 rifle
Made in China, its technical name was Type 88. It was a bolt-action 7.92 caliber rifle.
Grenade holder
It held four Chinese stick grenades based on the German Model 24.
Straps and cartridge holders
The parallel shoulder straps helped to sustain the weight of the cartridge holders full of bullets strapped to the belt.
Canteen
The diagonal strap held the brass canteen.
Douli hat
Premium symbol of the Chinese peasant; it was hung on the peasant's back and used when not engaged in battle.
Bayonet sheath
It housed a Hanyang M1935 bayonet.
Gaiters and footwear
Chinese peasant shoes were standard army footwear.

GUERRILLA WARFARE ACCORDING TO MAO

Mao Zedong distinguished three stages of development within guerrilla warfare:

Phase 1 Mobilize peasants.

Phase 2 Rural bases and guerrilla operations.

Phase 3 Transition to conventional warfare.

The Battle of Xuzhou

At the end of the 1940s, China found itself engulfed in civil war. On one side, well-armed and trained Nationalist troops, who wielded official power. On the other, Communist forces who advanced from the north. Between 1948 and 1949, the Communists unleashed the so-called Huaihai Campaign, which put them on the path to victory. The battle, fought on the outskirts of the railroad town of Xuzhou, represented a turning point in the outcome of the war.

The beginning of the end

On November 6, 1948, the Communist forces were making positive progress toward their targets: the main Nationalist cities of Nanjing and Shanghai. To this end, they believed that taking the railroad town of Xuzhou, a vitally important crossroads, was crucial.

BALANCE OF POWER

NATIONALISTS ▸ 800,000

COMMUNISTS ▸ 600,000

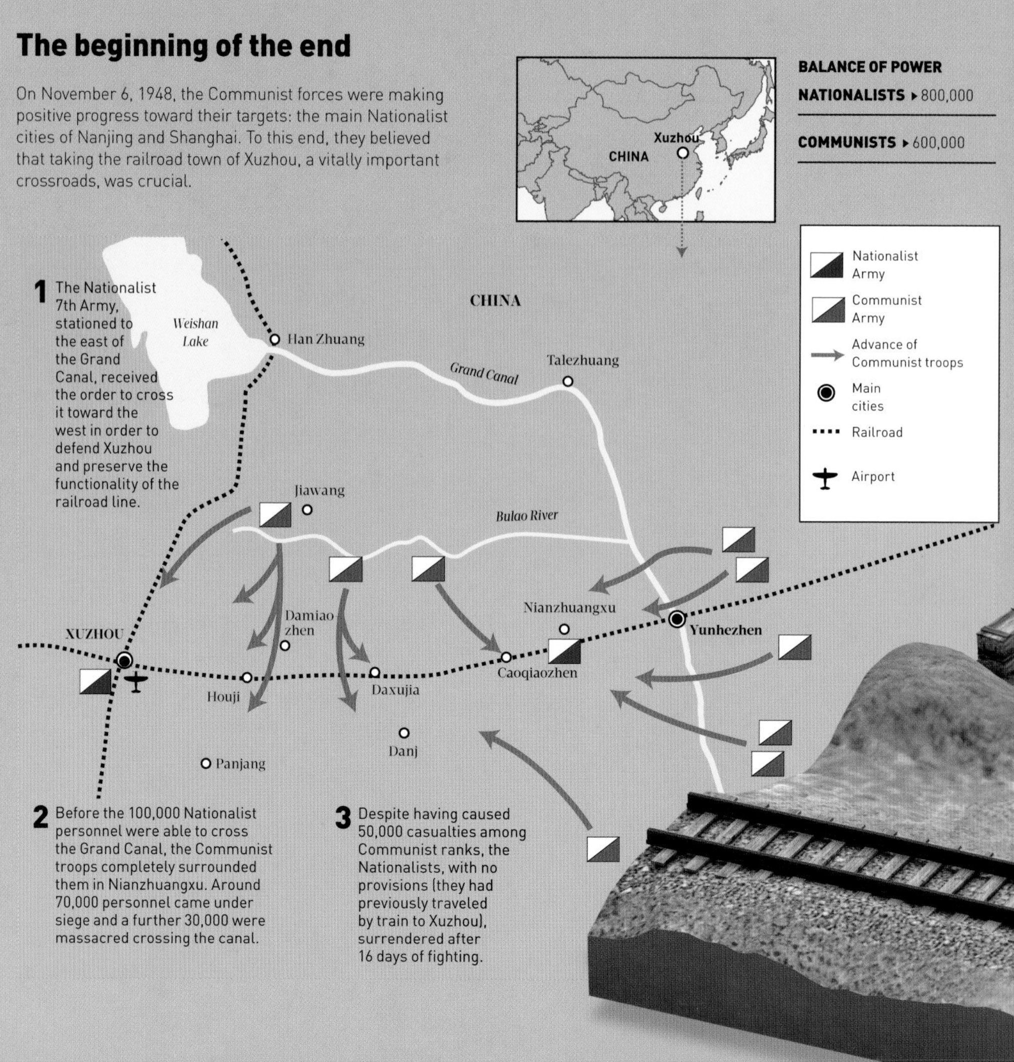
Xuzhou
CHINA
Nationalist Army
Communist Army
Advance of Communist troops
Main cities
Railroad
Airport
CHINA
Weishan Lake
Han Zhuang
Grand Canal
Talezhuang
Jiawang
Bulao River
Damiao-zhen
XUZHOU
Nianzhuangxu
Yunhezhen
Caoqiaozhen
Houji
Daxujia
Danj
Panjang

1 The Nationalist 7th Army, stationed to the east of the Grand Canal, received the order to cross it toward the west in order to defend Xuzhou and preserve the functionality of the railroad line.

2 Before the 100,000 Nationalist personnel were able to cross the Grand Canal, the Communist troops completely surrounded them in Nianzhuangxu. Around 70,000 personnel came under siege and a further 30,000 were massacred crossing the canal.

3 Despite having caused 50,000 casualties among Communist ranks, the Nationalists, with no provisions (they had previously traveled by train to Xuzhou), surrendered after 16 days of fighting.

Surprise factor

During the Battle of Xuzhou, Nationalist troops were totally surprised by the Communist forces and were surrounded. After the conquest of Xuzhou, the Red Army would enjoy further triumphs. The Huaihai Campaign resulted in the loss of half a million Nationalist men and the beginning of their eventual defeat.

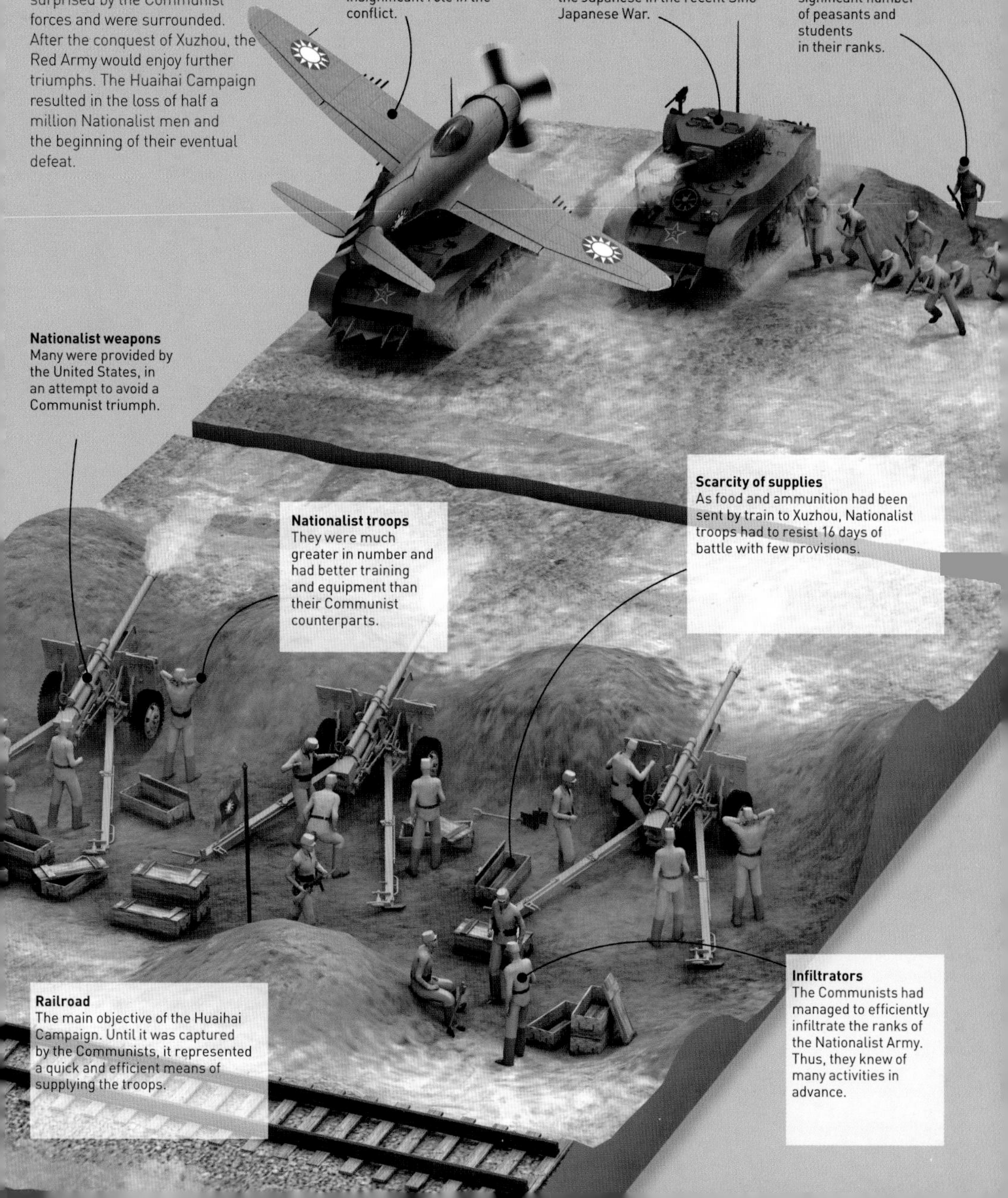

Aviation
Although the Nationalists had the upper hand in the air, aviation played an insignificant role in the conflict.

Communist weapons
The Red Army was supplied with weapons from the Soviet Union, and used others captured from the Japanese in the recent Sino-Japanese War.

Communist soldiers
Less professional, there were a significant number of peasants and students in their ranks.

Nationalist weapons
Many were provided by the United States, in an attempt to avoid a Communist triumph.

Nationalist troops
They were much greater in number and had better training and equipment than their Communist counterparts.

Scarcity of supplies
As food and ammunition had been sent by train to Xuzhou, Nationalist troops had to resist 16 days of battle with few provisions.

Railroad
The main objective of the Huaihai Campaign. Until it was captured by the Communists, it represented a quick and efficient means of supplying the troops.

Infiltrators
The Communists had managed to efficiently infiltrate the ranks of the Nationalist Army. Thus, they knew of many activities in advance.

THE MOST POWERFUL ARMY

The origins of the United States Army, responsible for ground operations and most branches of the U.S. Armed Forces, lie in the Continental Army. Created in 1775, its purpose was to fight during the American War of Independence, although it was dissolved after this conflict. Despite Congress shaping the United States Army in 1784, it was not actually until 1917 that it was created as a national force, as a result of a merger between the Regular Army and the National Guard to fight in World War I. It had already intervened on the Mexican border from 1910 to 1917, during the Mexican Revolution, but it was not until 1918 that the United States Department of War changed the name of all the country's ground forces to the U.S. Army.

In 1920, following the end of World War I, the U.S. Army was dissolved and its members who had not been demobilized were reintegrated back into the Regular Army, which had no more than 300,000 members. During the following decade, as a result of the Great Depression, its capacity and number of soldiers was gradually reduced. It was during World War II that the U.S. Army acquired the size and importance that made it, during the second half of the twentieth century, one of the best-prepared military organizations in the world. Its key role in liberating Europe from Nazi control, its actions in the Pacific, and its presence in Germany and Japan following the surrender of the Axis offered it a significant level of prestige among its allies. Furthermore, the progressive increase in the amount assigned to defense in the U.S. budget allowed the organization to equip itself with the best and most sophisticated weapons during the Cold War, during which it fought in Korea and Vietnam.

From the 1950s onward, the army reorganized, replacing its basic tactical unit, the regiment, with a battle group comprising five companies. However, its armed divisions would not be transformed until the 1970s, when they were divided into three brigades of three or four battalions able to organize themselves in response to the mission at hand or their likely enemy. However, following the Vietnam War, the army was reorganized again and, in 1973, a new command structure was established. During the 1980s, the U.S. Army based all its efforts around training and technology, creating combat units under geographically organized joint command structures. In 1989 it reduced the number of personnel from 750,000 to 580,000.

Generally speaking, it is fair to say that the U.S. Army, throughout its history, has made flexibility one of its main virtues. Furthermore, it is renowned for equipping its troops with the best and most sophisticated attack and defense systems, and to this day it remains at the cutting edge.

Marine Corps

The Marine Corps was founded in 1775 during the American War of Independence in order to defend and operate navy vessels and participate in landings. Thus, it served as a naval infantry force. Throughout its history, its responsibilities have been increased and it has become an amphibian force that incorporates marine military techniques and personnel in addition to ground troops and air forces. The marines are characterized by their speed in deployment and the effectiveness of their raids anywhere in the world.

Marine Air-Ground Task Force

The marines have a special structure, divided into three sections that cover land, sea, and air personnel under a single command unit. This organization, known as the Marine Air-Ground Task Force, can be flexible and its scope can vary, depending on the unit in question. The Marine Expeditionary Unit, comprising 2,200 marines, is the corps' smallest unit, especially trained to take action in a very short space of time.

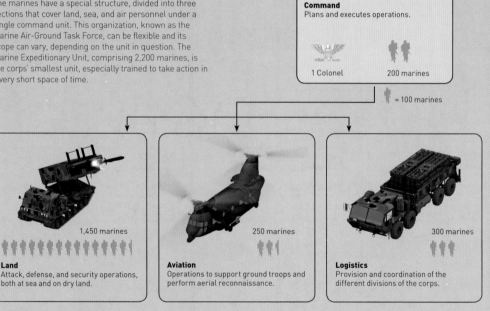

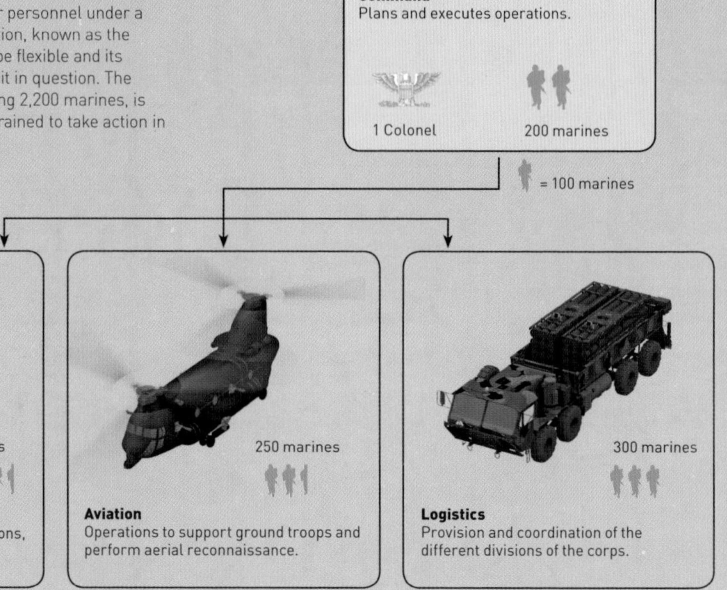
Command
Plans and executes operations.
1 Colonel
200 marines
= 100 marines
1,450 marines
Land
Attack, defense, and security operations, both at sea and on dry land.
250 marines
Aviation
Operations to support ground troops and perform aerial reconnaissance.
300 marines
Logistics
Provision and coordination of the different divisions of the corps.

BECOMING A MARINE
To become part of the corps, candidates must undergo a harsh 12-week training course.

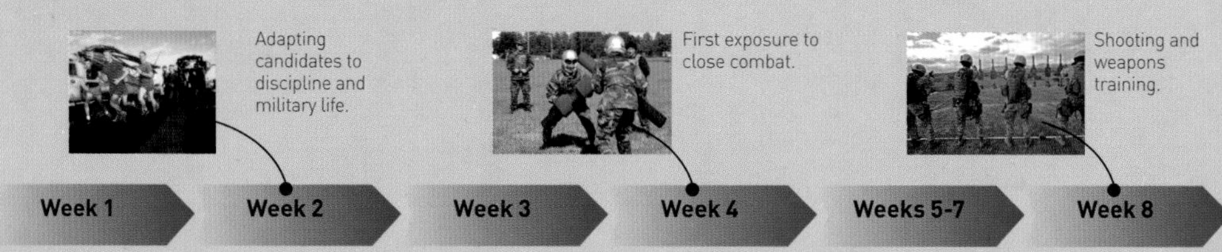
Adapting candidates to discipline and military life.
First exposure to close combat.
Shooting and weapons training.
Week 1
Week 2
Week 3
Week 4
Weeks 5-7
Week 8

THE UNIFORM

Collar
Originally designed to protect the marine against a sword attack, it is a reminder of the marine corps' past.

Rank
There are two hierarchies of rank. One is for officers commissioned after a program of training; the other is for noncommissioned officers, who begin their career in the military by means of the recruitment process.

The "line of blood"
The red line seeks to recall marines fallen in battle.

THE EMBLEM

This symbol has been used on the marines' uniforms since 1868, and in 1955 it was made the corps' official emblem.

An eagle, with its wings outstretched, represents the U.S.A.

A ribbon with the marines' motto *Semper Fidelis* (Always faithful).

UNITED STATES MARINE CORPS

The anchor represents the marine past of the corps.

The globe is a reference to the marines' global presence.

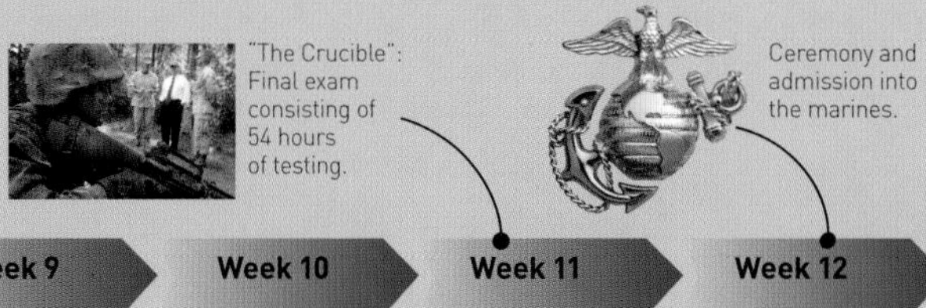
Week 9
Week 10
Week 11
Week 12

"The Crucible": Final exam consisting of 54 hours of testing.

Ceremony and admission into the marines.

RECENT OPERATIONS

JUST CAUSE (1989)
Operation against the Noriega regime in Panama.

DESERT STORM (1990)
Intervention in the Iraqi invasion of Kuwait.

INTERVENTION IN BOSNIA (1995)
Joint activities with NATO forces.

WAR ON TERROR (2001)
Ongoing operations since 9/11.

The Normandy Landings

On June 6, 1944 (known as "D-Day"), the Allied Forces, comprising British, United States, and Canadian troops, landed on the beaches of Normandy to liberate the Hitler-occupied territory. Under the code name "Operation Overlord," it was the largest naval operation of World War II and affected its course like no other.

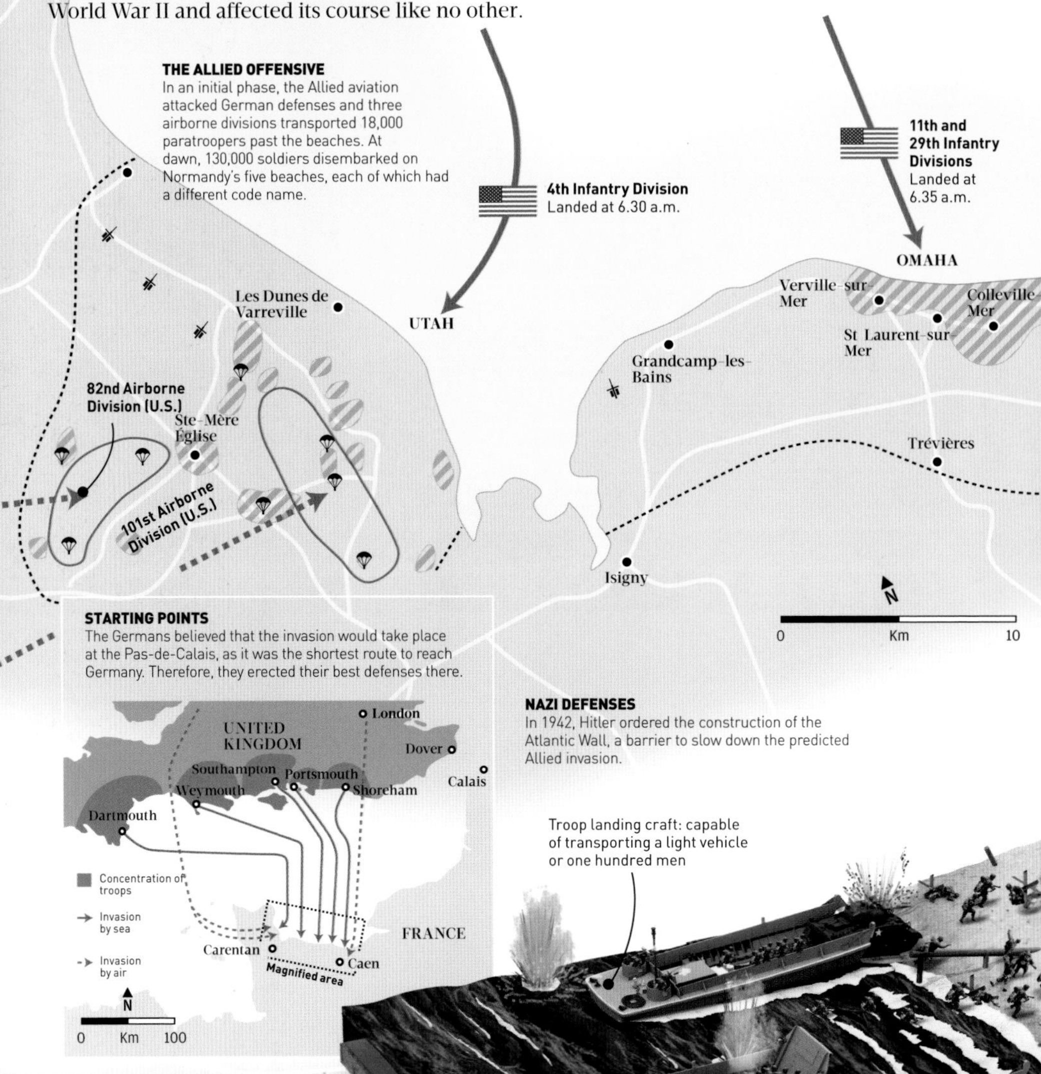
4th Infantry Division
Landed at 6.30 a.m.
11th and 29th Infantry Divisions
Landed at 6.35 a.m.
OMAHA
UTAH
Les Dunes de Varreville
Verville-sur-Mer
Colleville-s
Mer
St Laurent-sur-Mer
Grandcamp-les-Bains
82nd Airborne Division (U.S.)
Ste-Mère Église
101st Airborne Division (U.S.)
Trévières
Isigny
N
0
Km
10
UNITED KINGDOM
London
Dover
Calais
Southampton
Portsmouth
Shoreham
Weymouth
Dartmouth
Concentration of troops
Invasion by sea
Invasion by air
Carentan
Caen
Magnified area
FRANCE
N
0
Km
100
Troop landing craft: capable of transporting a light vehicle or one hundred men

THE ALLIED OFFENSIVE
In an initial phase, the Allied aviation attacked German defenses and three airborne divisions transported 18,000 paratroopers past the beaches. At dawn, 130,000 soldiers disembarked on Normandy's five beaches, each of which had a different code name.

STARTING POINTS
The Germans believed that the invasion would take place at the Pas-de-Calais, as it was the shortest route to reach Germany. Therefore, they erected their best defenses there.

NAZI DEFENSES
In 1942, Hitler ordered the construction of the Atlantic Wall, a barrier to slow down the predicted Allied invasion.

General Dwight D. Eisenhower
American
Supreme Commander of the Allied Forces. He was the tactician and was responsible for planning "D-Day."

Field Marshal Bernard L. Montgomery
British
Commander of the Allied ground forces. He was in charge of the 21st Army Group.

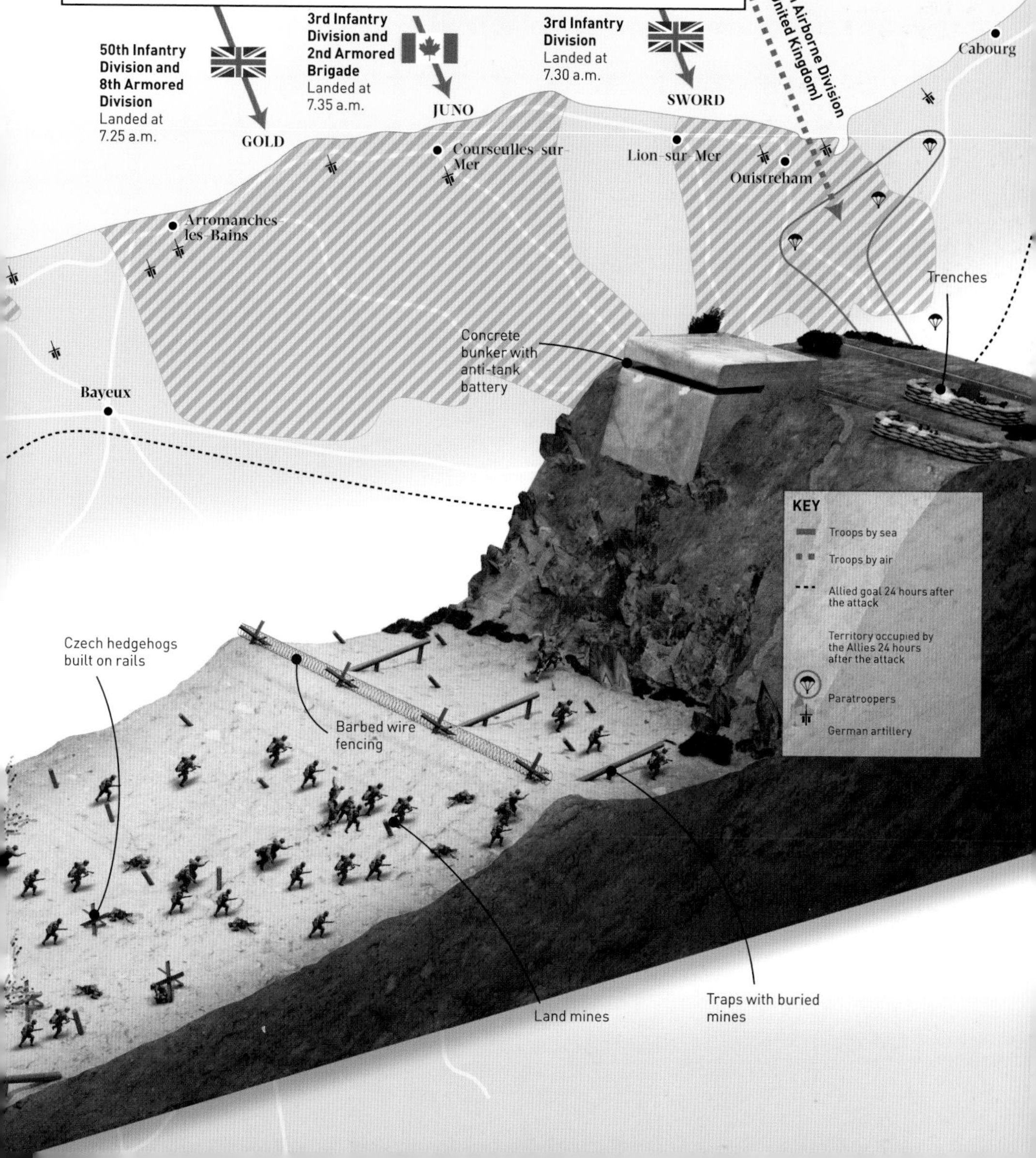

50th Infantry Division and 8th Armored Division
Landed at 7.25 a.m.

GOLD

3rd Infantry Division and 2nd Armored Brigade
Landed at 7.35 a.m.

JUNO

3rd Infantry Division
Landed at 7.30 a.m.

SWORD

6th Airborne Division (United Kingdom)

Cabourg
Courseulles-sur-Mer
Lion-sur-Mer
Ouistreham
Arromanches-les-Bains
Bayeux

Trenches

Concrete bunker with anti-tank battery

Czech hedgehogs built on rails

Barbed wire fencing

Land mines

Traps with buried mines

KEY
Troops by sea
Troops by air
Allied goal 24 hours after the attack
Territory occupied by the Allies 24 hours after the attack
Paratroopers
German artillery

Navy Seals

The U.S. Army has numerous Special Operations Forces, the best of which are the Navy SEALs, who specialize in nonconventional warfare, counterinsurgency, and counterterrorism. The SEALs were created in 1962, at the express request of President Kennedy in response to guerrilla warfare. A special infantry branch was therefore created, capable of operating at sea, in the skies, or on land, with the initials of *Sea, Air, and Land* used to baptize it.

All-terrain forces

The SEALs were created based on the British SAS using various bodies of the United States Navy. Since then, the SEALs have participated in conflicts in Vietnam, Grenada, the Persian Gulf, Panama, Operation Desert Storm, Somalia, Bosnia, Kosovo, Iraq, Afghanistan, and the operation to assassinate Osama Bin Laden, in Pakistan.

RIGOROUS TRAINING
Members of other special units are presented as SEAL candidates; however, only 40 percent pass the admission exams. Those accepted embark on a two-year training course, a veritable baptism of fire. It involves eight weeks' basic physical conditioning; a further eight weeks learning to dive and learning submarine tactics; nine weeks' land-conflict training and preparation; and the final three weeks dedicated to parachuting.

Diving The training is essential. Here, emerging from the sea.

GENERAL CHARACTERISTICS

The SEALs operate in small units, although numbers are not fixed; there can be up to eight, but numbers are always even.

Trident The SEAL insignia was created in 1970.

High command ▸ Navy Special Warfare Command

Structure ▸ 8 teams of 6 platoons

Personnel per team ▸ 96

Motto ▸ *The only easy day was yesterday*

M433 HEDP GRENADE
High-explosive dual purpose ammunition for grenade launchers.

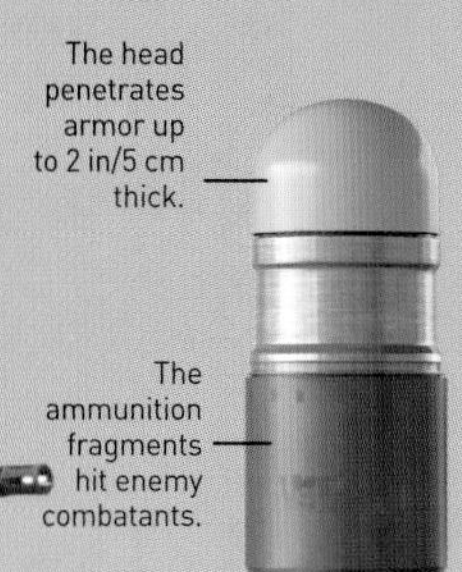

The head penetrates armor up to 2 in/5 cm thick.

The ammunition fragments hit enemy combatants.

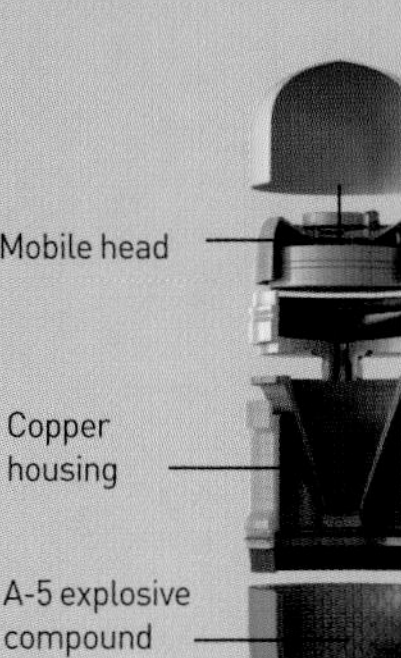

Mobile head

Copper housing

A-5 explosive compound

M-9 charge propellant

M-42 detonating cap

EQUIPMENT including survival and basic combat elements, in addition to everything needed for a given mission.
M203 grenade launcher Usually coupled to an M4 rifle, it fires 1.6 in/40 mm grenades to a distance of 500 ft/ 150 m.
Helmet Incorporates night vision.
Grenade Two cartridges are stored in the vest.
M4 rifle A 0.22 in/5.56 mm caliber carbine derived from an M-16 assault rifle. Designed for combat in enclosed spaces.
Tactical vest In addition to several cartridge holders, it is equipped with Kevlar protection.
SOG 2000 knife A tactical survival knife. Designed for both combat and daily use.
MK-23 pistol Manufactured by the German company Heckler & Koch, and adopted by the U.S. Special Forces. It is a 0.35 in/9 mm caliber.
Camouflage Following the Gulf War, desert camouflage was changed from six to three colors: green, earth, and sand.
Assault boots Light, water-resistant, and designed to withstand high temperatures.

THE U.N. PEACEKEEPING FORCES

UNITED ON A DIFFICULT MISSION

In 1948, three years after the creation of the United Nations (U.N.), the U.N. Security Council, comprising 15 voting members whose resolutions were mandatory in all member states, decided to create a multinational force that would end the conflict and supervise the ceasefire between Egypt and Israel. After that first mission, during which they participated as observers, the "Blue Berets" (their berets were blue and their vehicles white, in order for them to be easily identified as a peacekeeping force) intervened in the Korean War, actually participating in the conflict. This action did not in any way correspond with the original objectives of the organization, and many countries were harshly critical as a result. Among these objectives, the following are worth particular mention: the supervision and adherence to ceasefire agreements in armed conflicts; disarmament and immobilization of combatants; protecting civilians; safeguarding the maintenance of law and order; minesweeping territories at war, and supporting conflict resolution between countries and communities within a single country.

Its first mission was in 1956 during the Suez Canal crisis, and since then, it has been active in conflicts in Cambodia, the Middle East, Libya, Cyprus, Mozambique, Somalia, Sudan, the Democratic Republic of Congo, Serbia, Kosovo, and Bosnia, in addition to many other locations. Its personnel have traditionally been equipped with lightweight weapons and are under orders to use minimum force to legitimately defend themselves, or against anybody preventing them from performing the tasks with which they have been entrusted. However, in certain special situations, as occurred in the Congo between 1960 and 1964, they were ordered to use any force necessary, in this case to ensure the withdrawal of mercenaries who had contributed to the secession of the province of Katanga. Also, in 1996 they were authorized to use heavyweight weapons as a dissuasion tactic in SAO Eastern Slavonia, Baranja and Western Syrmia. The Blue Berets have come up against especially difficult situations on a number of occasions, when they have had to choose between maintaining peace and using force to restore peace, as happened in Bosnia and Herzegovina and Somalia in 1992 and 1995.

Despite having been awarded the Nobel Peace Prize in 1988 and the Prince of Asturias Award for International Cooperation in 1993, Blue Beret missions have not always been exempt from controversy and have even been subject to harsh accusations; this was the case during the extermination of the Tutsi at the hands of the Hutu in Rwanda in 1994, when the force was accused of abandoning the former, leaving them exposed to the latter.

Blue Berets

Since its creation in 1948, the U.N. Peacekeeping Force has participated in around 70 peacekeeping operations worldwide. However, the U.N. does not have its own troops. The Blue Berets, whose name is attributable to the color of their headgear, comprise units of soldiers from the United Nations member states. Thus, they are a multinational force that is controlled by the U.N. Security Council.

Multinational forces

The uniforms and the equipment of the Blue Berets widely vary depending on the country of origin of the troops sent to a given mission. Currently, 114 countries provide uniformed personnel, and each uses the standard equipment of their own national army. The blue beret which they all use identifies them as part of U.N. forces.

GENERAL CHARACTERISTICS

The troops deployed in areas of conflict are tasked with observing, controlling, protecting, and dissuading—thus preventing large-scale conflicts.

Insignia
Shield of the United Nations.

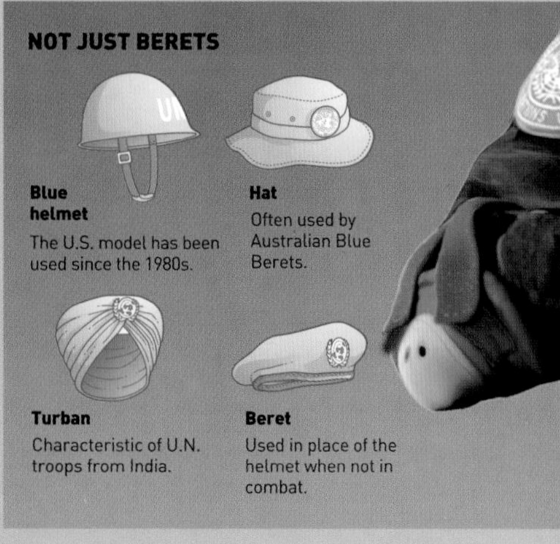

NOT JUST BERETS

Blue helmet
The U.S. model has been used since the 1980s.

Hat
Often used by Australian Blue Berets.

Turban
Characteristic of U.N. troops from India.

Beret
Used in place of the helmet when not in combat.

15 peacekeeping missions and a special policy mission in Afghanistan are currently ongoing.

PEACE MISSIONS AND WORLD LOGISTICS

Peacekeeping on a world scale demands the deployment not only of troops but also of equipment, communications systems, and transportation, both air and terrestrial.

Transportation and support
The vast majority of vehicles are used for support and transportation, and not for combat.

46
12
147
33,437

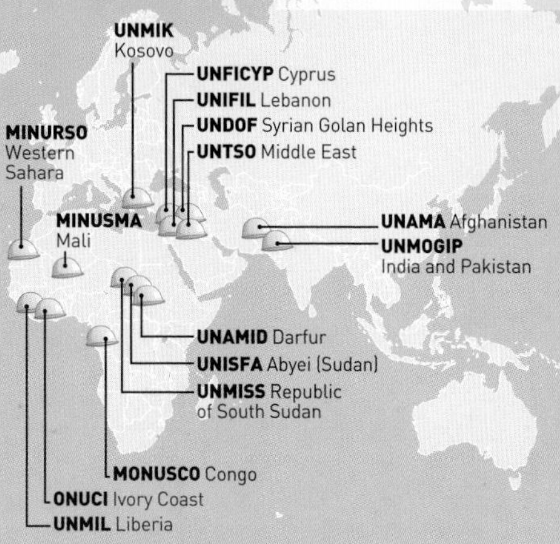
MINUSTAH Haiti
MINURSO Western Sahara
MINUSMA Mali
UNMIK Kosovo
UNFICYP Cyprus
UNIFIL Lebanon
UNDOF Syrian Golan Heights
UNTSO Middle East
UNAMA Afghanistan
UNMOGIP India and Pakistan
UNAMID Darfur
UNISFA Abyei (Sudan)
UNMISS Republic of South Sudan
MONUSCO Congo
ONUCI Ivory Coast
UNMIL Liberia

Bulletproof vest
Blue Berets are equipped with bulletproof vests like the ones used by the armies in their respective countries of origin. The outer layer is made from fire-resistant material.
Kevlar structure
Ceramic structure
SIZE MEDIUM
STRIKE FACE
HANDLE WITH CARE
Bulletproof plate
A ceramic or metala antitrauma plate is fitted in a pouch in front of the interceptor.
Interceptor
Inner structure, made from layers of resistant fibers that absorb the energy of the bullet.
FN FAL 50.61 rifle
The FAL, the M-16, and the AK-47 are the assault rifles most commonly employed by Blue Berets.
Uniform
Here, the combat uniform of the Brazilian Blue Berets can be seen.
Camouflage pattern
The camouflage pattern used as standard by each force for the type of warfare in question during the mission is employed.
Knee pads and shin pads
This type of protection, made using Kevlar, is regularly worn.
UN

LIMITATION TACTICS

Some forces find it difficult to complete their mission due to tactic-type limitations, such as a lack of sufficient weaponry or the number of troops required to keep the situation under control.

U.N. troops in Bosnia, in 1995, one of the most controversial missions.

Peace mission in Yugoslavia

Midway through 1991, Croatia declared independence from Yugoslavia, just as Slovenia had done a few months previously, unleashing one of the fiercest wars of the twentieth century between the Croats and the Serbs. To ensure the demilitarization of designated U.N.protection zones, the United Nations Protection Force (UNPROFOR) was deployed on a mission that involved dozens of countries, thousands of soldiers and expanded over land and over time to include Bosnia and Herzegovina.

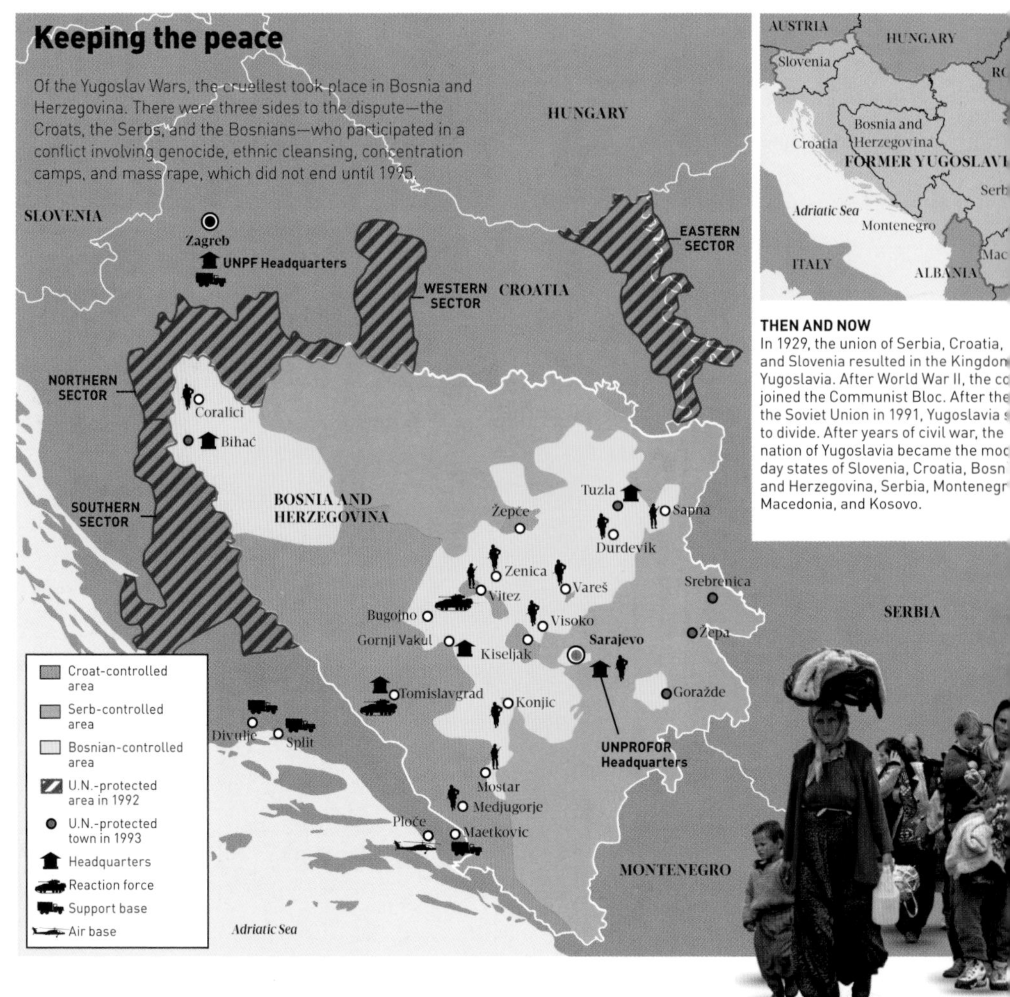
HUNGARY
SLOVENIA
Zagreb
UNPF Headquarters
WESTERN SECTOR
CROATIA
EASTERN SECTOR
NORTHERN SECTOR
SOUTHERN SECTOR
Coralici
Bihać
BOSNIA AND HERZEGOVINA
Tuzla
Žepče
Sapna
Durdevik
Zenica
Vitez
Vareš
Srebrenica
Bugojno
Visoko
Gornji Vakul
Kiseljak
Sarajevo
Žepa
SERBIA
Tomislavgrad
Konjic
Goražde
Divulje
Split
UNPROFOR Headquarters
Mostar
Medjugorje
Ploče
Maetkovic
MONTENEGRO
Adriatic Sea
Croat-controlled area
Serb-controlled area
Bosnian-controlled area
U.N.-protected area in 1992
U.N.-protected town in 1993
Headquarters
Reaction force
Support base
Air base
AUSTRIA
HUNGARY
Slovenia
Bosnia and Herzegovina
Croatia
FORMER YUGOSLAVI
Serb
Adriatic Sea
Montenegro
ITALY
ALBANIA
Mac

Keeping the peace

Of the Yugoslav Wars, the cruellest took place in Bosnia and Herzegovina. There were three sides to the dispute—the Croats, the Serbs, and the Bosnians—who participated in a conflict involving genocide, ethnic cleansing, concentration camps, and mass rape, which did not end until 1995.

THEN AND NOW

In 1929, the union of Serbia, Croatia, and Slovenia resulted in the Kingdon Yugoslavia. After World War II, the co joined the Communist Bloc. After the the Soviet Union in 1991, Yugoslavia s to divide. After years of civil war, the nation of Yugoslavia became the moc day states of Slovenia, Croatia, Bosn and Herzegovina, Serbia, Montenegr Macedonia, and Kosovo.

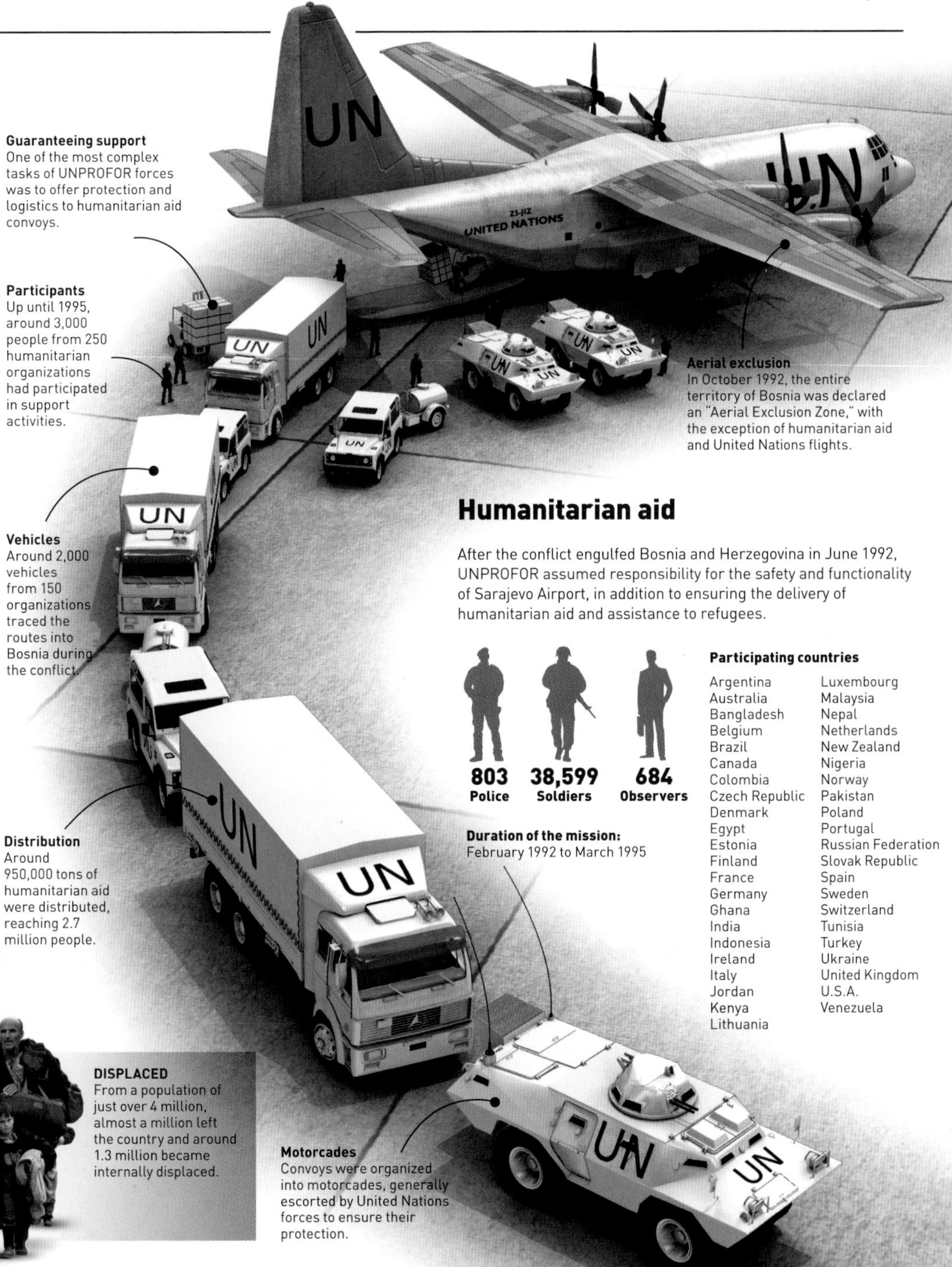
UN
ZS-JIZ
UNITED NATIONS
UN
UN

Guaranteeing support
One of the most complex tasks of UNPROFOR forces was to offer protection and logistics to humanitarian aid convoys.

Participants
Up until 1995, around 3,000 people from 250 humanitarian organizations had participated in support activities.

Aerial exclusion
In October 1992, the entire territory of Bosnia was declared an "Aerial Exclusion Zone," with the exception of humanitarian aid and United Nations flights.

Vehicles
Around 2,000 vehicles from 150 organizations traced the routes into Bosnia during the conflict.

Humanitarian aid

After the conflict engulfed Bosnia and Herzegovina in June 1992, UNPROFOR assumed responsibility for the safety and functionality of Sarajevo Airport, in addition to ensuring the delivery of humanitarian aid and assistance to refugees.

803 Police
38,599 Soldiers
684 Observers

Duration of the mission:
February 1992 to March 1995

Participating countries

Argentina
Australia
Bangladesh
Belgium
Brazil
Canada
Colombia
Czech Republic
Denmark
Egypt
Estonia
Finland
France
Germany
Ghana
India
Indonesia
Ireland
Italy
Jordan
Kenya
Lithuania
Luxembourg
Malaysia
Nepal
Netherlands
New Zealand
Nigeria
Norway
Pakistan
Poland
Portugal
Russian Federation
Slovak Republic
Spain
Sweden
Switzerland
Tunisia
Turkey
Ukraine
United Kingdom
U.S.A.
Venezuela

Distribution
Around 950,000 tons of humanitarian aid were distributed, reaching 2.7 million people.

DISPLACED
From a population of just over 4 million, almost a million left the country and around 1.3 million became internally displaced.

Motorcades
Convoys were organized into motorcades, generally escorted by United Nations forces to ensure their protection.

Based on an idea by Joan Ricart
Editorial coordination Marta de la Serna
Design Susana Ribot
Editing Alberto Hernández
Copy (supplied by) Federico Puigdevall
Historical documentation Frederic Puigdevall Claver
Graphic editing Alberto Hernández
Layout Paola Fornasaro
Copy Editor Stuart Franklin
Infographics Sol90Images
Photography AGE Fotostock, Getty Images, Corbis, ACI, Album, Granger